Praise for *The War Comes Home*

"In *The War Comes Home,* Aaron Glantz shows how the latest generation of American veterans, those from the highly unpopular war in Iraq, are getting the same shaft all their elder brethren got. Glantz's work is meticulously researched and glaringly frank in its depiction of the bum's reception these real heroes continue to get at home. The courage and honesty of *The War Comes Home* are a fitting tribute to what these men and women fought and risked their lives and well-being for."   **Gerald Nicosia,** author of *Home to War:*
A History of the Vietnam Veterans' Movement

"The treatment by the Bush administration of America's returning veterans from the wars in Iraq and Afghanistan is one of the saddest chapters in American history. This story is painfully documented by Aaron Glantz."

Max Cleland, former U.S. Senator

"*The War Comes Home* brings the reader into the personal hell that U.S. soldiers experience upon returning home from the meat grinder that is the U.S. occupation of Iraq. Glantz reminds us that the war soldiers bring home is intertwined with the evisceration of Iraq the occupation has caused, and this is precisely why soldiers are coming home shattered."

Dahr Jamail, author of *Beyond the Green Zone:*
Dispatches from an Unembedded Journalist in Occupied Iraq

"Aaron Glantz did not fight in Iraq, but he is a veteran of war's carnage and chaos. Living with Iraqis near Fallujah in 2004, Glantz—unlike many journalists at the time—put himself in harm's way to get his story, and brings this self-awareness to his analysis of war's homecoming. Although some military veterans may differ with his conclusions, we should all admire Aaron's courage, integrity, and commitment to discovering the truth."

David Danelo, former Marine Corps Captain and author of
Blood Stripes: The Grunt's View of the War in Iraq

THE WAR COMES HOME

THE PUBLISHER GRATEFULLY

ACKNOWLEDGES THE GENEROUS SUPPORT

OF THE BARBARA S. ISGUR PUBLIC AFFAIRS

ENDOWMENT FUND OF THE UNIVERSITY OF

CALIFORNIA PRESS FOUNDATION.

THE WAR COMES HOME

WASHINGTON'S BATTLE AGAINST AMERICA'S VETERANS

AARON GLANTZ

UNIVERSITY OF CALIFORNIA PRESS

BERKELEY   LOS ANGELES   LONDON

University of California Press, one of the most distinguished university presses
in the United States, enriches lives around the world by advancing scholarship
in the humanities, social sciences, and natural sciences. Its activities are supported
by the UC Press Foundation and by philanthropic contributions from individuals
and institutions. For more information, visit www.ucpress.edu.

University of California Press
Berkeley and Los Angeles, California

University of California Press, Ltd.
London, England

Library of Congress Cataloging-in-Publication Data

Glantz, Aaron.
    The war comes home : Washington's battle against America's veterans /
Aaron Glantz.
        p.   cm.
    Includes bibliographical references and index.
    ISBN: 978-0-520-25612-5 (cloth : alk. paper)
    1. Veterans—United States—Social conditions—21st century.   2. Disabled
veterans—United States—Social conditions—21st century.   3. Veterans—
Services for—United States.   4. Disabled veterans—Services for—United
States   5. Disabled Veterans—Rehabilitation—United States   6. Iraq War,
2003—Psychological aspects.   7. Afghan War, 2001—Psychological aspects.
8. Vietnam War, 1961–1975—Psychological aspects.   I. Title.

UB357.G56   2008
362.860973—dc22   2008035579

Manufactured in the United States of America

18   17   16   15   14   13   12   11   10   09
10   9   8   7   6   5   4   3   2   1

This book is printed on Natures Book, which contains 50% post-consumer
waste and meets the minimum requirements of ANSI/NISO Z39.48–1992 (R 1997)
(*Permanence of Paper*).

FOR NGỌC

With malice toward none, with charity for all, with firmness in the right as God gives us to see the right, let us strive on to finish the work we are in, to bind up the nation's wounds, to care for him who shall have borne the battle and for his widow and his orphan, to do all which may achieve and cherish a just and lasting peace among ourselves and with all nations.

Motto of the U.S. Department of Veterans Affairs,
from President Abraham Lincoln's second inaugural address,
March 4, 1865, after the conclusion of the Civil War

CONTENTS

List of Resource Boxes   xi

Preface: Returning Home from Iraq   xiii

Acknowledgments   xxiii

PART I   COMING HOME

1   A Soldier Comes Home   3

2   Trying to Adjust   16

3   A Different Kind of Casualty   28

PART II   FIGHTING THE PENTAGON

4   The Scandal at Walter Reed   49

5   Coming Together   61

6   Education   69

7   Drugs, Crime, and Losing Your Benefits   86

8   Losing Your Benefits—Personality Disorder   95

PART III   FIGHTING THE VA

9   Meet the Bureaucracy   105

10   Didn't Prepare to Treat the Wounded   118

11   More Bureaucracy   129

PART IV   **THE DOWNWARD SPIRAL**
            DRUGS, CRIME, HOMELESSNESS,
            AND SUICIDE

12   Crime   143

13   Homeless on the Streets of America   156

14   Suicide   167

15   Suicide after the War   176

PART V   **FIGHTING BACK**

16   A History of Neglect   193

17   Winning the Battle at Home   208

      Postscript: The War Inside   218

      A Note on Sources   227

      Notes   229

      Index   247

RESOURCE BOXES

Definition of PTSD   8

Transitioning to Civilian Life   15

Resources for Female Soldiers and Veterans   22

Resources for Families   27

Screening Test for Brain Injury   42

Veterans' Charities, Good and Bad   68

Finding Community at School   75

Rights and Responsibilities of Students
    Called Up to Active Duty   82

Finding Mental Health Care outside the
    Government System   92

Getting Help Filing a VA Claim   109

Further Reading on the VA Claims Process   113

Veterans for Common Sense Class Action Lawsuit   126

Storefront Help through the VA   135

Legal Help for Veterans Looking for
    a Fair Shake   148

Arts Programs by and for Veterans   151

Help for Homeless Veterans   159
24-Hour Suicide Helpline   188
The Joshua Omvig Suicide Prevention Act   189
Helping Vietnamese Agent Orange Victims   201
The National Gulf War Resource Center   203

RETURNING HOME FROM IRAQ

It's not easy to come home from war. Even if you're lucky enough to have survived mentally and physically, you still have to get used to the fact that most Americans can't relate to where you've been, what you think, what you've seen, how you feel, and what you've done.

I should know. I spent parts of three years as a journalist in U.S.-occupied Iraq, in Baghdad, Fallujah, Najaf, and other locales that have become more known for their battles, kidnappings, and car bombs than for their historic architecture, culture, or people. I existed in an atmosphere where I couldn't walk down the street, go to the grocery store, or eat in a restaurant without seriously considering the security situation. Explosions and gunfire were parts of my daily life. I saw the smelly, dirty remains of dead Iraqis before my eyes.

All the things that most Americans take for granted, like clean water and consistent electricity, were unavailable. No gym memberships. No sporting events. No hanging out at the neighborhood bar. No hiking or fishing or bowling. Just work, and the belief that by being there and reporting the news I was making some kind of difference.

As a journalist, I considered myself safer than most men and women who served in the military. I was in Iraq as an observer, interviewing regular people about their daily lives. This was something most Iraqis appreciated, and while there was always the chance that I would be killed or injured while caught in the cross fire, no one was targeting me directly and I was never ordered to shoot anyone myself.

I traveled in old, beat-up economy cars and station wagons that blended into the day-to-day of regular Iraqi life. Iraqi hospitality is legendary. So, despite war going on all around, wherever I went to conduct interviews, I was met with tea and snacks and often a complete lunch. Since I didn't carry a gun and presented myself as impartial, even most Iraqis who participated in attacks on American soldiers felt comfortable speaking and meeting with me. The work was dangerous, but more in the way that walking through a crime-ridden city at night is dangerous. I might get hurt, but I could also take precautions to keep myself relatively safe.

In April 2004, I was working west of Baghdad, interviewing Iraqis who had family in Fallujah, when I saw an American tank burst into flames on the highway, a dark red fire with black smoke spiraling toward the sky. More tanks sped past us and people shot at them. An ambulance rushed by, its sirens blaring. I ran toward a nearby mosque and hugged the wall to avoid the gunfire. Next to me stood a local sheik. When I told him I was a journalist, he told me his brother and sons were being held at Abu Ghraib. I took his mobile number and promised to call him to make an appointment later.

It was surreal. As I hugged the wall of the mosque, I met the head of a local relief agency who hold me about his charity's blood drive for civilian victims of the siege of Fallujah. He wanted to stay and talk, but I apologized and rushed back to my car. I sat in the old station wagon as my translator drove it through the back roads into Baghdad. It took an hour and a half to get home this way, but it was better than risking shrapnel from an exploding tank.

Those kinds of experiences weren't easy for me. While I was still in Iraq, I cried at the slightest provocation. Every afternoon, after my time in the field, I would sit transcribing interviews with my translator, tears running down my cheeks. At night it was worse. The tragedy unfolding on the streets of Baghdad and Fallujah began to invade my dreams.

In one recurring nightmare, I found myself at a bus depot in downtown Baghdad unable to get a ticket to Istanbul. From Istanbul, I would have been able to fly home to California. "I need to get to Istanbul," I would say with great urgency to a myriad of conductors, concessionaires, and drivers, but every time I would be denied.

"There are no buses to Istanbul," a conductor would say as a large 1970s superliner pulled out with ISTANBUL emblazoned on its front. When I ran to the driver of the bus, he turned to me. "All sold out," he would shrug. This would go on for some time until, eventually, a long-limbed man with a daffy smile and long tongue would approach me with a kitchen knife and cut off my head, in the style of the most macabre Hollywood slasher movie. Blood would spurt from the stump of my neck as my face looked on in horror. Finally, my translator Waseem would appear and wrestle the knife from my crazed assailant and I would wake.

I knew I had to get out of Iraq, especially after I went to Fallujah at the beginning of May 2004 and saw the aftermath of the U.S. siege there. In Fallujah, I watched as medical teams pulled the already decomposing remains of a middle-aged woman out of the ground before burying her in a makeshift cemetery in the municipal football stadium.

Back in Baghdad, I couldn't get her out of my mind. We had never met in life, but now that she was dead, she appeared to me as a vision over and over again. When I was awake, she hovered directly in front of my eyes with a kind of translucent quality. When

I was asleep, she appeared whole in the ground. I drank more and worried I was developing post-traumatic stress disorder, a psychological disease that often strikes soldiers and others close to severe violence.

I thought of broken Vietnam veterans I'd met back home in the States. I knew I didn't want to end up like them, tortured for decades by my wartime experiences. Every person has a breaking point, and I could tell that I was reaching my limit. So I called my editors, said goodbye to my Iraqi friends, and took a bus from Baghdad to Kurdistan in northern Iraq. From there, I took a taxi and then a bus back to Ankara where I spent a week "cooling off" with friends in the cafés and restaurants of the Turkish capital. I walked the streets of Aksaray, an old section of Istanbul, and relaxed in the heat of a Turkish bath. Then, with the war at least a little bit out of my system, I boarded a plane to the States. A week later, I was in California sleeping next to my fiancée in the back of her parent's house.

But I wasn't really happy back at home. Her parents lived a few blocks away from the local ABC-TV station's news helicopter pad. Every time I heard the chopper go by, I felt agitated. I woke up in the middle of the night and paced through the house and into their backyard. I had visions, usually during the daytime, of people and things I had seen in Iraq.

I'd left Iraq, but Iraq did not leave me. I'd left Iraq, but I knew civilians who lived there could not. I felt like I'd abandoned my Iraqi friends, my translators and their families, by coming back to the United States. How could I return to California and experience the "comforts of home" when death and destruction continued overseas? I tried to call Iraqis I knew as often as possible, but it still didn't seem right. My head told me I should relax and enjoy life, but the rest of my body pulled me back toward the Middle East.

My knees ached, but I couldn't figure out why. Perhaps it was from stress that had taken over my body. Perhaps it was weight I'd put on from too much drinking. I tried eating better and bicycling, but the pain wouldn't go away. I felt alone—I was surrounded by friends and family, but all of them saw the war in Iraq simply as a political debate—if they thought about it at all. How could they go on talking about such trivial things—iPods, celebrities, the latest fashions—when there was *A WAR GOING ON!?*

"I found that the most difficult part of this experience in Iraq was coming home," my friend, filmmaker Andrew Berends, said in his director's commentary on the DVD of *The Blood of My Brother.*[1] The award-winning documentary follows the family of a Shiite camera-store owner in Baghdad after he's killed by U.S. soldiers.

"The first two weeks back in New York were like a honeymoon," Andrew explained. "I was so happy. I was free. I was safe. I could walk around. But very quickly, I sunk into depression. I sent an e-mail to four or five other journalist friends I had in Iraq, all of whom happened to come back to New York the same month. I told them I couldn't sleep. I couldn't focus on my work. I felt depressed. I was having trouble in my relationship."

Andrew and I lived together during part of our time in Iraq and occasionally went out in the field reporting together. While we were together in Baghdad, I watched Andrew with a sort of envy. He was so calm, fearless. I was sure he was coping better than I was. When he saw an explosion or gunfire, he would get out of the car and stand silently, pointing his camera directly at the carnage, while I would avert my eyes and look for a safe place to stand until the fighting stopped and I could conduct interviews. Back at the hotel in the evening, Andrew would sit quietly listening to music on headphones for hours, before busting out with a wry comment that would cause the rest of us to erupt in laughter.

In August 2004, Andrew covered the Shiite uprising in the holy city of Najaf. In one scene he filmed for *The Blood of My Brother,* the Iraqi police and military gun down dozens of peaceful demonstrators who'd come out to protest during a break in the battle. Civilians and fighters alike fall down dead, shot right in front of his camera.

"I remember feeling very calm [with] some adrenaline," Andrew said of his experience filming the massacre. "I had been given a taste of how easy it is to kill. After that day I saw more violence: dead bodies in Sadr City, grieving brothers, grieving friends, and again I felt nothing. No emotions. No tears. I knew in my mind that what I was seeing was messed up, but I think that as a defense mechanism I couldn't process it at the time and still function. I was working and living. I had to make decisions."

When he got home, however, the bill came due. "It was almost like I couldn't find a reason to get up in the morning," he explained. "There were no car bombs. Nobody was being killed. It didn't seem like anything important was happening here. I felt such a strong desire to go back to Iraq but at the same time I knew that I needed to deal with what I'd seen and experienced. I knew that there are plenty of reasons to get up in the morning outside of a war zone and I just needed to relearn the job of living day-to-day without violence and death happening around me."

According to a study published in the September 2002 issue of the *American Journal of Psychiatry,* war reporters are much more likely to experience psychological trauma than journalists who never report on armed conflict. War journalists reported drinking more alcohol and were much more likely to show signs of depression or post-traumatic stress disorder (PTSD). Indeed, the study showed a lifetime rate of PTSD in war journalists of 28.6 percent, and the lifetime rate of depression was 21.4 percent—rates similar to those of combat veterans.[2]

Two months after I returned from Iraq, a friend suggested I go see a psychiatrist in San Francisco's Pacific Heights district. He was a specialist in PTSD, my friend told me, and would be able to tell me if something was wrong with me clinically or if I was just having "issues" that would pass. I found the experience infuriating. The shrink sat back and let me talk for an hour. Afterward, he asked for a check for $175 and scheduled an appointment for the next week. I wanted someone who would give me answers to my questions and help me learn ways of coping with my problems on my own. Instead, the psychiatrist promised me a mountain of bills but no guarantee of progress. That was the last thing I wanted, and I never returned.

What turned out to be most helpful to me was the continued practice of journalism. A few months after coming home in 2004, I got a contract to write a book, *How America Lost Iraq,* where I chronicled how and why Iraqis turned against the U.S. occupation even though they were initially happy about the overthrow of Saddam Hussein. For six months, I spent most of my days listening to the taped interviews I did in Iraq, transcribing them, and reinterpreting them into a coherent narrative that made sense to me.

Veteran crime reporter Bruce Shapiro, who heads the Dart Center for Journalism and Trauma at the University of Washington, told me many reporters find that their journalism can be a kind of therapy. "Our job is to make narratives, to take the fragmented shards of horrifying experiences that would be kicking around disorganized and confused and put them into some kind of shape, and though no one has done a study on this, the broader PTSD literature would suggest that this is a source of resilience," he told me. "I mean, trauma shrinks spend a lot of time with victims getting them to shape the story—to get some control over the experience to have the experience feel a little safer by putting it into narrative memory instead of kind of existential threat memory."

Another way the book helped was that it gave me the opportunity to process my experiences out loud. When it came out in hardcover in the spring of 2005, I toured the country, speaking at bookstores, churches, and college campuses. I also gave numerous radio and television interviews and was able to explain what happened around me and how I felt about it.

"Storytelling is not just about a narrative, but also about accountability," Shapiro explained. "We do have the ability to lay out lines of accountability for things that have happened, and that serves as a control for some people, and in my experience the experiences that most haunt journalists are most often the ones that we couldn't get adequate attention [for], get out there, get printed, or get to air."

During that book tour, I began to connect with veterans for the first time. They would come up to me at bookstores and ask about my experiences of a particular location where they had been stationed. "What did the Iraqi people there really think?" they asked. "How did they react when approached by a microphone instead of a gun?"

I especially enjoyed talking on overnight shows on AM radio. Soldiers and veterans called in when they couldn't sleep. During one interview, an active duty Marine stationed near Seattle called to talk about his experience shooting an innocent civilian at a checkpoint. At 3:00 A.M. on a talk radio station in Denver, a father called to tell me that his son, who had just returned from Iraq, was now addicted to drugs, as were many of his friends.

In Boston, I spoke on a panel with a former Navy lieutenant who bombed Iraq during the initial invasion. He told me he had become "completely dysfunctional" since returning to the States. He had two young children, "but was in no way able to be a father to them." He told me that since returning to his native Massachusetts in 2004, he had been in and out of the VA's mental facility.

The more stories I heard from American veterans, the closer I felt to them. In a way, I felt like we were alone in this country together—the only Americans to see the true horror that is the war in Iraq. I started seeking out vets, to tell their stories on the radio, in wire services, on the Internet, and in newspapers and magazines. I tried my best to make the war personal, to create an undeniable moral urgency inside my listeners and readers so they couldn't ignore the war—or pretend it was something that went on far away and didn't affect them.

That effort culminated in this book, one of the first attempts to systematically explain what Iraq and Afghanistan veterans face when they return home. In its pages, you will read about the difficulties soldiers have reintegrating into civilian life, living with disability and unemployment, dealing with the military bureaucracy, suicide, and homelessness—as well as more upbeat stories about families, communities, and fellow veterans pulling together to help each other.

While each veteran's case is different in its details, a clear pattern emerges overall. American soldiers return from Iraq and Afghanistan different from when they left. They have difficulty relating to their family and friends who never spent time in the war zone. But rather than help them adjust to civilian life, the federal government throws a series of bureaucratic barriers at them that make their problems worse. Injured veterans must battle Pentagon officials for an honorable discharge and then fight with a completely separate Department of Veterans Affairs bureaucracy to get their health care, education, and disability benefits. Oftentimes, that fight is so long and complicated that it pushes a veteran toward withdrawing, using drugs, suicide, or crime.

But the story doesn't need to go this way. While war is inherently damaging to a person's psyche and physical body, steps can be taken to make the transition from warrior to civilian easier. My hope is that I can show not only problems, but also solutions. As the Vietnam experience indicates, if we don't start addressing these problems now, they'll only get worse with time.

ACKNOWLEDGMENTS

The War Comes Home would not have been possible without the cooperation, patience, and interest of the veterans and their family members who allowed me to tell their stories. How a person processes his or her war experience is intensely personal, and I have done my best to be true to everyone who took the time to speak with me.

I am especially indebted to Paul Sullivan of Veterans for Common Sense, Dave Danelo, and Penny Coleman for reviewing this manuscript as I churned it out. Collectively, their feedback helped me keep the story real. Thanks also to Patrick Campbell of Iraq and Afghanistan Veterans of America, Jose Vasquez, Aaron Hughes and Garret Reppenhagen of Iraq Veterans Against the War, Todd Stenhouse of the National Veterans Foundation, Jim Cook of Veterans United for Truth, and Todd Dusenbery of Military Families Speak Out for being generous with their time and introducing me to others. Thanks also to journalists Sarah Olson, Salam Talib, and Dahr Jamail for being good friends and helping me sort through the difficult emotional territory one covers when writing on the reality of war as experienced by others. Thanks to my friend Kevin Brower for his feedback and for the long hours we spent together, both hunched over computers.

Thanks to Naomi Schneider, my editor at University of California Press. This book was her idea. After returning from multiple reporting trips to Iraq and Vietnam, I came to her with other suggestions, but she urged me to stay on the topic of the war. I am very happy she steered me toward this valuable endeavor. Thanks also to my agent Michael Bourret, who gave me feedback on my outline and helped me come up with a coherent narrative for this book. I also thank the editors of my regular freelance journalism work, who helped me keep these stories in the news while I worked on the book: Katherine Stapp at Inter Press Service, Jeffrey Allen at OneWorld, Jack Epstein and Bob Miller at the *San Francisco Chronicle,* Richard Kim at *The Nation,* Matt Rothschild at *The Progressive,* Kasia Anderson and Robert Scheer at Truthdig.com, and Monica Lopez, Sasha Lilley, and Aileen Alfanderry at KPFA Radio. Thanks also to Aimee Allison and Esther Manilla. Thanks to therapist Rachel Erwin for donating her services.

Finally, I'd like to give a big thank-you to my wife Ngoc. I know it's not easy to be married to someone who's always mired in the gunk of war and post-traumatic stress disorder. Just as writing this book has been difficult for me, I know it's been difficult for Ngoc as well. This book could not have been written without her support.

PART I

COMING HOME

1

A SOLDIER COMES HOME

Twenty-seven-year-old Melissa Resta remembers when she first met her husband. When she was growing up near Navy and Air Force bases in rural South Carolina, her father had always told her not to date cops or guys in the military.

Then Patrick Resta appeared at her door. "He showed up in full Army fatigues after going to drill," she recalled laughing. "It was a little awkward. I have to say that I giggled every time he put the beret on, but it was him that I loved."

Patrick had always loved the military. He'd signed up right after high school, but by the time he married Melissa he'd already finished his time on active duty and was in the Army Reserve. "I figured he's only in the Reserves so I'm not going to become an Army wife or anything," she told me, "but that definitely happened."

Patrick's aunt and uncle were killed in the World Trade Center on September 11, 2001, and about three weeks later Patrick was called to active duty as part of homeland security. A year later, the Bush administration started to advocate attacking Iraq. Patrick told me he "had questions from the start about some of the things that were being given as a rationale for the war," but considered it his patriotic duty to answer the call to service.

In the spring of 2004, the Army sent Patrick to Diyala Province, northeast of Baghdad near the Iranian border. One of the most dangerous places in Iraq, it's where al-Qaeda in Iraq leader Abu Musab al-Zarqawi was killed in 2006.

Patrick served as a combat medic. He went out on patrol and checked for roadside bombs. He says he saw American Humvees blow up in his face, but added the worst casualties he saw were Iraqi civilians—who he was often forbidden to treat.

"We could not treat Iraqi civilians unless they were about to die and we had done it," he said, noting the medic's primary (and nearly always exclusive) responsibility is to care for injured American soldiers. "When I would walk through these cities I had people bringing their children up to me who were ill and had to be treated, and we were threatened with being court-martialed if we took any medicine to treat these Iraqis in the city."

Patrick's experiences are hardly unique. In July 2004, a team of researchers from Walter Reed Medical Center published a report in the *New England Journal of Medicine* on the mental health of American troops before and after deployment. Ninety-five percent of those surveyed reported seeing dead bodies and remains, 95 percent had been shot at, and 89 percent had been ambushed or attacked. Another 69 percent had seen an injured woman or child and felt they could not provide assistance.[1]

On November 13, 2004, two days before he left Iraq, Patrick posed for a photograph that for him has come to symbolize his wartime deployment. "I went on my last patrol to the city where I was based," he told me. "I was walking through a market. I wanted to take a photo there because seeing the children probably had the most effect on me. So I handed the camera to a friend of mine."

Patrick said he didn't look at what the children were doing while the picture was being taken. He was too busy looking around, checking windows and rooftops to make sure no one was planning an attack.

When his friend handed the camera back after snapping the photo, Patrick saw something about the children he hadn't noticed. "One of them had his right arm extended in a kind of Hitler salute, and on the other side of me one of the children is holding up a local newspaper with the Abu Ghraib torture pictures on the front cover," he said. "That was the impression that I left Iraq with—that we've angered a lot of people and radicalized a whole generation of Iraqis to hate this country and hate Americans."

When Patrick returned home November 15, 2004, his wife Melissa quickly realized something was wrong. "That's when it was really bad," she said. "He was angry all the time and was drinking more than what I think someone normally should and at off hours. He wasn't sleeping. When I would lay down he wasn't there."

At first, Melissa blamed circumstances for Patrick's anger and mood swings. While Patrick was in Iraq, Melissa graduated from the University of South Carolina with a degree in sociology. Eager for work, the couple decided to move from South Carolina to Philadelphia, where they crammed into a family member's small apartment. Time passed and the anger continued. Melissa began to worry.

"Over the course of just two or three weeks, I started to notice that if I came into a room, he would just leave," she said. "If I said something to him, he would just snap. He didn't want to talk to me, he didn't want to talk to really anybody, and when I confronted him with us having problems I would get let into."

"Why do I have to do this?" Patrick would shout. "Why don't you have a job? Why haven't you done this? Why won't you go away?"

Six weeks later, at Christmas time, Melissa confronted her husband. "He just wasn't interested in even spending any time with me," she said. "Christmas morning he got up and went off with his brother and I didn't even see him the rest of the day. I knew there was something wrong there. So I finally said something. I asked him if he wanted to split up and he said he didn't care and then I realized something's not right. He wouldn't say this to me."

So Melissa talked to other veterans in her community, and a few months later a Vietnam War veteran helped Patrick get an appointment at the Department of Veterans Affairs, where he was diagnosed with post-traumatic stress disorder, an anxiety disease that can emerge after exposure to a terrifying event or ordeal in which grave physical harm occurred or was threatened. A person experiencing PTSD may lose touch with reality and believe that the traumatic incident is happening all over again. By March 2008, over 130,000 Iraq and Afghanistan war veterans had been diagnosed with a psychological illness by the VA's mental health services.[2]

Studies show that between 15 and 50 percent of all post-9/11 veterans (between 320,000 and 800,000 people) suffer from PTSD.[3] "It becomes a disorder when it causes dysfunction," explained Capt. Thomas Grieger, a doctor at the National Naval Medical Center in Bethesda, Maryland, and one of the military's leading researchers on traumatic stress, "to the extent that individuals change their activity patterns significantly or it changes their relationships with their family, or their employers, coworkers, or friends. . . . I've seen several soldiers and sailors who came back from combat, had serious symptoms, chose not to report them and continued to have severe symptoms through another deployment. Oftentimes, individuals try to manage it on their own, and regrettably it comes down to the use of alcohol."

Indeed, because many soldiers either don't realize their problems are linked to PTSD or don't want to admit to having a psychiatric illness, family members are often best positioned to point vets toward help.

"I'd be concerned if they weren't sleeping well," Dr. Grieger told me. "I'd be concerned if they'd given up activities that they previously enjoyed. Sometimes they call out in their sleep and wake up during nightmares. Often they have difficulty driving or flying or being in other kinds of confined spaces. Drinking too much over a long period of time would also be a red flag." Also of concern, Grieger said, would be if veterans were unwilling to talk about their war experiences or showed discomfort at reminders of war, like civilian aircraft or Hummers.

Even veterans who go in for therapy or psychoactive medication never fully recover. VA doctors can help patients manage their symptoms, but there's no cure for PTSD. After two years of therapy, Patrick Resta told me he's still "not the person I was before" experiencing combat in Iraq. "I was always laid back and relaxed, always cracking jokes and things like that," he said. "Now I'm anxious and tense. I have bouts of anger and pretty severe insomnia, some bad nightmares. It's pretty standard for the men and women who are over there. All the people I've talked to have pretty much the same symptoms."

Still, the group therapy sessions Patrick attends at the VA have been helpful. He's gone back to school and is working on an associates degree at a community college in Philadelphia. After that, he plans to transfer to Temple University to study nursing.

Melissa has also been able to move on in her life, securing a job as a contractor with the U.S. Department of Justice. The couple now has

Definition of PTSD

The American Psychiatric Association defines post-traumatic stress disorder from the *Diagnostic and Statistical Manual of Mental Disorders,* 4th ed. (DSM-IV) as follows:

A. The person has been exposed to a traumatic event in which both of the following were present: (1) the person experienced, witnessed, or was confronted with an event or events that involved actual or threatened death or serious injury, or a threat to the physical integrity of self or others, and (2) the person's response involved intense fear, helplessness, or horror.

B. The traumatic event is persistently re-experienced in one (or more) of the following ways: (1) recurrent and intrusive distressing recollections of the event, including images, thoughts, or perceptions, (2) recurrent distressing dreams of the event, (3) acting or feeling as if the traumatic event were recurring (includes a sense of reliving the experience, illusions, hallucinations, and dissociative flashback episodes, including those that occur on awakening or when intoxicated), (4) intense psychological distress at exposure to internal or eternal cues that symbolize or resemble an aspect of the traumatic event, (5) physiological reactivity on exposure to internal or external cures that symbolize or resemble an aspect of the traumatic event.

C. Persistent avoidance of stimuli associated with the trauma and numbing of general responsiveness that was not present before the trauma, as indicated by three (or more) of the following: (1) efforts to avoid thoughts, feelings, or conversations associated with the trauma, (2) efforts to avoid activities, places, or people that arouse recollections of the trauma, (3) inability to recall an important aspect of the trauma, (4) markedly diminished interest or participation in significant activities, (5) feeling of detachment or estrangement from others, (6) restricted range of affect (for example, unable to have loving feelings), (7) sense of a foreshortened future (for example, does not expect to have a career, marriage, children, or a normal life span).

D. Persistent symptoms of increased arousal that were not present before the trauma, as indicated by two or more of the following: (1) difficulty falling or staying asleep, (2) irritability or outbursts of anger, (3) difficulty concentrating, (4) hyper vigilance, (5) exaggerated startle response.

E. Duration for the disturbance (symptoms in criteria B, C, and D) is more than one month.

F. The disturbance causes clinically significant distress or impairment in social, occupational, or other important areas of functioning.

---

their own apartment. But Melissa says their lives have permanently changed. Patrick won't go to the grocery store because he feels unsafe amid so many shoppers. He gets upset when he sees a woman on the street in traditional Muslim dress.

"There's so many things that I never thought would be a problem and now I have to think them through," she said. "And at twenty-seven it's not really where I pictured myself." She told me she doesn't think about children now and has to take life, and her marriage to Patrick, one day at a time. I asked her what advice she would give to other couples in a similar situation.

"Just try to remember what you had with them before and realize that they're still there, but they're never going to be who they were before and you have to come to terms with what they need from you, what you need from them, and try to work out a happy medium," she said. "You can do a lot more than you think you can," she added sniffling, wiping away tears. "You're a lot stronger than you think you are and when you love somebody you can do a lot more than you ever dreamed you could."

And yet, the Restas are lucky. In many ways, their experience is a best-case scenario. Patrick survived his deployment to Iraq and within a few months of returning, the couple had found a support group of local veterans who helped get him care from the VA medical system. The couple has also stayed together—no small feat given the sharp rise in divorces among soldiers over the course of the Iraq War.

The couple is also lucky Patrick was not physically injured in Iraq. He has no symptoms of traumatic brain injury (TBI), which many call the "signature injury" of the Iraq War. The most common injury soldiers in Iraq experience is brain damage from blasts from roadside bombs, otherwise known as improvised explosive devices, or IEDs.

The military formally diagnosed more than 4,000 cases of traumatic brain injury from October 2001 through January 2007. But most observers believe the number is much higher, and a recent Army study found that 18 percent of troops who have been to Iraq likely suffered at least some brain damage from IEDs.[4] That means as many as 320,000 potential TBI patients.

Patrick is also lucky that he has all his limbs. In February 2008, the Pentagon reported that more than 1,000 Iraq War veterans had become amputees.

Finally, Patrick is lucky because he was released from the Army after only one tour and with full VA medical benefits. Many of Patrick's fellow soldiers are sent back to Iraq for multiple deployments—even after being diagnosed with conditions like PTSD. Others are being dishonorably discharged for destructive behavior brought on by their undiagnosed or misdiagnosed mental problems and are legally barred from getting the care they need from the VA.

But nobody comes back from a war the same, and even those who get the care they need often feel alienated on their return home. In August 2007, researchers at the University of Pennsylvania and the Philadelphia VA Medical Center looked at the family problems of 168 veterans who were referred for behavioral health evaluation and who had served in Iraq or Afghanistan since 2001. Forty-two percent told the researchers they felt like a guest in their own home, 22 percent said their children didn't act warmly toward them or were afraid of them, and 36 percent were unsure about their role in regular household responsibilities.[5] In interviews for this book, many veterans explained that distance and a lack of intimacy are caused by burdensome secrets they're afraid to share.

"When people ask you about your wartime experiences they usually don't want to know," former Abu Ghraib interrogator Joshua Casteel told me. The Iowa City native arrived at the prison in June 2004, a few months after photos surfaced showing grotesque abuse of Iraqis in American custody.

When he came home, he said, "people wanted to hear stories that either reaffirmed their patriotic notions or reaffirmed their belief that the person that they love was doing something worthwhile. They don't want to hear how their loved ones were harassing taxi drivers and devastating a country. They don't want to hear how soldiers came back and committed suicide. They don't want to hear that, but that is what it's like." Besides, he said, "the more you talk, the more you have to reconcile with pain, because if you start putting words to how pointless and hopeless the last year of your life felt . . . those things aren't very fun to think about."

According to a 2004 report by the International Red Cross, nearly 90 percent of Iraqis incarcerated by the U.S. military were picked up by mistake.[6] Because the military rarely releases detainees, Casteel said he was forced to interrogate innocent prisoners again and again.

"I was constantly being asked, 'Why am I being held here? I want answers!' " Casteel told me. "But that was my job. We were supposed to be finding answers to our questions, but we kept being put into situations that were incredibly puzzling because talking to people was like trying to get blood from a turnip. They were the ones that had a greater justification for the need to have answers."

Eventually, Casteel said, he did have the opportunity to interrogate a self-described jihadist. "I had an interrogation with a twenty-two-year-old Saudi Arabian who was very straightforward that he had come to Iraq to conduct jihad. . . . We started having a conversation about religion and ethics, and he told me that I was a very strange man who was a Christian but didn't follow the teachings of Jesus to love my enemy and pray for the persecuted. My nickname in my unit was 'priest' because I spent a lot of time in the chapel.

"So I had this moment with a man who was a jihadi and he was giving me a lesson on the sermon on the mount," Casteel said. "That was about five months into my time in Iraq, and I had already had about a hundred interrogations and I was so weary of the whole process. I told him that I thought he was right and that there was a massive contradiction involved with me doing my job and being a Christian."

In January 2005, Casteel left Iraq and was discharged from the Army as a conscientious objector. But in his mind, he wasn't free and clear. "There were days that I would hear a song that I heard when I was deployed and be emotionally devastated for a week," he told me. "One day I was watching the movie *The Godfather* and there's this line—'all politics is crime' and my mind just started racing around that idea and I didn't leave my apartment for four or five days except to buy food and was convinced that there wasn't such a thing as justice in the world."

In February 2006, pollster John Zogby conducted a survey of U.S. soldiers stationed in Iraq. Seventy-two percent said that U.S. troops should be pulled out within one year. Of those, 29 percent said they should be withdrawn "immediately."[7] After more than five years of war, most American soldiers know the same things about Iraq that the American people do: that the invasion of Iraq was based on lies, that there was no link between Saddam Hussein and the 9/11 attacks, and that Iraq had no weapons of mass destruction. Those facts—coupled with the Bush administration's disregard for the Geneva Convention and the guerrilla nature of the war that leaves many civilians killed by American arms—can only contribute to feelings of anger and guilt among U.S. soldiers and veterans.

Writing about their experience treating Vietnam veterans, psychiatrists Herbert Hendin and Ann Pollinger Haas wrote that "the moral ambiguity surrounding who should or should not be killed in Vietnam and the breakdown of codes of conduct, which at least to some degree govern behavior in other wars, created an inordinate number of guilt-generating situations."[8] But like other researchers, Hendin and Haas found that a sense of guilt and betrayal is less important to an individual soldier's mental health than the way he or she processes the trauma experienced abroad. Like war reporters, soldiers heal best when they can come up with a coherent narrative that puts their experiences in perspective.

Specialist Casteel told me the hardest, but most important, part of his healing process was learning to sit still. In Iraq, he said, "your senses are inundated. You're moving 99 miles an hour and when you're back . . . you haven't had time to really think about what you've done, but that's what you need to do. But that's the most terrifying thing. You have to ask yourself: was it my finger on a trigger that could have shot those eight-year-old boys? And it was my voice that did the interrogations? What does that make of me? What does it mean about me?"

After he returned from Iraq, Casteel entered the masters of fine arts program at the University of Iowa and the Iowa Playwrights Workshop and wrote two plays about his time abroad—"Returns: A Meditation in Post-trauma" and "Ishmael and Isa" (Isa is Jesus in Arabic). He said the plays weren't easy to write. "When I first started writing . . . I couldn't sit down for fifteen minutes at a time," he told me. "I couldn't think about arc or narrative structure or any of that. And I would just write in these bursts and then I'd go order a pizza with a friend and we'd just hang out. And eventually I began to realize that the way that I'm writing might be a way to figure out how PTSD works."

In Casteel's play "Returns," one of the interrogators allows his prisoner, a young boy, to take his gun from him and point it at his head. "If I can't make it right, then I want it to end," the interrogator says. "I want to make amends, but I can't. I don't know how to. Not when they're still in prison. Can't just be for me. But, with them! With you. You have to leave my mind and I have to gain back the power of my hands. I have to have ME back. And if that's not possible, then simply annihilate me. What's the point? I'm just a tool of duty. Of law. Exploited to exploit."

Another one of Casteel's characters, Jonathan, talks of sitting alone with his girlfriend after returning home to the United States. "Sarah was the only one to listen," Jonathan says. "She let me be quiet. As long as I needed. It must have been terrible for her. But she waited. That is all. It's all I really needed. After I returned I knew I had to be still. For a long time. Just stand in the sunlight. Feel the earth. I didn't need much."[9]

"Coming to the end of the road of PTSD is finding words to explain your experiences," Casteel explained, "but you can't have those words imposed upon you. They have to be self-generated, and I think

Transitioning to Civilian Life

The **National Veterans Foundation** operates a toll-free hotline for veterans having difficulty adjusting to civilian life. The line is staffed entirely by veterans and operates between 9:00 A.M. and 9:00 P.M. Pacific time seven days a week. Call 888-777-4443. Veterans can also make anonymous queries via the organization's Web site, www.nvf.org.

Vets4Vets (www.vets4vets.us, 520-319-5500) is a nonpartisan project in which of Iraq-era military veterans take part in and create veteran support groups. Veterans listen and take equal and uninterrupted turns telling their stories with an agreement of complete confidentiality. In this forum, U.S. military veterans can help and support each other and express problems and situations that family and/or friends may not understand or relate to. The forums are free of charge and Vets4Vets will pay veterans' transportation costs to and from support sessions.

that means more than anything a willingness to be quiet until they come and friends who are willing to stay with you but allow you to be quiet so they [the words] come on their own. It's instrumental to be able to talk about it with friends, but how and when and why it happens is different for each person."

2

TRYING TO ADJUST

Some soldiers' families and social networks can't survive the home-coming. In 2004, 3,325 Army officers' marriages ended in divorce—up 78 percent from the year before, and more than three and a half times the number in 2000, before the 9/11 attacks and the bombing of Afghanistan. In 2004, 7,152 enlisted soldiers got divorced, 28 percent more than in 2003 and 53 percent more than in 2000.[1]

No one is keeping track of the number of marriages that fail after Iraq or Afghanistan veterans leave the service, but history is not on their side. Close to 40 percent of Vietnam veteran marriages failed within six months of the vet's return from Southeast Asia.[2] Over the long term, federal surveys have found veterans with post-traumatic stress disorder have found it particularly difficult to stay married. According to the massive National Vietnam Veterans Readjustment Study, vets with PTSD were three times more likely than veterans without the disorder to divorce multiple times.[3]

Those statistics haunt Melissa Resta as she looks forward to her future with Patrick. "When you meet Vietnam veterans, nine times out of ten you're not going to meet a Vietnam veteran who's with his first wife," she told me. "That's something that I picked up pretty quick and it's scary."

Being married to a combat veteran can be frustrating, she said, "because you need some kind of concern or caring or compassion from them, but one of the big problems is that they're numb. There's nothing there. There's this complete and total apathy when it comes to your emotions, and it's because when someone has seen life and death every day for as long as they have, when you come home and you've had a bad day with your boss it's insulting for them to have to hear that.

"I try to understand that there are reasons why Patrick behaves the way he does, but it doesn't make it any easier on me," she said. "One of his big things that he used to say when he first came home is 'I don't know why you're freaking out. It's not the end of the world. Nobody died.' That bothered me so much that I've outlawed it and he's no longer allowed to say it. . . . That's frustrating. The temper is frustrating. All of these things weigh in on your relationship."

Sgt. Nicole Gordon grew up poor and black in Beaufort, an island on South Carolina's Atlantic coast. In 1996, she followed her sisters into college, receiving a full athletic and academic scholarship to North Greenville University, a Southern Baptist college whose mascot is the Crusaders. The school's slogan is "Where Christ Makes the Difference."

Gordon studied hard at North Greenville. She played on the school's basketball and tennis teams and graduated in four years with a degree in business administration. But when she looked for work after finishing college she couldn't find a job. "After 9/11 there was all kinds of economic downsizing," she told me. "No matter what kind of job you had you were getting laid off. Businesses were closing. So with that, I had no choice but to serve, because it was either not make it and wonder when I'm going to have a job or serve my country."

Gordon threw herself into her military career and she excelled, in just two and a half years rising to the rank of sergeant. While stationed at Fort Hood, Texas, she took online classes at Touro University. She wanted to make sure that when she finished her military service she'd have a masters in business administration and a leg up in a future job hunt.

Then, in January 2004, the U.S. Army deployed Gordon to Iraq. She served at Camp Victory, the giant U.S. military headquarters located at Baghdad's airport just west of the capital. There, she carried out numerous duties, from running convoys to processing newly arrived prisoners. Occasionally, she was put on "escort duty"—supervising Iraqi workers as they moved around the base changing the sewage of the facility's portable toilets.

"When you are on escort duty, they send only one of you out there with two Iraqis," she explained. The first Iraqi worker drives the truck while the other one empties the waste using the same system local garbage companies use to pick up trash back in the States. Gordon's role was to supervise the operation and provide security. It was a routine duty, but one day, it had to be done in a blistering sandstorm.

"During the process of the day, the sand got into my eyes and I was slowly losing my vision," she said, speaking quickly, almost shouting the words because it was the only way they would come out. "The problem was I didn't trust the Iraqis and they didn't trust me neither. So I couldn't let [the Iraqi I was escorting] know, because I can't let someone I don't trust see that I can't see. But I had a weapon there on escort duty, because if they do anything there are rules of engagement that you go by to protect yourself if you feel like you're being threatened. So it came to this point that I couldn't see and I didn't know what to do because I didn't want to display any fear to this man and I'm a female. He's driving. And I realized that he was taking me the wrong way and I told him to turn around and he started yelling at me, telling me I couldn't see, but even though I was already losing vision . . . , I knew I was going the wrong way. So I actually had to lock and load my weapon and say I was going to shoot him. Even though I was scared, I didn't want to have to kill that man. And he threw up his hands at that point because he could see that I was getting delirious and called to his partner who was in the other vehicle behind us, and that person drove me back to my quarters."

When Gordon got back to her unit, she was immediately evacuated to the combat support hospital in Baghdad's Green Zone. She stayed there for a week and slowly regained her ability to see. When she returned to Camp Victory, she learned the Iraqi driver had been fired. He was surely embittered by his experience, she thought. Perhaps he had gone home and become an insurgent.

As Gordon's tour continued, her commanders began to require a buddy system for female soldiers—even on base. The impetus was a government report showing that between November 2003 and April 2004, eighty-three female American soldiers were raped in Iraq and Kuwait.[4] Gordon said some of those rapes took place at Camp Victory.

It became difficult to even go to the bathroom. "I'm already over here by myself fighting a battle," Gordon told me. "A battle in myself and a battle against these people and then suddenly there are all these other things you have to deal with like the rape issues that started to happen. We couldn't walk home or walk to the bathroom because people started to file complaints about their being raped."

Brig. Gen. Janis Karpinski (who oversaw operations at Camp Victory and nearby Abu Ghraib) confirmed that the rapes took place. The latrine for female soldiers at the base was located away from the barracks, she explained, and women had to go outside if they needed to go the bathroom. "There were no lights near any of their facilities, so women were doubly easy targets in the dark of the night," Karpinski told retired Army colonel David Hackworth in a September 2004 interview.[5]

Karpinski told Hackworth she complained to Brig. Gen. Michael J. Diamond, then commander of the 377th Theater Support Command in Kuwait. But he refused to do anything. "When I tried to discuss the gravity of the situation with him, he responded, 'It's not always easy being me, you know,' " Karpinski said. "My recommendations for some easily implemented actions to reduce this serious problem fell on deaf ears."

The male latrines, on the other hand, were well-lighted. "A female soldier coming off night shift took a shower and was standing at the sink brushing her teeth," Karpinski said. "A male soldier entered the tent brandishing a long blade knife. He had a scarf . . . over his head. He threatened her, and she tried to run. Another female soldier heard her scream and nearly bumped into the would-be attacker as he was running out of the tent. They actually cornered him, but CID (military cops) released him the next day because the intended victim was not certain she could identify him."

The large number of female soldiers on the battlefield is one of the key differences between the Iraq War and previous conflicts. More than 160,000 female soldiers have been deployed to Iraq and Afghanistan, compared with the 7,500 who served in Vietnam and the 41,000 who were dispatched to the Gulf War in the early 1990s. In March 2007, one of every ten U.S. soldiers in Iraq was female.[6] Female soldiers and veterans say the fear of sexual assault is widespread throughout the ranks.

Nicole Gordon told me that neither she nor any of the women in her unit was personally assaulted, but that didn't take away her fear.

"I had a good master sergeant," she told me. "He drove us all back to our quarters at night and made sure we were safe. But that meant that we couldn't go to the bathroom because it was hard to coordinate a buddy system."

Many women refused to drink in the late afternoon so they wouldn't have to urinate at night. They didn't get raped, Brig. Gen. Karpinski told me, but some of them died in the desert heat: "The women, in fear of getting up in the hours of darkness to go out to the port-a-lets or the latrines, were not drinking liquids after 3:00 or 4:00 in the afternoon. And in 120-degree heat or warmer, because there was no air conditioning at most of the facilities, they were dying from dehydration in their sleep. And rather than make everybody aware of that, because that's shocking—and as a leader, if that's not shocking to you, then you're not much of a leader—so what they told the surgeon to do was, 'Don't brief those details anymore. And don't say specifically that they're women. You can provide that in a written report, but don't brief it in the open anymore.'"

In September 2004, Nicole Gordon was medically evacuated a second time. Months of sleepless nights and demanding military operations were aggravating an old basketball injury and causing blood to pool in the lower half of her legs. On Labor Day weekend, Gordon was flown to Germany for medical treatment, processed, and then flown back to America.

A year later, on November 28, 2005, Gordon was given a medical discharge from the Army with the full array of health and education benefits. A masters degree in hand, she moved to put her Iraq experience behind her. "I was bitter," she said. "When I got out of the military I never wanted to look at that uniform anymore because all I wanted to know was, how can I move on in life after this?"

Resources for Female Soldiers and Veterans

The private, nonprofit **Miles Foundation** has a toll-free advocacy helpline (877-570-0688) for victims of military sexual assault and domestic violence. The organization also furnishes professional education and training to civilian community-based service providers and military personnel, and conducts research to ensure that public policy on military sexual assault and domestic violence is well informed and constructive (www.hometown.aol.com/milesfdn, 203-270-7861).

The **Service Women's Action Network** (www.servicewomen.org, info@servicewomen.org) supports and develops the leadership of veterans, mentors young women considering military service, works to solve problems facing women in uniform, and provides and promotes services that are healing to women after their military service experience.

As the months went by, Gordon started having nightmares; she dropped to the ground at the slightest provocation. She didn't talk to anyone about her demons, though. "I definitely take pride in serving my country. It was a pride for me to join," she told me. "It was a [point of] pride to be accepted. It was an honor for me to serve, but in serving I never thought it would make my life like this. Never. I didn't bargain for it."

As a way of moving on, Gordon and her husband decided to start a family. Their first child, Shaneeka, was born in October 2006. It was Shaneeka's birth that pushed Gordon to turn to the VA for professional help. "When I look at my child, I remember when I was over there with another female [soldier] . . . I remember going into one of the markets and you know you can't let the younger kids get close to you. They're not supposed to come near you or in your vicinity. Even on a convoy when you get out and the kids come walking up to you,

you have to point your gun at them. Those are some of the issues I have to deal with when I look at my child. I think about pointing my weapon at my own child," she told me crying. "That's one of the things that bothers me is that I think about how I pointed my weapon at somebody else's child."

In September 2007, Gordon filed a disability claim for post-traumatic stress disorder with the Department of Veterans Affairs. The process of filing the claim put her in touch with the Texas Veterans Commission, a state agency that helps former soldiers present their best case to the VA.

A month later, she was employed at the agency as a veterans' counselor, helping those with similar experiences fight their way through the VA bureaucracy. Now, she comes home every day after eight hours of listening to other soldiers' war stories. When she closes her eyes at night, the stories replay themselves as dreams inside her mind. "I'm still dealing with my issues," she said, "but at least I'm not where I was."

She's proud of her job at the Texas Veterans Commission. "It's some kind of way to fight," she told me. "I can encourage people, I can understand and I'm in a position to help. I feel like instead of being a victim of this thing in some way I am a victor over it."

Finances can also be a problem. In addition to psychological and physical injuries, many of the soldiers being deployed must endure a loss in pay. A recent government study found that more than 40 percent of National Guardsmen and Army Reservists lose income when they're called to active duty.[7]

When forty-three-year-old Will Beiersdorf joined the Illinois National Guard, he never imagined the military would play such a significant role in his life. "I'd initially thought I'd just do six years, get my college and get out," the Chicago native told me. But after he graduated with an accounting degree from DePaul University, Beiersdorf decided to reenlist for another term of service. Six years later, he re-upped again.

"I always wanted to be a part of something bigger than myself," he said. "Even though I was a professional and climbing up that corporate ladder, I still wanted to be a part of that [the Guard] because not many people have an opportunity to serve. Part of it was the friendships and the camaraderie that comes with being part of something that's bigger than myself, and part of it was being there to defend my country if something bad should ever happen."

During his eighteen years in the Guard, Beiersdorf was called up many times. He took part in the 1991 invasion of Iraq, was sent on relief missions to Africa and Central America, and helped save communities in southern Illinois after historic floods on the Mississippi River.

One of his favorite memories comes from a 1993 call-up, when the National Guard was deployed to prevent a riot after Michael Jordan and the Chicago Bulls won their third straight NBA Championship. "We had a chance to meet some revelers and just encourage them to settle down," he said laughing. "Some of them became our friends later on."

When al-Qaeda attacked the World Trade Center and the Pentagon in 2001, Will Beiersdorf was thirty-six years old. He had been married nine years and fathered three sons, ages six, four, and two. He'd also landed a good day job in the sales department of Siebel Systems, a high-tech company headquartered in Emeryville, California. The job paid close to $100,000 a year, enough for his family to buy a two-bedroom house in Chicago's middle-class northern suburbs. The family lived comfortably and his wife, Mary Beth, who worked in marketing, could stay home and raise the kids. To set an example for his young children, Will continued his service by joining the U.S. Navy Reserve. In many ways the Beiersdorfs were living the American Dream.

The 9/11 attacks threw that dream into question. After 9/11, the Navy called Will up and sent him on a thirteen-month deployment guarding newly arrived detainees at Guantanamo Bay, Cuba. Under federal law, his employer, Siebel Systems, was required to offer Will his job back when he returned. But the company refused to go the extra step and pay the difference between his white-collar salary and the $25,000 a year Will earned in the Reserves.

"They said turn in your computer, turn in your stuff, and let us know when you get back. That was it," Will told me. "It was ironic, because they were very patriotic from a marketing perspective." After 9/11 the company had draped a nine-story American flag over the side of its corporate headquarters. By January 2002, Siebel was buying full-page ads in the *New York Times* arguing it should be given lucrative government contracts by the Department of Homeland Security.[8]

"The employees were the best part," Mary Beth remembered. "When Tom Siebel and Siebel Systems made the decisions to offer us a loan at 5.5 percent, the employees came back and said 'Hey we'd like to donate some vacation time.' But that was denied, so the employees got together gave us a large gift at Christmas time. The company didn't want to set a precedent for this one guy out of six thousand, and fortunately for us we took the high road and built something really great out of this bad experience."

It wasn't easy. "With three kids in Catholic School and a house and a car and all of those things, we were struggling very strongly financially," Mary Beth said. "We had to remortgage the house and borrow money from family members. Some of our neighbors helped us with lawn care. One neighbor volunteered for babysitting duties so I could do freelance marketing work. It was really a community effort."

Money wasn't the only challenge the family faced. "The little one was only two years old when Will left," Mary Beth told me. "The first month he started biting and kicking me and saying, 'Where's daddy? Where did he go? I hate you! I hate you! I hate you!' How do you explain all this to a two-year-old? It just got worse and worse and worse. Eventually, we had to send him to a therapist."

But with the help and support of their family, friends, and their church the Beiersdorfs were able to continue to stand on their feet. Time and time again, the community came to their aid—a process that continued even after Will returned from Guantanamo.

In August 2003, one of the Beiersdorfs' neighbors hosted an outing at a local golf club. "We walked in there and everyone was acting kind of weird," Mary Beth told me. "There were about thirty or forty people and there was a buffet, food, all kinds of stuff including raffle gifts. And they wouldn't sell us any raffle tickets and I said, 'God, that's rude. How come they're not letting us in on this?' And they turned around and said, 'This is for you guys. This whole event is for you.' And they raised three thousand dollars and they gave us three thousand in cash, which was just unbelievable."

Later that year, Will and Mary Beth founded Salute Inc., a nonprofit organization dedicated to providing direct financial support to military men and women who might otherwise fall through the cracks. They raise money primarily through community events like golf outings and pizza parties, and by sponsoring teams that run in races like the Chicago marathon. The organization's slogan is "Honor the service. Remember the sacrifice."

Resources for Families

Salute Inc. (www.saluteinc.org, 847-749-2768) is a project started by Will and Mary Beth Beiersdorf to provide financial support and direct assistance for service members and veterans.

The **National Military Family Association** (www.nmfa.org, 800-260-0218) provides resources and support to spouses and children of the U.S. Air Force, Army, Navy, Marine Corps, Coast Guard, National Oceanic and Atmospheric Administration, and the Public Health Service. The NMFA runs Operation Purple Camp, a series of free, week-long summer camps around the country for children of soldiers deployed overseas. A special Operation Purple Camp for Children of Wounded Service Members incorporates additional mental health support into the daily camp activities—without losing the focus on fun. The NMFA also provides college scholarships for military spouses.

"We were very, very supported and very grateful, and that has motivated us to where Salute has become a 24/7 job for our family," Mary Beth said. "We live it. We breathe it. It's our passion because we know so many people are in need of this help and they can't do it themselves."

3

A DIFFERENT KIND OF CASUALTY

Since the start of the Iraq War, it's been fashionable to compare America's invasion and occupation of Iraq to the war in Southeast Asia thirty years before. As with the Vietnam War, American soldiers face a determined guerilla opponent in unfriendly territory. As with Vietnam, the mission of the war is unclear. Soldiers fight to hold the ground they stand on from an elusive enemy and continue to fight without a clear definition of "victory." No one on the front lines is really sure when the war is going to end or what they can do to end it.

"In World War II, the soldiers knew the fastest way home was straight through Berlin or Tokyo," Sgt. Ronn Cantu told me in a phone conversation from Baghdad. "Once a paper was signed saying they were surrendering unconditionally, we were coming home. But we don't have any of that this time around. There's just no representative force that's going to surrender to us and our win conditions are in the hands of another entity."

Like most American soldiers, Sgt. Cantu has served more than one tour in Iraq. When I interviewed him in January 2007, the intelligence officer was already on his second deployment—with the possibility of more in the future.

"When you go back to the States or wherever you're stationed, you're just so ecstatic that Iraq is behind you," he said. "You just want to put it completely behind you. But then you come back. That's when you start asking yourself: 'Where is the end? Is the end in sight?' "

As of December 2006, fully half of the approximately 140,000 troops in Iraq were enduring their second tour, while another quarter were in their third or even fourth tour. In addition, a stop-loss policy, which some call a "backdoor draft," is forcing tens of thousands of members of the country's volunteer armed forces to remain in service beyond their contractually agreed-upon term. For example, many soldiers with a two-year enlistment contract have been forced to serve three years.[1]

In January 2007, the Bush administration revoked a policy that had capped a National Guard or Reserve soldier's cumulative time on active duty for the Iraq or Afghanistan wars at twenty-four months. As of this writing, the only current limit to protect these service members is the length of a single mobilization, which may not exceed twenty-four consecutive months.[2]

From the soldier's perspective, this is one of the biggest differences between the Iraq and Vietnam wars. Because of the draft, the vast majority of servicemen and women served only one tour in the conflict zone—departing by airplane exactly one year to the day they arrived. From the government's perspective, stop-loss and multiple combat tours have a number of advantages over the Vietnam-era draft. Stop-loss reduces the number of new recruits the military needs and saves the government money by retaining experienced troops in the force. Sending soldiers on multiple combat tours cuts down the cost of training new soldiers and lowers long-term war costs by reducing the number of veterans who would have earned benefits from their service.

From the soldier's perspective, however, these developments are a disaster. Unlike Vietnam vets, Iraq War veterans "are getting layered with PTSD," explained Shad Meshad, a mental health counselor who served on the front lines of the Vietnam War and returned to found the first veterans resocialization unit at the VA hospital in Los Angeles. "We've never seen guys go back so many times," Meshad said, "and if they have PTSD from their first tour and then they're back within a year of their second tour, most of them aren't getting treated for a number of reasons so they're caught in this vicious loop and their lives start to go south."

Another key difference is that Iraq—on the whole—is much more dangerous than Vietnam was for an American soldier. Each of the 1.7 million U.S. soldiers who has served in Iraq has essentially spent his or her entire deployment engaged in round the clock combat operations. Insurgency, terrorism, and sectarian violence are daily facts of life in all but a handful of provinces in the Kurdish north.

American soldiers are not allowed to leave their bases unless they're on a combat mission. Special "soldier villages" with bars, clubs, video arcades, and dens of prostitution exist outside nearly every overseas U.S. military base in the world—from South Korea to Turkey—but not in Iraq. According to a November 2006 report by the United States Army Medical Command, only 5 percent of soldiers were able to take R&R while in theater.[3] By contrast, a large percentage of Vietnam War veterans served in support conditions and did not experience combat in the same way. "Whereas some areas in both the North and South [of Vietnam] were crushed by bombings, suffering, and death, in other parts of the South, where large numbers of Americans were stationed, life was often like a massive out of control party," wrote journalist Trin Yarborough in her book *Surviving Twice: Amerasian Children of the Vietnam War.* The book chronicles the lives of an estimated 100,000 children born of Vietnamese women and American soldiers.

Reading Yarborough's description of wartime South Vietnam, it's difficult to image a scene more different from the reality of today's Iraq.

> In southern cities of Vietnam, particularly Saigon, bars, dance clubs, and brothels quickly sprang up to serve the growing number of Americans entering the country, as well as the large number of Vietnamese military, officials, and others enriched by American spending and aid. Prostitutes crowded streets and alleys, especially in the Ton Dan area of Saigon soon famous for its pleasures. Bars tended to become known as 'black' or 'white,' drawing almost entirely one or the other racial group of American troops. . . . American soldiers bought Vietnamese women gifts and took them to restaurants and clubs, which most Vietnamese men couldn't afford. Many American soldiers lived with Vietnamese girlfriends.[4]

The behavior of American soldiers in Vietnam created outrage around the world, and since then the Pentagon has taken numerous steps to reign in prostitution. Fearing a repeat of Vietnam-era lawlessness would create a devastating violent backlash among the Iraqi populace, the U.S. military banned all fraternization and alcohol consumption in Iraq (although some make moonshine, obtain illegal drugs, or abuse over-the-counter medicine). The idea of an American soldier spending time off base with anyone, least of all an unattended Iraqi woman, is impossible to even imagine, and has been since the beginning of the war. In October 2005, the U.S. military banned soliciting a prostitute anywhere in the world. In 2006, the Department of Defense began requiring "Trafficking in Persons" training for all soldiers deployed overseas. The most important thing for soldiers to learn, *Stars and Stripes* reported: "No buying, selling or renting people."[5]

This increased insistence on sex education, sexual hygiene, and prostitution avoidance is good for soldiers' health and for the United States' image overseas. American soldiers' treatment of Vietnamese women was one of the more despicable aspects of the Vietnam War and it's good that the Pentagon has learned from this experience. But there is a downside for American soldiers deployed to the war zone. Whatever the morals and ethics of Vietnam-era debauchery, it's clear that it provided a kind of noncombat recreational release for American soldiers that is not available in Iraq. American soldiers in Vietnam were able to blow off steam. American soldiers in Iraq, on the other hand, are in a pressure cooker and they have to experience that stress over and over again.

Early on in the Iraq War, the Bush administration was regularly raked over the coals for failing to "support the troops" by denying them urgently needed body armor and armored Humvees to protect them from death in the event of an attack. Pressure built during the first year of the war and boiled over in December 2004, when an active-duty soldier confronted Defense Secretary Donald Rumsfeld during a town hall meeting in Kuwait.

"We're digging pieces of rusted scrap metal and compromised ballistic glass that's already been shot up, dropped, busted, picking the best out of this scrap to put on our vehicles to take into combat," Specialist Thomas Wilson of the Tennessee National Guard said, applauded by the soldiers around him. "Now why do we soldiers have to dig through local landfills for pieces of scrap metal and compromised ballistic glass to up-armor our vehicles, and why don't we have those resources readily available to us?"[6]

Rumsfeld's flippant response, that "you go to war with the Army you have" sparked a furor in Washington policy circles, as did his minimization of the importance of armor: "If you think about it, you can have all the armor in the world on a tank and a tank can be blown up," he told the troops. "And you can have an up-armored Humvee and it can be blown up."

Rumsfeld was widely denounced for this comment, with everyone from Republican senator Trent Lott to *Weekly Standard* editor William Kristol calling on him to resign. Other members of Congress called for investigations. At the time, a Scripps Howard News Service survey reported that 275 American soldiers had died while in Humvees.[7]

But the controversy over body armor obscured a key fact about the war: that U.S. soldiers who patrol Iraq's streets have been at great risk, not only because their Humvees lacked armor but also because they are the most visible—and therefore the easiest to target—portion of an unpopular military occupation. "Every night, a group of us get together and wait for the Americans to drive by in their Humvees," an auto repairman in Baghdad's Sunni-majority Adamiya neighborhood told me when I worked as an unembedded journalist in 2004. "Then, when the Humvees come, we hit them."

The repairman told me he took up arms when it became clear the U.S. military wouldn't be leaving Iraq quickly after the fall of Saddam Hussein. "We have to fight for our country and our religion," he told me, "so when an American Humvee goes by, we attack it. Sometimes there are American snipers on top of the police station, so we hit the police station. Sometimes there are no Americans around, so we just hit the police. When anyone puts himself on the Americans' side, he's a traitor."

Why are the Americans on patrol to begin with? Officially, we're told they are patrolling the streets, hunting down insurgents. My experience in Iraq led me to believe that the Humvees themselves create the insurgents. "We have a problem," former Iraqi general Farouk Mu'aden told me in April 2004, "which is that the American military goes door-to-door and captures people for cooperating with the resistance. This causes more people to join the resistance and makes it more difficult for us to make a peace here."

At that time, Gen. Farouk was part of a team of notables from Diyala Province (where Patrick Resta was stationed) who tried to negotiate a ceasefire with the Americans. His group told the local American commander that if he stopped his patrols and gave jobs to the local people, his group would stop the insurgency in Diyala. But the offer was refused.

Some soldiers understand this. Chanan Suarez-Diaz is a Navy hospital corpsman who was deployed to Iraq's western Anbar Province with the Second Battalion, Fifth Marines Division from September 2004 until February 2005. He would have stayed longer, but on February 26, 2005, the Seattle native was hit by a rocket-propelled grenade (RPG) fired by an insurgent in Ramadi. His Marine Corps unit fired back, killing the seventeen-year-old boy who had launched the rocket.

Even though Suarez-Diaz was almost killed by the RPG fire, he nonetheless feels guilty about the death of his adversary. "I don't know how it is to be occupied and have your country devastated by another country," he told me. "He was a freedom fighter. He died fighting an occupation and I almost died for this lie that this war is based on. I told my Marines that I didn't agree that they killed him, but they did what they did and I respect them for it."

At the time, Suarez-Diaz said most of his Marine Corps buddies thought he was odd. They called him the "hippy doctor," and he was tolerated only because he saved their lives. But by the time his battalion was redeployed to Iraq in March 2007, many of them had come to agree with him. "They had changed their minds," he told me. "The prior Republican conservatives had turned left on the war. They came to see it as an occupation, and the war would not end until we—the foreigners—leave."

But political leaders in Washington have kept U.S. troops in Iraq. And so, over the ensuing years, the number of attacks on American soldiers steadily increased—from just over 1,000 a day in June 2003 to close to 4,000 daily in June 2007[8]—and while improved military technology has kept the number of soldiers killed in action from sky-rocketing, it has dramatically increased the number seriously wounded.

When the United States invaded Iraq in 2003, most soldiers were wearing Kevlar vests developed by military contractors in the 1980s. Those vests were a big improvement over Vietnam, when American troops wore nylon vests that couldn't stop a bullet. Body armor improved again as a result of controversy in Washington, and now nearly all U.S. soldiers in Iraq wear massive sixteen-pound Interceptor body armor, which uses ceramic plates that can stop small-arms rounds.[9]

The result? Fifteen out of every sixteen seriously wounded service members survive injuries that in previous wars would have been fatal. During the Vietnam era, only five out of eight injured soldiers survived.[10] "If you lost an arm or a leg in Vietnam, you were also tremendously injured in your chest and abdomen, which were not protected by the armor plates back then," explained Dr. Col. Vito Imbasciani, a urologist and state surgeon with the California National Guard. "Now, your heart and chest and lungs are protected by armor, leaving only your extremities exposed."

In 2006, Dr. Imbasciani spent four months at Landstuhl Regional Medical Center in Germany, where he treated the worst of the U.S. war wounded. He noted that an extremely high number of wounded soldiers were coming home with their arms or legs amputated. Imbasciani said he regularly amputated soldier's genitals.

"I walk into the operating room and the general surgeons are doing their work and there is the body of this Navy SEAL, which is a physical specimen to behold," he explained. "And his abdomen is open, they're exploring both intestines. He's missing both legs below the knee, one arm is blown off, he's got incisions on his thighs to relieve the pressure on the parts of the legs that are hopefully gonna survive and there's genital injuries, and you just want to cry."

By August 1, 2008, the Pentagon listed more than 78,000 service members as wounded, injured, and ill; 324,000 Iraq and Afghanistan veterans had already visited a VA facility to receive health care for their injuries, and close to 300,000 (more than 30 percent of eligible veterans) had filed for disability.[11] Physical brain damage is perhaps the most common injury; the RAND Corporation estimates that more than 320,000 veterans have experienced traumatic brain injury while deployed in Iraq or Afghanistan.[12] Many observers call TBI the "signature injury" of the Iraq War because it happens so often after a soldier is hit with a gunshot or a blast from a roadside bomb.

On March 19, 2004, Corporal Justin Bunce was partway through his second tour in Iraq, patrolling the city of Husayba on the Syrian border, when an IED exploded in the wall of a cemetery. The blast sent shrapnel into nearly every part of his body and knocked him into a coma for four days. With the high quality of Army field medicine, military doctors were able to keep him alive while they medically evacuated him to Landstuhl in Germany. There, doctors found some of the shrapnel had lodged in the left frontal lobe of his brain.

"Because of my injury, making new memories is hard as hell," twenty-five-year-old Bunce told a gathering on war and brain damage in Washington, D.C. "I've been leaving myself a dozen voice mails every day." Bunce also leaves a lot of messages on his parents' voice mail and writes reminder notes constantly on his left arm. "By the end of the day it looks like it's tattooed," he said. "My left side is paralyzed so I put it to good use. At least I can write on it."

Despite the severity of his injury, Justin Bunce is lucky. His father is retired Air Force colonel Peter Bunce—a politically connected lobbyist who now works as president and CEO of the General Aviation Manufacturers Association. With his income and connections in the military and Congress, he has been able to navigate the myriad Pentagon and Department of Veterans Affairs bureaucracies necessary to get his son top-notch care at Walter Reed Medical Center and the National Rehabilitation Hospital in Washington, D.C.

After that, Col. Bunce arranged for his son to receive treatment at the Defense and Veterans Brain Injury Center in Charlottesville, Virginia—a Pentagon-funded transitional home for soldiers and veterans who've suffered physical brain damage. "The quality of care has, throughout his process, been phenomenal," the elder Bunce said. "They started to get him walking again and it was truly incredible to see that happening."

Getting that care has been a hassle, though. Col. Bunce has had to call in his connections on Capitol Hill to help him leap bureaucratic hurdles. Even then, staffing shortfalls at each of the facilities have been so great, and the bureaucracy so complicated, that navigating the maze has proved difficult even for a well-connected person like Col. Bunce. At one point, for example, his son Justin had been discharged from the military, but not yet admitted to the VA health system. As a result, the family had to pay $20,000 of their own money to ensure that Justin's care, and recovery, would continue uninterrupted.

"I know my father has been through a lot of people trying to get the care all sorted out, and I'm so grateful," Justin said. He noted that quality health care has made a big difference. "Now I'm actually horseback riding," he said. "One of the first things I said when I got out of my coma was that I wanted horseback riding and acupuncture and I'm getting both now. . . . It's incredible. I ride the same two horses every time we go there. They see me and they actually walk toward me. They come toward me and lick me on the cheeks. They're my buddies. My balance has just shot through the roof because of horseback riding."

Yet even with all that care, Justin is still blind in one eye. He still walks with a cane. Parts of his body remain paralyzed. His father told me that Justin still dreams of a recovery that would allow him to re-join his unit and redeploy and help his buddies fight the war in Iraq, but that seems like an impossibility.

"He still has shrapnel is his brain and he lost his right eye over there," the elder Bunce told me. "The other shrapnel wounds from the rest of his body have healed, but when you have a left frontal lobe in-jury, part of the governor that keeps you and I from saying things that we might be thinking but not vocalizing kind of goes away. When you take a twenty-five-year-old man—especially when there are young ladies around—the things he says are unpredictable and definitely a lot of the time not appropriate."

Justin's medical needs now dominate the Bunce family's lives. They sold their home in Washington, which had stairs Justin could no longer navigate, and moved into a more horizontal house in suburban Virginia. Justin has doctors' appointments at the VA in Washington at least four days a week and must be taken to and from each visit. Col. Bunce knows his son will probably never fully recover, but he nonetheless considers "the glass half full."

"The alternative is that I wouldn't have my son," he said. "And I would do anything for him and his buddies who sacrificed so much for our freedom. That's just something you do as a parent. Had it been the Vietnam War, these guys wouldn't be coming home."

Corporal Justin Bunce has a severe traumatic brain injury. According to George Zitney, cofounder of the Defense and Veterans Brain Injury Center, only about 10 percent of Iraq and Afghanistan vets with TBI had "severe and penetrating" wounds to the head.

Many more soldiers likely suffer undiagnosed, mild, or moderate traumatic brain injury. In April 2007, military doctors released a report showing that 18 percent of soldiers deployed to Iraq and Afghanistan from Fort Carson, Colorado, exhibited at least one of the symptoms associated with mild TBI, which include headaches, memory loss, irritability, difficulty sleeping, and balance problems.[13]

In their survey, Fort Carson doctors relied on a special screening three to four months after a soldier's return home and on input from family members and the chain of command.[14] "Symptoms can present themselves at different points in time," Col. John Cho, who commands the Evans Army Community Hospital at Fort Carson, told the Associated Press. "You might ask why," he said. "I can only surmise that when a soldier returns to the United States and is subjected to the activities of daily living—traffic, making formation . . . perhaps the stressors then bring some of these symptoms to light."[15]

This study's results, if extrapolated across all soldiers and Marines deployed in the war (and there's no reason to expect soldiers from different bases had different experiences in Iraq), would mean more than three hundred twenty thousand Iraq and Afghanistan war veterans suffer from some form of traumatic brain injury. These statistics from Fort Carson are consistent with the RAND Corporation figure mentioned above. Yet only a few thousand cases have been diagnosed.

Like most veterans, Sgt. Patrick Campbell has never been screened or treated for TBI. On the surface, he doesn't appear to need treatment. A former student body president at the University of California, Berkeley, Campbell now works as legislative director for Iraq and Afghanistan Veterans of America, the first and largest group supporting post-9/11 vets. He's also in law school, finishing up his JD at Catholic University in Washington, D.C.

But Campbell said he's changed below the surface in ways only he can see. During his tour in Iraq, the National Guardsman experienced multiple concussions. "I was exposed to my first possible traumatic brain injury when a pound tank catch fell on my head," he told me. "I knocked myself out, and because I was the medic I told everyone 'I'm good. Let's go.' But I knew that I wasn't."

It was one of many head injuries Campbell sustained in Iraq. "While I was in Iraq I was involved in many motor vehicle accidents," he said. "We flipped a tank. We flipped a Humvee. While I was there, I had a mortar rocket land about fifteen feet from me. Thankfully, I was standing on the other side of a wall, but just the wave of air [from the explosion] almost knocked me over."

Despite the lack of a diagnosis, Campbell has noticed a change since his service in the war: "I have a real trouble remembering things," he said. "If I'm going somewhere I have to write it down. I write things on my hand all the time."

At the urging of health care advocates, Campbell took an online test for traumatic brain injury, which revealed he now has "severe short term memory loss." He hasn't gone into treatment for the condition, but nonetheless found the test helpful. "It helped me understand what was going on in my life," he said. "For a lot of these guys coming back who are trying to deal with who they've become, that understanding what happened to them will begin that process."

Medical professionals are also concerned that if cases like Campbell's aren't caught early on, they could become more debilitating over time. "I think everyone has probably heard of the shaken baby syndrome," explained Dr. Gene Bolles, who served as the former chief of neurosurgery at Landstuhl from the 9/11 attacks until March 2004. "That's a syndrome whereby if you shake up the brain or just have a concussive effect with a change in barometric pressure, that you can have an injury to the fibers within the brain itself, within the neurofibers. And these unfortunately do not show up on the tests that we use many times, and yet these patients do have injuries that end up being less obvious at least initially and it's only [apparent] as they begin to function—they may have headaches, dizziness, the inability to learn, they may lose ability to recognize words."

Also of concern, Bolles said, is that physical brain damage from roadside bombs can cause psychological illness like post-traumatic stress disorder. The psychological injury then makes it harder to cope with the physical one.

For these reasons, Bolles believes veterans should be screened for traumatic brain injury not only when they first get back from the front, but regularly over the years. "There are rather subtle changes that show up as time goes on," he said. "Often these patients are seen by doctors and appropriate tests are done and you don't see anything so you're told that well, can't find anything abnormal it must be emotional or this or that or the other, but these patients go on and often can remain permanently disabled in this way."

On April 13, 2007, the Department of Veterans Affairs issued a directive that, going forward, all troops returning from Iraq and Afghanistan who seek care at the VA would be screened for TBI.[16] The screening would consist of a questionnaire similar to the one in the Fort Carson study, with VA staff asking veterans about events that may have

Screening Test for Brain Injury

The Pentagon-funded **Defense and Veterans Brain Injury Center,** or
DVBIC (www.dvbic.org, 800-870-9244), has developed a simple, three-
question survey to help service members and veterans learn if they're
suffering from undiagnosed, mild traumatic brain injury.

1. Did you have any injury(ies) during your deployment from any of the
   following? (check all that apply):

   A. ☐ Fragment

   B. ☐ Bullet

   C. ☐ Vehicular (any type of vehicle, including airplane)

   D. ☐ Fall

   E. ☐ Blast (improvised explosive device, RPG, land mine, grenade, etc.)

   F. ☐ Other   specify: _____

2. Did any injury received while you were deployed result in any of the
   following? (check all that apply):

   A. ☐ Being dazed, confused, or "seeing stars"

   B. ☐ Not remembering the injury

   C. ☐ Losing consciousness (knocked out) for less than a minute

   D. ☐ Losing consciousness for 1–20 minutes

   E. ☐ Losing consciousness for longer than 20 minutes

   F. ☐ Having any symptoms of concussion afterward (such as headache,
       dizziness, irritability, etc.)

   G. ☐ Head injury

   H. ☐ None of the above

3. Are you currently experiencing any of the following problems that you
   think might be related to a possible head injury or concussion? (check all
   that apply):

   A. ☐ Headaches   E. ☐ Ringing in the ears

   B. ☐ Dizziness   F. ☐ Irritability

C. ☐ Memory problems   G. ☐ Sleep problems

D. ☐ Balance problems   H. ☐ Other specify:_____

According to the DVBIC, a service member or veteran who endorses an injury (any positive response to question 1), as well as experiencing an alteration of consciousness (question 2, A–E], should be further evaluated via clinical interview because he/she is more highly suspect for having sustained a traumatic brain injury or concussion. Endorsement of any item under question 3 can be used to verify symptoms that may be related to a traumatic brain injury if the screening and clinical interview process determines that such an injury occurred.

increased their risk of TBI and any symptoms experienced immediately following or slowly developing after such an event. A veteran who answers "yes" to any of those questions would be given a follow-up appointment for a physical examination and further evaluation.

Since then, the military itself has followed suit. Landstuhl Regional Medical Center has begun screening all patients airlifted to Germany for traumatic brain injury. The military has also implemented a series of new protocols in the war zone designed to catch brain injuries among soldiers still stationed in Iraq.

"The new set of guidelines involve screening all folks who've undergone any incident which might have put them at risk of having a traumatic brain injury," the head of the Defense and Veterans Brain Injury Center, Lt. Col. Mike Jaffee told me. "Part of that management would include putting them on a profile which would not allow them to go outside the wire into harms way until there's evidence that they have recovered from that concussion."

There's little evidence that's happening in practice, however, as you'll see in cases throughout the rest of this book. "The pressures on commanders in the field are so strong," explained Sgt. Patrick Campbell. "If the commander allows a soldier to sit out and recover, it means some other guy is going to have to do double duty and not sleep for two days. That also puts pressure on the soldier. You don't want to be screwing your buddies by not doing your duties."

Campbell's organization, Iraq and Afghanistan Veterans of America (IAVA), argues that what's really needed is pre- and postdeployment cognitive tests to make sure that soldiers' brains have not changed as a result of their service overseas. Those screenings are already mandated by a 1998 federal law, but as with many laws designed to protect America's fighting men and women, the Bush administration has refused to implement it.

On the eve of the invasion of Iraq, President Bush's assistant secretary of defense for health affairs, Dr. William Winkenwerder, told a congressional committee that a predeployment "screening" could be as simple as asking a soldier to fill out a pile of paperwork. A medical examination, he said, is simply "a gathering of information to determine a person's health." Dr. Winkenwerder added that the bulk of service members are "young, healthy individuals who don't necessarily need a hands-on physical . . . [and] a physical examination generally does not add an amount of useful information about the health of a group of young, healthy people."

Needless to say, most soldiers' brains are not screened before deployment. "They need to take a look at people before they go, just like we do with vision, and hearing and then after you come home," IAVA's Campbell said. "Right now, they don't do that because it saves them a lot of money—not only the costs of additional screenings, but also the costs of caring for us. They can say 'We just think you were dumb before and you don't have any paperwork to prove you weren't.' " Campbell believes Pentagon officials have not ordered the screenings because they're afraid of what they might find—especially since the vast majority of servicemen and women are currently on their second, third, or fourth tour in Iraq.

"If they were to say anyone with mild TBI could not be sent back [to Iraq], it would sink the force," Campbell noted. "It's just like post-traumatic stress disorder. The reason we're not doing mass scale screenings is that the Pentagon doesn't want the answers to these questions. Traumatic brain injury and PTSD shouldn't disqualify you from further military service, but they shouldn't be able to deploy you again without treating your wounds."

PART II

FIGHTING THE PENTAGON

4

THE SCANDAL AT WALTER REED

On Sunday, February 18, 2007, the headline "Soldiers Face Neglect, Frustration at Army's Top Medical Facility" splashed across the front page of the *Washington Post*. The article, which described unsafe conditions and substandard care at Walter Reed Army Medical Center, began with the story of Army specialist Jeremy Duncan who was airlifted out of Iraq in February 2006 with a broken neck and a shredded left ear, "nearly dead from blood loss."[1]

"Behind the door of Army Spec. Jeremy Duncan's room, part of the wall is torn and hangs in the air, weighted down with black mold," the article read. "When the wounded combat engineer stands in his shower and looks up, he can see the bathtub on the floor above through a rotted hole. The entire building, constructed between the world wars, often smells like greasy carry-out. Signs of neglect are everywhere: mouse droppings, belly-up cockroaches, stained carpets, cheap mattresses."

The *Post* reported that patients inside Walter Reed, which sits just five miles from the White House, found it difficult to receive the care they were promised and felt they deserved. "On the worst days, soldiers say they feel like they are living a chapter of 'Catch-22,'" Dana

Priest and Anne Hull wrote. "The wounded manage other wounded. Soldiers dealing with psychological disorders of their own have been put in charge of others at risk of suicide. Disengaged clerks, unqualified platoon sergeants and overworked case managers fumble with simple needs: feeding soldiers' families who are close to poverty, replacing a uniform ripped off by medics in the desert sand or helping a brain-damaged soldier remember his next appointment."

An amputee who had lived at Walter Reed for over a year, twenty-six-year-old Marine Sgt. Ryan Groves, told the paper his life had turned into a daily fight with the military bureaucracy. "We don't know what to do," he said. "The people who are supposed to know don't have the answers. It's a nonstop process of stalling."

When the story broke, politicians from both parties expressed outrage and promised solutions. Walter Reed's commander, Maj. Gen. George Weightman, was fired almost immediately. Following him out the door was the secretary of the Army, Frances Harvey.

On Capitol Hill, a barrage of hearings ensued, with politicians tripping over each other to denounce the deplorable conditions described by the paper. At one hearing, Republican congressman Tom Davis of Virginia produced an internal Army memo dated October 12, 2006, that described problems with housing and staffing at the facility. "You knew these were problems," Davis said to the Army surgeon general, Lt. Gen. Kevin Kiley, wondering aloud why nothing was done to improve the situation.[2]

In response to such withering critique, military brass were contrite: "Our counselors and case managers are overworked," the Army's vice chief of staff, Gen. Richard Cody, told one congressional committee. "We do not adequately communicate necessary information. Our administrative processes are needlessly cumbersome, and quite frankly, take too long. Our medical holding units are not manned to the proper level, and we do not assign leaders who can ensure proper accountability, proper discipline, and well-being of our wounded soldiers and their health, welfare and morale, and our facilities are not maintained to standards we know are right."[3]

On March 6, 2007, President Bush announced the formation of a bipartisan independent commission led by former Republican senator Bob Dole and the Clinton administration's Health and Human Services secretary, Donna Shalala. "It's unacceptable to me, it's unacceptable to you, it's unacceptable to our country, and it's not going to continue," Bush told the American Legion in a speech announcing the commission creation. "My decisions have put our kids in harm's way. And I'm concerned about the fact that when they come back they don't get the full treatment they deserve."[4]

Three weeks later, on March 30, Bush paid a visit to Walter Reed and apologized again: "I was disturbed by their accounts of what went wrong," Bush told the hospital staff after a tour of the facility. "It is not right to have someone volunteer to wear our uniform and not get the best possible care. I apologize for what they went through, and we're going to fix the problem."[5]

But the allegations raised in the *Washington Post* were not actually new. In February 2005, the exact same conditions had been exposed in a damning series in the online magazine *Salon*. Wounded soldiers at Walter Reed, reporter Mark Benjamin wrote, were "overmedicated, forced to talk about their mothers instead of Iraq, and have to fight for disability pay. Traumatized combat vets say the Army is failing them, and after a year following more than a dozen soldiers at Walter Reed Hospital, I believe them."[6]

It's not that top Bush administration officials didn't know about Walter Reed's problems. It's just that they had other priorities. Indeed, before the *Washington Post* put the facility's substandard conditions on its front page, President Bush's appointees at the Pentagon had strenuously lobbied Congress *against* funding military pensions, health insurance, and benefits for widows of retirees. They argued that money spent caring for wounded soldiers and their families could be better spent on new, state-of-the-art military hardware or enticing new recruits to join the force.

In January 2005, Bush's Undersecretary of Defense for Personnel and Readiness David Chu (the official in charge of such things) went so far as to tell the *Wall Street Journal* that veterans' medical care and disability benefits "are hurtful" and "are taking away from the nation's ability to defend itself."[7] Before the scandal at Walter Reed broke, the Bush Administration ran programs for injured soldiers much the same as it did the rest of the war: for the benefit of a narrow group of well-connected contractors.

In 2005, with tens of thousands of casualties already reported, a Pentagon commission recommended closing Walter Reed by 2011. When the commission report became public, the Bush administration moved to privatize the facility for as long as it would remain open, turning management of the hospital over to IAP World Services, a politically well-connected firm with almost no experience in military medicine. The Florida-based IAP had also faced scrutiny from Congress for unseemly profiteering after Hurricane Katrina. After the levees broke, FEMA ordered IAP to deliver 211 million pounds of ice for cooling food, medicine, and sweltering victims of the storm. Instead, the company trucked the ice in circles around the country at taxpayers' expense, with much of it ending up in storage 1,600 miles away in Maine.[8] But in January 2006, this was the company that won the military's five-year $120 million contract to operate Walter Reed.

The IAP leadership had an extensive record of corruption. Before becoming the company's CEO, Al Neffgen was a top executive at Halliburton's subsidiary, Kellogg, Brown & Root, where he was responsible for "all work performed by KBR for the U.S. government."[9] That included testifying before congressional committees about why Halliburton (which had earlier been run by Dick Cheney) had overcharged American taxpayers by hundreds of millions of dollars while providing support for U.S. troops in Iraq. Neffgen wasn't the only well-connected person at IAP. The company's president, aptly named David Swindle, was also a former Halliburton executive. And one of IAP's directors was former Republican vice president Dan Quayle.

Employees started to leave Walter Reed before the deal was even finalized, figuring they would lose their jobs anyway. When news of the proposed contract first surfaced in 2005, three hundred federal employees provided facilities-management services at Walter Reed. That dropped to fewer than sixty by February 3, 2007, the day before IAP took over. The company then proceeded to replace the remaining sixty federal employees with fifty private workers.[10]

Inside Walter Reed, alarm bells were sounding. On September 21, 2006, Garrison Cdr. Peter Garibaldi wrote to the installation's commanding general, saying that privatization had put "patient care services at risk . . . of mission failure." Garibaldi's memo said, "We face the critical issues of retaining skilled personnel for the hospital and diverse professionals for the Garrison, while confronted with increased difficulty in hiring."[11]

No one took notice then, and nothing significant has been done since to improve care or lessen bureaucracy at Walter Reed or at the nationwide network of Pentagon and VA hospitals. Military hospitals are still short staffed. Injured soldiers are still left alone for hours, or even days.

In September 2007, a congressionally mandated report by the non-partisan Government Accountability Office (GAO) found that Pentagon and VA care for service members suffering from PTSD and traumatic brain injury was "inadequate," with "significant shortfalls" of doctors, nurses, and other caregivers necessary to treat wounded soldiers. According to the GAO, "46 percent of the Army's returning service members who were eligible to be assigned to a [medical] unit had not been assigned due in part to staffing shortages." Over half of the military's special "Wounded Warrior Transition Units" had staffing shortfalls of more than 50 percent. Key bases like Fort Lewis in Washington State and Fort Carson in Colorado were short massive amounts of doctors, nurses, and squad leaders.[12] In short, the Bush administration was simply not hiring enough doctors and nurses to care for what had become a tidal wave of soldiers wounded in Iraq and Afghanistan.

Gerald J. "G. J." Cassidy was drawn to the military from a very young age. As the youngest of six children growing up in suburban Indianapolis in the early 1980s, he enjoyed playing Army around the family home. "He and his cousin Ryan would roam around, finding 'bunkers' and attacking here and there," said his uncle, Mike Cassidy. "It was always the USA versus the Soviet Union, or G. I. Joe versus Cobra."[13]

As a teenager, G. J. became more interested in battle strategy. He painstakingly painted tiny toy soldiers in historically accurate uniforms and positioned them atop the family's ping-pong table, reenacting battles with his friends. "They spent hours, month after month, year after year, painting figures of the different wars," his mother, Kay McMullen told me. "His favorite was the Civil War. They would refight the Civil War over and over again. He always had an affinity for strategy and always wanted to have something to do with the military."

G. J. spent his summers at Culver Military Academy in northern Indiana, where he became a member of the Black Horse Troop, an elite equestrian detail. By age seventeen, he had achieved the title of adjutant commander, and he convinced his mother to sign a waiver allowing him to join the U.S. Army Reserve. He went through basic training between his junior and senior year of high school. Over the next fourteen years, as G. J. graduated from the University of Alabama, married, and fathered two children, the Army remained an important part of his life.

After finishing his commitment to the Army Reserve, he switched to the Indiana National Guard and served in Bosnia in 2004 and also in New Orleans after Hurricane Katrina in 2005. "He loved being in Bosnia, even though he missed his wife and children, because he felt like he was really doing something," his mother remembered. "The Serbs were trying to annihilate the Muslims and the Muslims would come up to him and thank him. They wanted to hug the soldiers because they knew that without the American soldiers they would face being killed. He felt like he served a real purpose and he loved it."

In March 2006, G. J. volunteered for a tour in Iraq—motivated to serve and help others the same way he had done in Bosnia and Louisiana. Because the Indiana National Guard wasn't scheduled to be sent until 2007, he was reassigned to the Minnesota Guard before being deployed overseas.

In Iraq, he was assigned to Camp Scania, a truck stop along the main supply route from Baghdad to Kuwait. American convoys heading north to Baghdad stop at Scania, where they refuel and use the PX and head north. According to the well-regarded military affairs Web site GlobalSecurity.org, the camp is isolated, far from any Iraqi towns and cities: "It has all the ambiance of a land fill. Scania is a walled community, a lot like a prison in reverse. There is a high wall topped with razor wire and guard towers. The walls are to keep the bad guys out and the good guys protected. One end of the base is the fuel point; the other is living, and logistics."[14]

As a sergeant, G. J. regularly commanded small groups of soldiers who went outside the base to hunt down and kill the fighters who mortared the base and planted roadside bombs. It was grueling work, much more dangerous than his service in Bosnia.

"On June 28, 2006, he was in a convoy and there was a Humvee ahead of them and his gunner said 'Sir, I'm almost sure there is a roadside bomb over there,'" his mother Kay told me. "And my son, being in charge of those eight men, turned to look at it and it exploded. The Hummer ahead of them took the full brunt and there were men killed in that." The blast sent G. J. flying and knocked him unconscious. When he woke up, his family said he was not given medical attention, but kept on in his duties—conducting raids, escorting convoys, and guarding the perimeter of Camp Scania.

When he returned to the United States in April 2007, G. J. was finally given a medical evaluation. Doctors at Fort McCoy, Wisconsin, diagnosed the sergeant with post-traumatic stress disorder, noting he had sustained a concussion and suffered from memory loss, severe migraines, and permanent partial hearing loss.

Following procedures developed after the scandal at Walter Reed, the doctors put a "medical hold" on G. J.'s discharge from active duty and sent him to Fort Knox, Kentucky, where he was assigned to one of the Army's newly created Wounded Warrior Transition Units, where injured soldiers are each supposed to be assigned a doctor, a nurse care manager, and a squad leader to manage treatment.

The new unit didn't work well for G. J. On September 21, 2007, five months after arriving home from Iraq, Sgt. G. J. Cassidy was found dead in his room at Fort Knox.

"This is something that is serious to Fort Knox and to the Army," base spokeswoman Connie Shaffery told the Associated Press after G. J.'s family complained to the media. "Every aspect of his death is being investigated," she added.[15]

But G. J.'s family wasn't satisfied with the Army's response. "He died from lack of care," his mother told me tearfully. "He came back from Iraq, and the Army killed him." According to his family, the medical ward at Fort Knox was so understaffed that G. J. was lucky to have one doctor appointment and one psychiatrist appointment a month. "The young men, including him sometimes, would go and sit in chairs all day outside their doctor's office, waiting for a chance that someone wouldn't show up for an appointment, or if he could fit them in for a few minutes between appointments," Kay said.

Most of the time, Kay said, her son was left alone in his third-floor room, where he sat unattended playing games on his X-Box and laptop computer. One time, he passed out in his room by himself and woke up three or four hours later, lying in a pool of blood that he said had come from his mouth or nose. "He blacked out and fell forward and something in his head started bleeding. He doesn't know what, he was unconscious," Kay told me. "Another time, he was climbing the steps to his third-floor dormitory and he blacked out and hit his head against the wall and had abrasions all over his forehead. They knew that and they still let him stay in this third-floor room by himself with no buddy system, no hospitalization, no nothing."

On Wednesday, September 19, 2007, Kay had her final conversation with her son. G. J. complained of flashbacks brought on by maintenance work being done on his building at Fort Knox. The base's staff was replacing the shingles on the roof above his dorm room, and every time a new shingle went up or an old one was ripped off he felt like a bomb had exploded. He told his mom he hadn't slept in days.

Then, two days passed and neither Kay nor G. J.'s wife Melissa heard a word from him. The silence was eerie. G. J was bored at Fort Knox and called them three or four times a day. He almost always answered his phone and told them many times he couldn't wait for his medical hold to end so that he could get back to Indiana, where he planned to help raise his children and reenter the civilian workforce as a high-school teacher.

G. J.'s family knew something was wrong. At 8:00 A.M. on Friday, September 21, 2007, they got on the phone and called Fort Knox, trying to reach anyone who might be willing to go up to G. J.'s third-floor room to check and see if he was alright. At 7:00 P.M. on September 21, a soldier entered Sgt. Gerald Cassidy's room and found him sitting in a chair dead.

"They let a young man who had passed out in his room in a pool of blood, who had passed out and hit a wall—they let a young man like that live in a dormitory room all by himself, and when he didn't show up for [daily] roll call nobody went up to check on him for at least two and a half days," G. J.'s mother raged. "It's criminal negligence."

Military officials declined to comment on the specifics of G. J.'s death until a full investigation is completed, but an independent autopsy performed at the request of his family found that G. J. had died hours before being found and may have been unconscious for days.

On Monday, October 1, 2007, G. J. Cassidy received a full military funeral, which was attended by many of his state's most prominent officials. The commander of the Indiana National Guard, Gen. R. Martine Umbarger, gave the eulogy.

"Sgt. Cassidy represents citizen-soldiers everywhere who sacrifice family and career to serve their state and nation," the general said. "What a great American. What a fine young man. How blessed we are as a nation and as a state to have soldiers like Sgt. Cassidy who are willing to volunteer and to go in harm's way serving their country."[16]

Indiana governor Mitch Daniels also spoke at the funeral, presenting G. J.'s widow Melissa with a posthumous Purple Heart. "A free nation cannot survive, freedom cannot survive without people like Sgt. Cassidy," he said.[17]

Three weeks after his death, G. J.'s family got support from another source. One of Indiana's U.S. senators, Evan Bayh, wrote to Secretary of the Army Preston Geren (a former Democratic congressman from Texas who had been appointed to the position after his predecessor resigned because of the Walter Reed scandal). In his letter, Senator Bayh noted the September 2007 Government Accountability Office report (mentioned earlier this chapter), which demonstrated staffing shortfalls as high as 50 percent at the Army's Wounded Warrior Transition Units. The senator voiced concern that the Army was insufficiently caring for soldiers who, like Sgt. Cassidy, suffered physical brain damage while serving in Iraq.

"The GAO report also found that the Army is not properly screening and treating soldiers with TBI [traumatic brain injury], due in part to staffing shortfalls," the senator wrote. "I am aware that the Army has established policies to provide training on TBI to all of its nurse case managers and psychiatric nurses, among others. Yet as of September 13, 2007, only 6 of the Army's 32 Warrior Transition Units had completed TBI training for all staff.

"I ask that you share with me the Army's decision-making process behind sending SGT Cassidy to Fort Knox for treatment," Bayh continued. "Was this an appropriate facility? Also, what steps are being taken by the Army to determine the circumstances surrounding his tragic death? What is the Army doing to improve its Warrior Transition Unit program, especially for those who have suffered brain injuries? How often are wounded soldiers put into situations similar to that of SGT Cassidy? How might the current inadequacies of the Warrior Transition Unit program have contributed to his death? How might a properly functioning program have prevented it?"[18]

Like Senator Bayh, G. J. Cassidy's family is waiting for answers.

5

COMING TOGETHER

It is possible for wounded soldiers to get both quality and prompt care from the Pentagon and Department of Veterans Affairs' medical systems, but getting that care usually means a fight. Families who have received proper care for their sons and daughters report that forcing the government health care bureaucracies to give proper care can be a full time job.

According to the bipartisan Dole-Shalala Commission (formed to investigate the Walter Reed scandal), 21 percent of active-duty soldiers, 15 percent of reservists, and 24 percent of Iraq and Afghanistan veterans had "friends or family [that] gave up a job to be with them or act as their caregiver." In addition, 33 percent of active-duty soldiers, 22 percent of reservists, and 37 percent of recent veterans told the commission "that a family member or close friend relocated for extended periods of time to be with them while they were in the hospital."[1]

"Get to know the system," advises fifty-two-year-old Ed Edmundson, who quit his job as ConAgra Foods plant supervisor after his son Eric was severely wounded in an IED attack. "You have to do lots of research. Understand what the VA and Department of Defense are all about. Information empowers you and gives you options. Don't wait for things to come to you. You want to go out and seek them. If you don't, in many cases things are a long time coming."

On October 2, 2005, Specialist Eric Edmundson's Stryker unit was supporting a major Marine Corps offensive in a rural area along the Euphrates River near the Syrian border when one of their vehicles hit a landmine. No one was hurt in the explosion, and Eric's vehicle was sent to assess the damage.

"We were on our way to the damaged vehicle on a road that was between two large hills, in order to avoid detection from the nearby people," Capt. John Hawbaker wrote of the incident. "There was a small cornfield in the valley that was across a dirt road from the only house in the valley. Apparently, a terrorist was hiding in the cornfield to watch over a bomb in the road, and when we drove over his buried bomb he detonated it with a remote control." The Stryker vehicle was destroyed, sustaining a large hole right behind Eric's seat. According to Capt. Hawbaker, Eric was conscious but not aware of his surroundings.

"While we conducted casualty evacuation procedures and first aid, the rest of the troop spotted the terrorist and chased him into a house," Hawbaker said. Apache helicopters flew in and fired on it. "The triggerman/terrorist survived," Hawbaker added, "but was severely wounded and taken into custody."

While that was happening, a Marine gunship flew down and airlifted Eric and a wounded staff sergeant to al-Asad Airbase in western Iraq. There, doctors found shrapnel wounds to Eric's chest (which required the removal of his spleen) and his right leg. His back was broken in two different places.

Military doctors saved his life, but they could not work a miracle. Two days later, while Eric was still in Iraq awaiting transport to Germany, he had a heart attack and fell into a coma. It took doctors thirty minutes to revive him, during which time his brain was starved of oxygen, resulting in what's called an anoxic brain injury. When he finally arrived at Walter Reed, Eric could not walk, talk, eat, or drink. His family said he started to recover, but when he was transferred to the VA hospital in Richmond, Virginia, his family said his condition started to deteriorate.

The VA claims its hospital in Richmond is one of the best in the county. Bureaucrats have dubbed it a "polytrauma" center that specializes in patients with multiple serious wounds and injuries. But the Edmundsons quickly found the facility to be understaffed and overburdened. Most of the patients were geriatric veterans of World War II and Korea. "They weren't able to meet Eric's challenges medically and rehabilitatively," his father Ed told me. "They weren't set up staffwise, trainingwise, to deal with him and so Eric started to disintegrate."

The entire family, including Eric's mother, wife, and baby daughter, temporarily relocated to Virginia. Ed quit his job as a supervisor at Con-Agra Foods so he could work full-time as his son's caretaker and advocate. "He suffers a lot of cognitive issues, he can't speak, he really needed an advocate and we were trying to battle our way through that labyrinth of bureaucracy called the government," Ed remembered.

The decision put the family in a difficult spot. Ed's abrupt departure from the workplace left them completely dependant on his wife's income as a social worker. In addition to their son's injury, the family now had their own financial problems. And Ed himself no longer had health insurance.

But it was necessary, Ed said, because without the family's strenuous efforts their son might have never recovered. After Eric's health declined at the VA, officials there recommended he be transferred to a nursing home. The family was told that Eric, then twenty-six, would never emerge from what had become a persistent vegetative state. "We had to get Eric out of that system," Ed explained. "We took him out and took him home and he was home for about six months."

While caring for Eric at home, Ed began researching his options. He knew that if the Army discharged his son, he would be purged from the Army's TRICARE insurance system. TRICARE, unlike the VA, covers specialized care outside the government system. So Ed insisted that his son be left on active duty. It was a hard-fought battle.

Ed and Eric's sister, Anna, got on the phone. They called their representatives in Washington, attended meetings and conferences, and met with advocates at long-standing organizations like the American Legion and Veterans of Foreign Wars—as well as new groups like the Jacksonville, Florida–based Wounded Warrior Project, which was founded after 9/11 by John Melia, a Marine Corps veteran whose helicopter exploded and crashed into the seas off Somalia in 1992. Through their research, the Edmundsons learned what no one at the VA or the Pentagon wanted to tell them: that Ed was eligible for treatment at the Rehabilitation Institute of Chicago, one of the nation's premier hospitals for treatment of traumatic brain injury. During Eric's stay, he would be the only veteran there.

In Chicago, Eric's condition improved dramatically. Dr. Joanne Smith, head of the institute, told the *New York Times* that the hospital's first step was to use drugs, technology, and devices "to reverse the ill effects of not getting adequate care earlier." For example, the *Times* reported, Eric's hips, knees, and ankles were frozen "in the position of someone sitting in a hallway in a chair." Doctors helped straighten him out to help him stand. They also taught him to express his basic needs using a communication board, and he learned to chew and swallow. "He has a profound cognitive disability," Dr. Smith told the paper. "But he can communicate, albeit not verbally, and can express emotions, including humor and even sarcasm."[2]

On June 29, 2007, Eric left the Rehabilitation Institute after making steady progress. He donned his uniform and, with the help of hospital staff, walked into the arms of his wife Stephanie and daughter Gracie, who by now was two and a half years old.

"Before he went to Chicago, his daughter would come up to him with a toy and he couldn't participate with her. He was unable to move anything and interact," his father Ed told me. "Since he came back from Chicago he can propel his wheelchair around the house with his legs. So he follows his wife and his daughter around the house. They go into the kitchen to cook something, he goes into the kitchen with them. He'll kick a ball around with his daughter. She climbs up on his lap. It's helped him tremendously."

Eric's recovery made headlines across the country. *ABC News* named Eric and Ed Edmundson its Person of the Week. "This is about a father and a son waging separate battles for the same cause," anchor Charles Gibson intoned. "It began when one of them was badly wounded in Iraq. The healing has taken them both further than they ever imagined."[3]

Ed Edmundson knows he could not have done it alone. In January 2007, after Eric was admitted to the Rehabilitation Institute, Ed was in a bind. He wanted to stay with his son to keep his spirits up, but he had already cashed out his retirement and had no idea how to pay for an extended stay in the Windy City.

That's when Will and Mary Beth Beiersdorf stepped in to help. After Will's 2001 deployment guarding Guantanamo Bay strained their family's finances, the north Chicago couple founded a charity called Salute Inc. to help families in similar situations. After seeing Eric in a local TV news story, the Beiersdorfs decided that their next family pizza party would benefit the Edmundsons. It was held at the Arlington Park Race Track and raised over $10,000.

"What Ed did with that was incredible," Mary Beth told me. "He used that to fly back and forth to Washington lobbying for help, pay bills back home in North Carolina, and get a place here in Chicago where he could stay with Eric for the next seven months."

The Edmundsons also received help from Homes for Our Troops, founded by contractor John Gonsalves in 2004. After the 9/11 attacks, Gonsalves had a surge of patriotism. He had more than twenty years of experience in construction and wanted to give back.

As the Iraq War began, he was watching the news when he witnessed a wounded soldier and thought, "What now? What will happen to this soldier?" When he researched the realities for injured soldiers, he learned the VA's largest help for disabled vets was a $50,000 grant to help make an existing home more accessible. That amounted to a small percentage of the money needed to overhaul a building, and the VA was only willing to give the grant to families that owned their home. Since many injured service members come from modest backgrounds, this meant that the people who needed help the most got no help at all.

According to the Homes for Our Troops Web site, Gonsalves began searching for an organization in his field of construction and home building where he could volunteer his services. When his search came up empty, he decided to create his own organization, and within months he founded Homes for Our Troops. The group has since built dozens of homes specifically designed for newly disabled war veterans. One of those homes, for M.Sgt. Luis Rodriquez, was featured on ABC's *Extreme Makeover: Home Edition.*

In 2006, Gonsalves met the Edmundsons at a steakhouse in Washington, D.C. At the time, Eric was at the VA hospital in Virginia. "There was one table open in the restaurant," Gonsalves told the *New Bern Sun Journal.* "The Edmundsons took it. I came in and sat down at the table with them."[4]

A year later, on October 5, 2007, Eric Edmundson rode his wheelchair up the ramp of his new home. The house has no stairs, and every doorway is wide enough for his wheelchair to pass through. It has a low counter in the kitchen so he can help cook and a front-loading washer-dryer so that he's able to help with the laundry. "Now he's able to participate in many things," his father Ed told me. "It's a great thing and he's really excited."

Homes for Our Troops had pledged $250,000 to help build the Edmundsons' home, but so many community members and business people stepped forward, the organization only used $5,000 of that. "Local people and businesses gave so much money," Gonsalves said. "The $245,000 we didn't use will go to the family of another troop on the waiting list."

With an accessible house taken care of, Ed Edmundson is looking forward to more relaxing days with his son. The two of them have started taking fishing trips on North Carolina's Atlantic coast. Soon, Ed hopes, father and son will open a bait and tackle shop.

Through his joy, Ed told me there's a lesson in his son's journey from the Richmond VA hospital to the Rehabilitation Institute of Chicago to his specially built home on North Carolina's Atlantic coast. "It's important to plan ahead," he said. "Look at Eric's home. We've been working on it for a year. If we would have waited until it was this point, it could have been a problem. But now when he's ready for the home, the home is ready for him."

Veterans' Charities, Good and Bad

Homes for Our Troops (www.homesforourtroops.org, 866-7-TROOPS) and the **Wounded Warrior Project** (www.woundedwarriorproject.org, 877-TEAM-WWP) are just two of many excellent charities that help injured veterans adjust to civilian life. But not every group that says it supports Iraq and Afghanistan spends its money wisely.

According to the American Institute of Philanthropy (www.charitywatch.org) many veterans' charities spend less than 60 percent of their budgets on bona fide charitable programs. Among the worst offenders: Paralyzed Veterans of America, Disabled American Veterans, American Veterans Coalition, the Military Order of the Purple Heart, and Help Hospitalized Veterans.

By contrast, **Fisher House Foundation** (www.fisherhouse.org, 888-294-8560) and **Intrepid Fallen Heroes Fund** (www.fallenheroesfund.org, 800-340-HERO) spent virtually all their money on helping veterans. Fisher House constructs facilities to house families temporarily while visiting patients in military and veterans' hospitals, and provides financial and other assistance to armed services personnel and veterans. The Fallen Heroes Fund provides cash assistance to severely injured veterans and their families. In 2007, the fund completed construction of a $40 million state-of-the-art physical rehabilitation center at Brooke Army Medical Center in San Antonio, Texas.

He added, "There are a lot of people who want to help, but you have to seek them out. They don't just walk up to your door and say 'Can I help you?' You have to seek them out. You have to take the initiative. There are people out there willing to help. They want to help. They just have to know who to help and what they need to do."

6

EDUCATION

The Edmundsons' story is heartwarming. It shows how regular Americans, pulling together, can overcome an indifferent bureaucracy and a Congress and president preoccupied with fundraising dinners with corporate fat cats. For many, Eric Edmundson's recovery gives hope. For me, it's also cause for concern.

The families of American soldiers injured in the line of duty should not have to go, hat in hand, looking for charity. A veteran like Eric Edmundson should not have to depend on the kindness of strangers, but should be cared for as a matter of course. A father like Ed Edmundson should not have to sacrifice his income and health and insurance to care for a son wounded in war. This is the very definition of the job of government.

People like Will and Mary Beth Beiersdorf, who reach out to help their fellow Americans, are happy to give back to their community, but they don't see their efforts as a replacement for the obligations of the government. By spotlighting what it takes for an injured veteran to make a full and successful recovery, the Beiersdorfs hope to push the government to provide more for those who sacrifice for their country.

"All the people that we've gotten involved with in our organization have never been involved in the military, and in all honesty if they had never gotten to know us they would never have imagined that this situation for the veterans exists, because the assumption is that the government, Uncle Sam, takes care of everything," Will said.

"The media does quick hits here and there," he continued, "but do you really think we're going to see Eric Edmundson on the TV in the next year or two? He'll be forgotten just like the rest of the people. That's why we want to keep them in the forefront. We've got to make sure the government fulfills its obligations to care for these guys when they're hurt, and give them good living conditions when they're not hurt."

Most people believe that this kind of government apathy is unique—if not to the Iraq war alone, certainly to Vietnam and the conflicts that followed. America no longer has a draft, some argue, meaning that the sacrifices of war are no longer shared across society but are instead borne by a new "military class" of warriors who come primarily from rural America and our country's inner cities. There are few people like the Beiersdorfs—comfortable, suburban families who nonetheless choose a life of military service. No wonder military families are being ignored.

The truth is that this kind of neglect goes back a lot farther. After World War I, tens of thousands of veterans had to camp on the National Mall in Washington to get their promised bonuses. Even during the Good War, World War II, journalists wrote of the "legion of the disabled, who had come home in mid-war to delay, neglect and dissolution."[1]

Writing in *American Legion Magazine,* David Camelon noted that official Washington essentially ignored soldiers wounded in World War II until veterans' groups made such complacency unpalatable.

His words, penned close to sixty years ago, read like they could have been written yesterday.

> War and its harsh truths were far away. . . . Casualties were unpleasant—but we accepted them as necessary. They were statistics. Part of the costs of war—and they happened to other people; people far away from the Pentagon building, the Mayflower Cocktail Lounge or the House and Senate Office Buildings. . . .
>
> Everybody was going to 'do something' for the veterans 'after the war.' It was a nice thought, but hazy. Meanwhile, soldiers, sailors, Marines were being shot and discharged. But the public had forgotten that before a war ends it has its veterans. It seems impossible to believe, now, that thousands of disabled men discharged during the war were forced to depend on charity for their very existence for months before the country they had fought to defend got around to caring for them.[2]

To combat that apathy, the American Legion presented Congress with the story of the "Forgotten Battalion" in 1943. Among the veterans profiled was Bill Smith, a Marine who had been declared unfit for service after a grenade at Guadalcanal destroyed nerves in his brain and paralyzed his left side. When he was discharged six and a half months later, no one helped him file for disability compensation. He was entitled to up to $100 a month, free hospitalization and medication, and vocational retraining. But the benefits didn't come because the paperwork hadn't been filed. Instead, Smith was turned out onto the street with a warning: find civilian clothes to replace his military uniform within ninety days. Smith went home paralyzed and penniless, waiting four months before his disability claim was adjudicated and vocational rehabilitation recommended.

"How did Bill and his mother live during those months?" Camelon asked. "No one seemed to know, or, apart from the Legion, to care. Perhaps he was able to drag his paralyzed body to his neighbor's door for a handout."[3] In his book, *When Dreams Came True: The GI Bill and the Making of Modern America,* journalist Michael Bennett notes that "the road to the passage of the GI Bill had to be built over the broken bodies, and sometimes broken minds, of thousands of early casualties of the war."[4]

Fear was also a factor that turned out to be instrumental in the success of the GI Bill. The Great Depression had only been stopped by the advent of a war economy, and politicians in Washington worried that another depression might ensue if the twelve million serving in 1944 were dumped on an economy potentially on the verge of bankruptcy when the mills of war stopped churning.

In April 1942, for example, Eleanor Roosevelt warned that veterans could "create a dangerous pressure group in our midst." The nation would have to "adjust our economic system so that opportunity is open to them, [or] we may reap the whirlwind."[5] Both sides of the political spectrum shared this concern, especially with communism and fascism on the rise in Europe. Republican congressman Fish, of New York told his U.S. House colleges that unless something was done to provide for returning veterans, "I believe we would have chaotic and revolutionary conditions in America." Unless returning veterans could find jobs, warned Representative Maury Maverick, a liberal Democrat, the country could become a "dictatorship."

The result was that, for one of the only times in American history, the U.S. government did right by its veterans. In 1944, President Franklin Roosevelt signed the GI Bill into law, calling it the final part of his New Deal program. The law, officially known as the Servicemen's Readjustment Act, promised veterans the government would pay the entire cost of tuition and books at any public or private college or job-training program. It also provided unemployment insurance and loans to purchase homes and start businesses.

All told, 7.8 million World War II veterans received a full ride at a four-year college or university. As a result, thousands of veterans graduated from Harvard and Yale. Humorist Art Buchwald used the GI Bill to attend the Sorbonne in Paris. On March 18, 1946, *Time* magazine asked, "Why go to Podunk College, when the Government will send you to Yale?"[6]

Since then, however, the power of veterans waned in Washington, and the GI Bill was systematically weakened. The American Legion didn't fight for a strong GI Bill after the Korean War ended in a stalemate and so, unlike World War II veterans, Korean War vets were forced to pay their own college tuition out of a small monthly stipend—which was only enough to pay the bills at the cheapest public universities. As a result, there were only 78,000 veterans in college in 1954, and only 42,000 in 1955.[7]

Vietnam War veterans received similarly small stipends, and after Vietnam the value of the GI Bill continued to deteriorate. While a major overhaul of the GI Bill improved education benefits for veterans starting in July 2008, for the first seven years after 9/11 returning Iraq and Afghanistan war veterans had access to benefits outlined in the 1984 Montgomery GI Bill, which demanded active-duty members accept a pay reduction of $100 per month through twelve months of military service. If veterans returned to school after service, they were eligible to receive up to $1,100 a month for a maximum of thirty-six months of education benefits. It's an amount that didn't come close to covering most of a modern college education, but it did help some veterans—if they could get through the red tape.

In July 2005, twenty-three-year-old Paris Lee was honorably discharged after serving just under three years in the Army. A native of California's rural, picturesque North Coast where towering old-growth redwoods grow, he returned home and enrolled in a free ten-week college prep program called Veterans Upward Bound at Humboldt State University.

Lee was preparing to enroll in a bachelor's program at Humboldt State in September 2007, but in May of that year, he received a letter from the Department of Veterans Affairs denying his application for the GI Bill. "They said I'm not eligible because I served thirty-five months and two days in the Army," he told me. "Normally, you have to serve thirty-six months to get education benefits, so they're trying to deny me based on twenty-eight days."

Lee is comparably lucky. Veterans Upward Bound at Humboldt State was one of only forty-four college prep programs in the nation geared specifically for veterans, and it employed a Vietnam veteran as a counselor. He helped Lee send an appeal letter to the VA regional office in Muskogee, Oklahoma. While Lee waited for the response, the U.S. Army veteran worked dealing cards for black jack, pai gow, and Texas hold 'em at the Blue Lake Indian Casino east of Arcata. (In August 2007, the Department of Education cut the funding for Veterans Upward Bound at Humboldt State. The successful program shut its doors a few months later.)

According to the VA, veterans seeking GI Bill benefits must fill out a twelve-page form, which is then submitted to the college or university of choice. On its Web site the VA says it's not uncommon to receive an additional letter from the agency requesting more information. Questions must be answered to the VA's satisfaction to complete the application process. A notice of eligibility usually takes between four and eight weeks.

When the system is working properly, checks arrive a few months later, forcing most veterans to take out loans so they can pay tuition up-front before reimbursement by the government. With a process

Finding Community at School

A nationwide list of **Veterans Upward Bound** college prep programs can be found online at www.veteransupwardbound.org.

Veterans at Sierra Community College in Northern California have founded the first **Veterans Club** in the nation (www.sierracollege.edu, look under Student Services, then Campus Life, then Clubs; 916-789-2879). The club provides a community for student veterans with similar experiences. The club also encourages student veterans to broaden their self-image and fosters lifestyle management principles that contribute to success with veterans' academic, community, spiritual, and emotional needs.

like that, it's little wonder that, according to the federal Department of Education, veterans are much less likely to graduate from college than students who have never served in the military. The department's most recent data show that just 3 percent of veterans who entered a four-year college in 1995 graduated by 2001, compared with a 30 percent overall graduation rate.

Another reason for that gap is the military experience itself. The headquarters of the TELACU Foundation rise off the south side of Olympic Boulevard in the heart of East Los Angeles. Founded in 1968 as a series of nonprofit companies to bring vitality to the run-down, mostly Latino section of Southern California, TELACU is home to the state's only other Veterans Upward Bound program.

Thirty-two-year-old Jorge Reyes Jr. is one of its students. Trained as a machine gunner, he served ten years in the Army and had considered a career in the service. But after his first tour in Iraq, he decided to leave the military when his term was up. "There were too many close calls, too many signs," he told me.

Because of his experience and dark skin, the Army offered him a $32,000 bonus to re-up in a special operations unit. His superiors wanted to teach him Arabic, dress him up in local clothing, and send him out to infiltrate "the insurgency." They made the offer while Reyes was still in Iraq. At the time, he was working as a rear gunner on Humvees sent on patrol in Diyala, Najaf, and Baghdad. "I called my mom on the satellite phone," he said, "and I told her and she just yelled at me and told me I was crazy, and it was funny because while I was on the phone with her a couple of bullets whizzed by my ear, and I don't know if that was an omen or a sign or what, but later that day I told my commanding officer that I didn't want to do it."

Reyes said his commanding officer told him to "think it over," but the "signs" kept coming. "On my way out, on my last day there, an RPG [rocket-propelled grenade] shattered our Chinook [helicopter] and it just missed us," he said. "I was like, fuck, on my last day in Iraq I almost get blown up, and it was just a week before that that twelve people were killed in a Chinook."

Reyes needed reconstructive knee surgery after his first tour in Iraq, but he considers himself lucky. Four soldiers in his division were shot in the head and lived. One of his closest friends was blinded for life. "You see these things, and movies don't even come close to what it is to be there," he said, "but it's those kinds of things that make you understand that there's more out there for you."

Still, it was difficult for Reyes to get on with his life after a decade in the armed forces. He had become addicted to the rush of battle and had become used to the camaraderie. By his own admission, he spent his first two years as a civilian "doing nothing." His first year out of the Army he didn't even return to the United States. Instead, he hung out in Germany near a U.S. military base where he became romantically involved with a Russian immigrant. When he finally flew home

to Los Angeles and enrolled in the local community college, he found
himself adrift and failing.

"The hardest thing for me was computers," he told me. "I joined
the military in 1997, and from 1997 until 2007 technology has changed
dramatically, while the only thing I learned during those years was
how to clean my M-16 or how to mount up a .50-caliber machine
gun."

He also had trouble relating to the other students. At eighteen to
twenty years old, most of his classmates were a decade younger than
him. They had not been to war, had not been in the military, and their
lack of discipline grated on him during class. His break came when a
girlfriend introduced him to the Veterans Upward Bound program
after she received a scholarship from a different program at the
TELACU Foundation. There, he found a friendly atmosphere of fellow veterans and teachers who taught him computer skills and helped
him brush up on the material he had learned, but forgotten, from high
school.

"We're finding that a lot of veterans who don't have a stepping-
stone program don't complete it [college prep], or they enroll into college and they're placed into remedial English and remedial math,"
TELACU's Nani Escudero told me. "It's not because they're not
savvy," she said, "but because they've been away from school for five,
ten, or fifteen years so they don't have that foundation that they had
in high school, so we academically prepare them for college-level English and college-level math and also just prepare them for the class-
room environment."

With the help of TELACU and Veterans Upward Bound, Jorge
Reyes began passing his classes at Glendale Community College and
planning to transfer to a certificate program in gerontology at the University of Southern California or California State University, Los

Angeles. In the meantime, he's working as a site manager for Casa Maravilla senior center in East LA—on-the-job experience he hopes will prepare him for his postmilitary career.

The Pentagon sells an educational dream to new recruits. In addition to luring future soldiers with promises of tens of thousands of dollars for a college education, recruiters also promise that soldiers will be able to "attend college anywhere they are based and even in the combat zone through internet classes offered from the college they are enrolled in."[8] But most Iraq War veterans say that promise only exists on paper. They say it's difficult to study while in the military— especially in combat zones.

Take twenty-three-year-old Alejandro Rocha. The Los Angeles native joined the military in 2002 at age eighteen. After graduating from high school, he started to drift, and when his father's hours were cut at the pen factory, Rocha dropped out of community college and took a minimum-wage job loading and unloading merchandise in the shipping and receiving department of Macy's department store in Pasadena.

"I wanted to escape," he told me. "The money wasn't good and I said to myself I can't just be doing this my whole life. So I joined the Marine Corps. They sent me on three tours in Iraq."

Rocha was assigned to an infantry unit and spent most of his five-year commitment either in Iraq or in training. After taking part in the initial invasion in 2003, he was called back for the brutal siege of Fallujah in November 2004 (more than 100 Americans and 4,000 Iraqis died in the battle). In 2005, he was back in Fallujah again.

"I don't know how they expect us to take classes in Iraq," he said. "Maybe some people can. Maybe some people have desk jobs, but I was a machine gunner. I manned a Humvee and rolled around in Humvees patrolling. Sometimes we went house to house in combat, going door by door and knocking down doors." He added, "When we were back in the U.S., we were just training and training. Training was the priority for commanders. It wasn't really part of my job to study."

According to Pentagon guidelines, active-duty soldiers are guaranteed six months at home between deployments abroad. But, observers note, soldiers usually spend five of those six months in training—leaving very little time for classes, family, or anything else.

A different set of issues confronts members of the National Guard and Reserves. Many of these "weekend warriors" signed up before the war in Iraq started. Until 2004, the Guard's slogan was "One weekend a month, two weeks a year," and recruits were told they would be called up primarily in the case of natural disasters like earthquakes and floods or social disturbances. Service could be tough, but it would be brief and close to home. Many members of the Guard signed up before 9/11 and never dreamed they would be sent abroad. As of June 2007, there were about 90,000 U.S. military reservists enrolled in college, and about 25,000 of them have been deployed at least once to either Iraq or Afghanistan.

Juggling school and military service isn't easy. Just ask Marine Corps reservist Todd Bowers. He was halfway through his degree in Middle Eastern studies at George Washington University when the Pentagon pulled him out of school and sent him on two combat tours to Iraq.

The tours were tough. On October 17, 2004, Bowers was shot in the face while conducting a patrol on the outskirts of Fallujah. The sniper's round penetrated the scope he was using and sent fragments into the left side of his face. When he returned home, he found his student loans had been sent to collection.

"I had notified my lenders that I was leaving on a combat deployment," he told me. "Something went awry while I was gone and [when I returned] I had tremendous amounts of letters saying: 'You owe this money.'" Eventually, Bowers said he was able to get the difficulty "squared away, but the damage had already been done and my credit history was ruined."

Under federal law, there are no protections guaranteeing that a school must accommodate a student-soldier who's been deployed. Universities and colleges are not required to readmit a student, are not required to refund tuition for a soldier pulled out midsemester, and are even allowed to flunk students for not attending classes—even if they're in Iraq.

"When I returned from a twelve-month deployment on my second tour, I was given just two weeks to complete my finals," Bowers complained. "I hadn't seen the course work in nearly twelve months." So Bowers dropped out of school. He now works as government affairs director for Iraq and Afghanistan Veterans of America (IAVA)—the first and largest member organization for veterans of recent U.S. wars. In July 2007, IAVA convinced Congresswoman Susan Davis (Democrat from California) and Senator Sherrod Brown (Democrat from Ohio) to introduce a bill called the VETS Act, which would require colleges to refund tuition for service members sent overseas, would cap student loan interest at 6 percent while the student is deployed, and would extend the period of time during which a student-soldier may reenroll after returning from abroad.

The bill was written by Patrick Campbell, a former student-body president at the University of California, Berkeley, who was sucked into a maelstrom of bureaucracy after serving as a combat medic in Iraq with the Louisiana National Guard in 2005. "I spent my first semester back at law school exchanging over forty letters with my student loan lender trying to stop their harassing phone calls saying that I was defaulting on my student loan payments," he said in comments posted on IAVA's Web site. "According to my lender, due to my deployment, I had used up all of my permissible grace period."[9]

Campbell added, "Unlike my non-veteran classmates, I will be required to start repaying my loans the day after I graduate. I was told the only way I could be restored to my pre-deployment status was to rewrite the laws. So I spent my last year of law school finding ways to change the law to help returning student-soldiers."

The VETS Act received a positive response from university administrators. Calling around, I found most officials had a positive read on the legislation. "Anything that would help the students be able to pick up their studies if they're interrupted, or to begin their studies if they hadn't done it before—sounds like those are all good things," Jo Volkert, an assistant vice president at San Francisco State University told me.

Volkert said veterans may believe that universities are hostile to student-soldiers returning from a deployment, but she said administrators legally have very little wiggle room. "Basically, the rules are dictated by the education code we have to follow," she said. "So if this is something that would cause the education code to be more lenient to students who are deployed, that's positive."

As of this writing, the VETS Act has passed the house and Senate and veterans groups are optimistic about the bill becoming law. They believe that a bill that costs taxpayers very little money while helping veterans finish their degrees should pass both houses of Congress relatively easily.

Indeed, education is perhaps the only area where veterans have made major progress since the start of the Iraq War. In January 2007, newly elected Democratic senator James Webb of Virginia (one of a handful of congresspeople with a son or daughter serving in Iraq), introduced legislation that would create a new GI Bill that would provide

Rights and Responsibilities of Students Called Up to Active Duty

Iraq and Afghanistan Veterans of America (www.iava.org, 212-982-9699) publishes a *Student to Service Deployment Guide* detailing the rights and responsibilities of students being called up for active duty. The *Deployment Guide* has information about what happens to a student's tuition, student loans, housing, credit cards, and cell phone when he or she is called up.

college tuition, room and board, plus $1,000 a month stipend to veterans who have served at least two years on active duty since 9/11.

"By contrast," Webb told the Senate, "existing law under the Montgomery GI bill provides educational support of up to $1,000 [actually $1,100] per month for four years, totaling $9,000 per academic year. This benefit is simply insufficient after 9/11. For example, costs of tuition, room and board for an in-state student at George Mason University located in Fairfax, Virginia, added up to approximately $14,000 per year. In addition existing law requires service members to pay $1,200 during their first year of service to even qualify for the benefit."[10]

Webb noted the benefits in his bill essentially mirrored the widely popular benefits allowed under the GI Bill enacted in the waning months of World War II. According to a 1986 Congressional Research Office study, each dollar invested in the World War II GI Bill yielded five to twelve dollars in tax revenue, the result of increased taxes paid by veterans who had achieved higher incomes made possible by a college education.[11] "That bill helped spark economic growth and expansion for a whole generation of Americans," Webb told Congress. "As the post–World War II experience so clearly indicated, better educated veterans have higher income levels, which in the long run will increase tax revenues."[12]

Initially, Webb's colleagues in Washington didn't share his enthusiasm for veterans' education. The Bush administration quickly declared its opposition to the bill, warning it would cost tens of billions of dollars and prove cumbersome to administer. Respected Republican senators agreed and, by June 17, 2007, Virginia's *Daily Press* newspaper reported that Webb's new GI Bill had "wilted" and was "fading fast."[13]

But Webb and the veterans groups didn't give up. They convinced House speaker Nancy Pelosi and Senate majority leader Harry Reid to fold the new GI Bill of Rights into a massive, $162 billion warspending bill they believed President Bush was sure to sign. They reached across the aisle and gained the support of Republican senators like Chuck Hagel of Nebraska and John Warner of Virginia. The mounting pressure caused dozens of other Republican lawmakers to abandon their president and support the popular program. On May 15, 2008, Webb's GI Bill passed the House of Representatives, and on May 22, by an overwhelming 75-22 margin, the Senate passed the "Post-9/11 GI Bill" as part of the war supplemental funding bill.

Even then, however, the future of the GI Bill was far from certain. The two houses of Congress needed to negotiate their differences in a conference committee and President Bush still opposed the bill, as did John McCain, the Republican nominee for president. So veterans and Democratic interest groups threatened to make the GI Bill an issue in the 2008 election.

Major national newspapers also weighed in to support the bill, slamming President Bush for the emptiness of his rhetoric about "supporting the troops." The *New York Times*'s editorial was particularly pointed. "Having saddled the military with a botched, unwinnable war, having squandered soldiers' lives and failed them in so many ways, the commander in chief now resists giving the troops a chance at better futures out of uniform," the editorial read. "So lavish with other people's sacrifices, so reckless in pouring the national treasure into the sandy pit of Iraq, Mr. Bush remains as cheap as ever when it comes to helping people at home." The administration's approach, the *Times* noted, was not to provide a real education benefit to veterans, but to make the benefits of service *seem* attractive to soldiers when they enlist while extracting as little money as possible from the federal treasury. The GI Bill had withered into a recruiting tool that could be used to persuade skeptical young people to join the military, and Bush and McCain "would prefer that college benefits for service members remain just mediocre enough that people in uniform are more likely to stay put."[14]

Eventually, the pressure simply became too great. On June 19, 2008, the president reached a compromise with congressional leaders; and on June 30, 2008, Bush signed the new law into effect. Speaking from the Oval Office, Bush praised the expanded GI Bill for paying "a debt of gratitude to our nation's military families," which "will help us to recruit and reward the best military on the face of the earth."[15] The bill Bush signed was essentially the same as the one he opposed for close to two years; it guarantees a full scholarship at any in-state public university, along with a monthly housing stipend and a stipend for books and materials, to Americans who serve in the military for at least three years. It more than doubles the value of education benefits— from $40,000 to $90,000.[16]

Veterans were ecstatic. "It's hard to actually picture that it's done," IAVA's Patrick Campbell told me the day the bill was signed. "There are veterans all across this country and in Iraq and Afghanistan who are dreaming bigger dreams now. When we were in Iraq we were always talking about what we were going to do when we got home and I know that now they're over there thinking 'I can go to any college I want to now. I can go to the best school I can get into not just the school that I can afford.' That's a big difference and that's going to change who comes into the military; it's going to change who people become after they separate from the military. This is going to change generations."

Campbell also noted that the GI Bill will allow veterans to graduate from school debt free, changing the arcs of their careers. "I have over $100,000 in student loans that I have to worry about paying back and that's going to dictate what kind of jobs I can have in the future," he said. "Future veterans won't have that problem. Now veterans can go into public service jobs and dedicate themselves to service and not have to worry about having to pay back these crushing student loans."

7

DRUGS, CRIME,
AND LOSING YOUR BENEFITS

Thirty-four-year-old S.Sgt. Don Hanks had served fifteen years in the U.S. Army before he spent a year running patrols in the heart of Iraq's Sunni triangle. He always considered himself a career soldier and planned to spend his life in the service, but when he got back to the Untied States, Hanks was a broken man. He told me he couldn't continue in the military.

"I lost friends over there and some of those friends I'd had for my whole frickin' adult life," he said. "You're over there at their houses and barbequing with their kids and you get to know them and their families and then one day they're not there anymore because of something really bad. . . . It's just a really sad experience."

After his return to the States, Hanks said, he couldn't visit the mall or other crowded places. He broke off friendships and spent most of his days emotionally numb. "You start to forget shit," he said. "I can't tell you how many times I'd get up in my house and go into my kitchen or my bathroom or my bedroom and just forget why I was in the room." He added, "It started to affect my interpersonal relationships, and when that happened, I bottled it up. I didn't go talk to somebody when I should have because of the stigma, because I didn't want them to know I was having problems because that is not the sign of a top performer. That is not the sign of a good soldier."

Hanks said he became completely nonfunctional. He started smoking marijuana to cope with his mental problems. When he was hospitalized at a military mental institution, he failed a drug test. Then the military expelled Don Hanks, a move he did not fight because the alternative was another tour in Iraq. Formerly stationed in Fort Lewis outside Seattle, he landed a job washing windows in the city's downtown skyscrapers. He finds the job relaxing, since he can spend his days alone on scaffolding above the cityscape.

Don Hanks's story is hardly unique. Between September 30, 2001, and September 30, 2007, 11,407 soldiers have been discharged for drug abuse after serving in Iraq or Afghanistan; 6,159 have been kicked out for "discreditable incidents"; 6,436 have been discharged for "commission of a serious offense"; and 2,246 have been discharged for "the good of the service," according to Pentagon data I obtained through a Freedom of Information Act request.[1]

"A lot of guys really want to get out," explained Garrett Rappenhagen, a scout sniper in the First Infantry Division who later served as chairman of the board of Iraq Veterans Against the War. "And the military, rather than take the responsibility that this guy has actually just fought in a war and is possibly damaged from that, is just allowing these guys and almost helping these guys get these discharges just to get them out of the military and get rid of a problem."

The Pentagon admits that this happens. In June 2007, the congressionally mandated Department of Defense Task Force on Mental Health reported that "returning service members were pressured by commanders and peers to accept an administrative discharge so they could be expeditiously cleared from the unit and replaced with a fully functional person."[2]

It's not known how many soldiers have been forced out this way since the Iraq War began. In response to a written query, the Pentagon told me it didn't keep this data. But, slowly, different branches of the service are releasing information that sheds light on the size and scope of this problem.

In the first four years of the Iraq War, for example, 1,019 Marines were dismissed with less than honorable discharges for misconduct committed after overseas deployments. In June 2007, Navy captain William Nash, who coordinates the Marines' combat stress program, told *USA Today* that at least 326 of the discharged Marines showed evidence of mental health problems, possibly from combat stress. Nash told the paper he hoped that "any Marine or sailor who commits particularly uncharacteristic misconduct following deployment . . . [would] be aggressively screened for stress disorders and treated. . . . If a Marine who was previously a good, solid Marine—never got in trouble—commits misconduct after deployment and turns out they have PTSD, and because of [that] they lose their benefits, that may not be justice."[3]

Soldiers and Marines often agree to a dishonorable discharge in part because being diagnosed with a mental disease like post-traumatic stress disorder does not necessarily mean they won't be sent abroad again. In November 2006, the Pentagon released guidelines that allow commanders to redeploy soldiers suffering from post-traumatic stress disorders. Service members with "a psychiatric disorder in remission, or whose residual symptoms do not impair duty performance" may be considered for duty downrange. The guidelines list PTSD as a "treatable" problem and set out a long list of conditions for when a soldier can and cannot be returned for an additional tour in Iraq. Those on lithium, for example, would not be allowed to deploy, while those on another class of medications similar to Prozac may be sent to the front.[4]

"As a layman and a former soldier, I think that's ridiculous," Steve Robinson, a Gulf War veteran who works as director of veterans affairs for Veterans for America, argued after the guidelines' release. "If I've got a soldier who's on Ambien to go to sleep and Seroquel and Klonopin and all kinds of other psychotropic meds, I don't want them to have a weapon in their hand and to be part of my team because they're a risk to themselves and to others," he told me. "But apparently, the military has its own view of how well a soldier can function under those conditions and is gambling that they can be successful."

"It's just terrifying," said Dr. Karen Seal, a clinician at the San Francisco VA Medical Center who treats soldiers suffering from PTSD and other psychological illnesses. Seal told me that patients under her care are regularly redeployed despite serious mental health conditions. "I feel like writing them a medical excuse," she said, "but that's not my responsibility as a VA clinician. Because I'm a VA provider, I don't have the authority to do that."

The Pentagon doesn't keep data on the number of soldiers and Marines redeployed after being diagnosed with PTSD or a related disease after serving a tour abroad. Veterans' groups joke that the Bush administration has instituted a policy of "don't look, don't find" in order to absolve itself of criminal, financial, and medical liability for its treatment of veterans.

Soldiers thrown out of the military for drug and alcohol abuse are usually not eligible for veterans' benefits because they've gotten a less than honorable discharge. That extends not only to health care, but also to the housing and college education programs usually available to returning service members.

It's a condition familiar to Specialist Shaun Manuel. When the North Carolina native signed up for the Army in December 2003, his father, who directs the organization Veterans for Peace, tried to talk him out of it. But Manuel wouldn't listen to his father's admonitions. After completing boot camp, he was assigned to the 101st Airborne Division stationed at Fort Campbell, Kentucky, and in September 2005 he deployed for a year-long tour running convoys and warehouse operations in Tikrit.

As he dealt with the daily danger of mortar rounds and roadside bombs, Manuel said, he began to share his father's perspective. "It was like I was over there for no reason," he said. "We weren't accomplishing anything. It was like we were doing the same thing every day and they wouldn't tell us nothing about what was going on at the Pentagon." Manuel said he repeatedly asked his chain of command, "Why am I over here?" but no one gave him an answer. It was "like they were ready to come home too," he said. "What I was thinking—it was on their face."

While Manuel was in Iraq, his wife gave birth to their third son, Jeremiah. But the joyous occasion turned sour when Jeremiah was diagnosed with a genetic disease called muscular spinal atrophy and died in January 2007. Manuel said the situation was made even more painful when his superiors ordered him to begin training for a second tour in Iraq.

"My son passed away," he said. "You gonna send an emotionally distressed soldier to Iraq—who knows what he's going to do? I'm ready to just blow the whole world up because I didn't see my son being born and then he just passed away on me with no warning." He said he complained to his chain of command, but was told "just forget about all that, keep training. You're going back over." He added, "I wanted to cuss them out, but out of respect I kept my trap shut."

Manuel never filed paperwork to medically excuse himself from the deployment. Instead, he withdrew and buried himself in alcohol. He estimates he drank three fifths of liquor a day. At one point, his wife had to call the police during a domestic disturbance. In response, the Army threw him in a local county jail and kicked him out of the military with a bad-conduct discharge, which will deny him medical benefits he might have been able to use to get his life back together again.

Like many soldiers who have returned from Iraq, Manuel has never seen a military psychiatrist. "I tried to go see mental health," he told me, "but by the time I tried to see them the Army had put me in pretrial confinement for my court-martial."

Because Manuel has been dishonorably discharged from the Army, he won't be able to see a government psychiatrist in the future. He and his wife and their two surviving children have been forced to give up their home in Kentucky and move back in with his mother in North Carolina. A year after being expelled from the Army, Manuel is now working as a laborer on the construction of big box stores.

Often it takes public pressure to get a distraught serviceman his benefits. Cody Miranda joined the Marine Corps when he was seventeen years old. He loved the military and hoped to spend his entire career in the service. During his sixteen years in the Marines, Miranda was deployed to the Middle East six times, including stints in the 1991 Gulf War and the 2003 invasion of Iraq.

But when he returned from a tour in Iraq in 2003, his stepmother Jodie Stewart told me, he was a changed man. "He always used to be overfocused on time, as the military trains you to be," she said as an example. "He's never on time for anything anymore. I don't know how to explain it to you. How do you explain it when a man who used to behave one way has gone abstractly and profoundly different?"

After returning from Iraq, Miranda divorced his wife and pulled away from his son. He started drinking too much and was found in

Finding Mental Health Care outside the Government System

A number of mental health organizations have stepped forward to provide psychiatric and psychological help to active-duty service members, veterans, and their families regardless of where the vet stands with the VA.

The nonprofit **Give an Hour** (www.giveanhour.org) is developing a national network of mental health professionals and reaching out to U.S. troops and families affected by the military conflicts in Afghanistan and Iraq. Those looking for services can search for a volunteer provider in their area through listings on the group's Web site.

The nonprofit **Coming Home Project** (www.cominghomeproject.net) is devoted to providing compassionate care, support, and stress-management tools for Iraq and Afghanistan veterans and their families. It is a group of veterans, psychotherapists, and interfaith leaders committed to helping "veterans and family members rebuild the connectivity of mind, heart, body and spirit that combat trauma can unravel; renew their relationships with loved ones; and create new support networks." The project offers a range of free services: workshops and retreats, psychological counseling, training for care providers, and community forums. Its programs address the mental, emotional, spiritual, and relationship challenges faced by veterans and families before, during, and after deployment.

The **Soldiers Project** (www.thesoldiersproject.org, 818-761-7438) is a group of licensed psychiatrists, psychologists, social workers, and marriage and family therapists who volunteer to help military personnel and their loved ones prior to, during, and after deployment to Iraq or Afghanistan. The project is a program of the Trauma Center of the Los Angeles Institute and Society for Psychoanalytic Studies and serves the Southern California area.

possession of cocaine. "He never received any of the postdeployment questionnaires that now are mandatory for all troops," said Amanda Newman, a licensed family therapist who's been seeing Miranda on a pro-bono basis. "He couldn't understand why all of a sudden his life was falling apart."

In 2005, Miranda went AWOL from Camp Pendleton in California for nearly a year and lived homeless on the street. When he returned to the Marine Corps, military doctors diagnosed him with severe post-traumatic stress disorder, bipolar disorder, insomnia, and sleep apnea. But rather than give him treatment for his illness, his commanders at Camp Pendleton lowered his rank to private from staff sergeant, threw him in the brig multiple times, and began court-martial proceedings that can lead to a dishonorable discharge—which would have denied the medical benefits Miranda needs to get his life right again.

While he was in the brig, Miranda's therapist argued Camp Pendleton officials should have given Miranda inpatient care at a military medical institution. "Ordering Pvt Miranda to the brig has significantly exacerbated his psychiatric condition," Newman wrote to Miranda's military lawyer on June 29, 2007. "Behavior such as that . . . could easily be the trigger that results in suicide." She also complained that Miranda had never been screened for traumatic brain injury.

What irked her more than anything, though, was that her attempts to see him were delayed as a result of military orders. "I asked immediately to see him in the brig and was told that it was not possible," Newman wrote. "This is absolutely unacceptable: if a Marine was experiencing a medical emergency and had cut an artery and was bleeding profusely, he surely would not be denied treatment simply because he was in the brig. In fact I would assume and hope that he would be transferred to the hospital for appropriate treatment. There is no difference regarding the severity and crisis nature of Pvt Miranda's psychiatric condition and that of a medical condition: both are life threatening."

Initially, Camp Pendleton brass rebuffed Newman's concerns. But, working together, Miranda's supporters were able to bring public pressure against the base commander, Col. James B. Seaton. Veterans' groups helped Miranda file formal complaints with California congressman Ken Calvert and Senator Barbara Boxer. They arranged for Miranda's story to be featured in local TV and radio programs and in the pages of *USA Today*. I covered the story as well, broadcasting it nationally on Pacifica Radio and writing it up for the Inter Press news wire.

Shortly after that, base command relented. According to military defense lawyer Capt. Bart Slabbekorn, Miranda was brought before the base commander on July 3 and given "nonjudicial punishment."

"As a result of today's proceedings, Pvt Miranda may be retained in the Marine Corps or he may ultimately leave active duty," Slabbekorn wrote in a letter to supporters. "Either way, at this point, he will be looking at a discharge making him eligible for VA treatment down the road." If Miranda does remain in the military, it's likely he will be assigned to a Wounded Warrior Transition Unit, where he would work with other soldiers facing similar issues. "The future is up to Miranda," Slabbekorn said.

But the story doesn't really end there. According to Slabbekorn, 10 to 20 percent of soldiers imprisoned in Camp Pendleton's brig suffer from some kind of combat-related mental illness. Most of them don't have the support network Cody Miranda has, making it likely that few will receive the care they need.

8

LOSING YOUR BENEFITS

PERSONALITY DISORDER

Eventually, Camp Pendleton put a different spin on Cody Miranda's case. While the case was pending, Camp Pendleton officials had refused to talk to me. But after Col. Seaton granted leniency, the base's spokesperson, Maj. Alan Crouch, wrote me an e-mail. In it, he disputed my conclusions and said the colonel's decision was made "independent of letters or media interest, [and] was taken in the best interest of the Marine Corps and of Pvt Miranda."

He added, "The issue of PTSD is very significant, and has the attention of commanders here at Camp Pendleton, across the Marine Corps and, I'm sure, in the other services. We're all doing a lot, but can certainly do more. Speaking for Camp Pendleton, PTSD is a wellness issue and commanders at all levels are obligated to ensure the wellness of their Marines."

Maj. Crouch listed off eight programs available to returning Marines at Camp Pendleton, including:

- Operational Stress Control and Readiness (OSCAR), which embeds mental health professionals inside of combat units while the unit is deployed.
- The Naval Hospital at Camp Pendleton.

- The Deployment Health Clinic, which was founded in 2006 to meet the needs of returning combat veterans. It includes three therapists and a psychiatrist as well as support personnel to help provide treatment for combat-related mental illness.
- The Military One Source Program, which helps Marines who want to get care from a civilian provider.
- Marine and Family Services, which provides counseling to families of soldiers who've returned from deployment.
- The Mental Health Self-Assessment Program, a Department of Defense program that allows a service member to seek psychiatric help while maintaining anonymity.

But the long list of programs is in many ways misleading. The Pentagon's own data shows the military actually has fewer mental health professionals now than it did when the United States invaded Iraq in 2003. Between 2003 and 2007, the number of active-duty Air Force mental health professionals dropped by 20 percent; the Navy reported a 15 percent decline between 2003 and 2006; and the Army an 8 percent drop between 2003 and 2005.[1]

Indeed, the Department of Defense Task Force on Mental Health found young psychiatrists and psychologists no longer want to work for the military, for the same reasons the military itself is having trouble meeting its recruiting goals. According to the government task force, young mental health professionals are concerned about the negative effects of "protracted deployments on family life" and believe they can be paid better to do more rewarding work outside of the military. As a result, young people are no longer applying for psychology internships with the armed forces and the positions remain vacant.

"The number of highly qualified applicants has dropped off dramatically," the task force reported. In 2007, for example, the Army filled only thirteen of thirty-six slots, while the Air Force filled only thirteen of twenty-four positions. "Given the four-year military ser-vice commitment of these interns," the task force said, "this shortfall in the major pipeline feeding the psychology corps will have ramifi-cations for years to come."

In 2007, the American Psychological Association surveyed thirty-eight military installations around the world and found that "current mental health staff are unable to provide services to active members and their families in a timely manner; do not have sufficient resources to provide newer evidence-based interventions in the manner pre-scribed; and do not have the resources to provide prevention and training for service members or leaders that could build resilience and ameliorate the long-term adverse effects of extreme stress."[2]

Given the falling number of military mental health professionals, it's hardly surprising that only a small percentage of soldiers' psycho-logical problems are diagnosed and treated. In August 2007, the *Hartford Courant* obtained documents showing just 3.2 percent of sol-diers who had served in combat since 2003 had been diagnosed by the Army with post-traumatic stress disorder—even though the Penta-gon's own studies show between 15 and 50 percent of Iraq and Afghan-istan veterans suffer from the disease. Even the combined total of Army and Department of Veterans Affairs' diagnoses of PTSD—which at the time the *Courant* article was published stood at 76,000—represented only about 5 percent of the more than 1.5 million troops who have served in Iraq or Afghanistan.[3]

In the *Courant*'s report, a spokesperson for the Army surgeon gen-eral blamed the gap on sick soldiers, who she said fail to come forward because of the stigma surrounding mental health issues. "For PTSD and acute stress disorder, we think, and we're pretty sure about this, that soldiers are worried about being perceived as weak and don't want to have people in their unit find out," Col. Elspeth Ritchie told the paper. "The training program emphasizes the importance of leaders taking care of their soldiers, buddy aides [caring for fellow soldiers] and soldiers recognizing the symptoms in themselves, with all of those knowing where to go for assistance."[4]

But while stigma definitely plays a role, my own experience interviewing veterans and clinicians shows that even when soldiers seek help they usually can't get it. That leaves military commanders in a difficult spot. The lack of military psychologists, psychiatrists, and other mental health professionals means that damaged soldiers can't get the care they need. But commanders on the ground have to find some way of dealing with ill service members. With so many soldiers being mobilized so often, the military can't very well maintain a state of "readiness" if large numbers of soldiers have literally been driven crazy by the war.

Enter the "personality disorder," two magical words that helped the U.S. Army, Air Force, Navy, and Marine Corps discharge more than 23,275 people between 2001 and 2007.[5] Unlike Cody Miranda and Shaun Manuel, these soldiers haven't necessarily broken any laws or military regulations, but like Specialist Manuel they will live the rest of their lives damaged by war and unable to use medical services or receive disability benefits they would have otherwise earned through their service.

That's because the military considers a "personality disorder" to be the soldier's fault, a preexisting condition—and all commanders need to get someone out for a personality disorder is a psychologist's assessment that the service member has shown "a deeply ingrained maladaptive pattern of behavior that interferes with a soldier's ability to perform duty."[6] Soldiers discharged for a personality disorder are supposed to be dishonorably discharged for lying about their mental health when they joined the military. But the truth is that many soldiers with so-called personality disorders only started acting out after finishing a deployment to Iraq.

Consider the case of Specialist Jonathan Town of Findlay, Ohio. On April 9, 2007, *The Nation* magazine published a front-page story titled "How Specialist Town Lost His Benefits."[7] Three months later, on July 25, 2007, Town testified before the House Committee on Veterans Affairs, telling them he had served four and a half years in the Army before he was deployed to the western Iraqi city of Ramadi in August 2004.

"On October 19, 2004, I was running mail for our battalion when incoming rounds started exploding across the street from where my vehicle was parked," he told the committee. "While running for shelter in our S-1 shop's office, a 107-mm rocket exploded three feet above my head leaving me unconscious on the ground. After regaining consciousness, I was taken to the battalion's aid station where I was treated for various wounds including a severe concussion, shrapnel wound in my neck and bleeding from my ear. I was given quarters for the rest of the day and went back to work the next day."[8]

Suddenly, Town said, everything went downhill. After the attack, he remained in Iraq for nine additional months, battling severe headaches, bleeding from his ear, and experiencing insomnia. Then, when he got back to the States, he started experiencing symptoms of post-traumatic stress disorder. "My ability to adjust to loud noises, large groups of people, and forgetting what had happened to my unit and myself while we were in Iraq was going to be yet another battle," he said.

About forty-five days after coming back to Fort Carson, Colorado, Town said, he was finally able to see a military psychologist. "The first few meetings with the doctor were good and it seemed like he actually cared about helping me get through my issues if it were possible," he said. "Then word came down that our unit was going to be redeployed. The next time I went to see the doctor he informed me that he was going to push a personality disorder chapter and explained why. The doctor said 'You have the medical issues that call for a medical board but the reason I am going to push this chapter is because it will take care of both your needs and the Army's. You will be able to receive all of the benefits that you would if you were to go through a medical board; get out of the military; and focus on your treatment to get better. For the military they can get a deployable body in to fill your spot.' "

In written correspondence to *The Nation* magazine, Town's psychologist, Mark Wexler, denied the conversation ever took place. "I don't presume to know all the details about benefits," *The Nation* quotes him as writing, "and therefore do not discuss them with my patients."[9] Regardless of what Wexler did or didn't say, the question remains: why would a military psychologist diagnose a soldier with a history of good conduct with a personality disorder after that soldier served nine months in Iraq and took a 107-millimeter rocket to the head?

The answer is that nearly everyone in the military system has an incentive to short-change the soldier. Military psychologists are overworked because of understaffing and an ever-increasing torrent of soldiers suffering from PTSD. At the July 2007 House Veterans' Affairs Committee hearing, Jason Forrester of the advocacy group Veterans for America described the results of his organization's investigation of psychiatric care at Fort Carson, Colorado: "We found soldiers who had been diagnosed with chronic PTSD who were only receiving one hour of individual therapy a month," he told the committee. "Often, these soldiers saw a new therapist each visit. In an attempt to compensate for this deficiency, many soldiers were prescribed medicines to help them deal with their PTSD. It was not uncommon for us to meet soldiers on over fifteen to twenty different medications at once."[10]

Since psychologists can't possibly properly care for all the damaged soldiers sent to them, there is an incentive to thin some of the backlog by quickly diagnosing soldiers with personality disorder. Indeed, Forrester said the diagnoses for a preexisting-condition personality disorder discharge were often made "in under an hour—regardless of the fact that they [the soldiers] were deemed fit when they entered the service and regardless of the fact that they had been diagnosed with PTSD post-deployment to Iraq and/or Afghanistan."

Commanding officers also have an incentive to push for personality disorder discharges. As the war drags on, officers are under increasing pressure to keep their units strong and ready for yet another deployment to Iraq. As soldiers serve more and more deployments, burning out and fraying evermore at the edges, this task gets more and more difficult. The commander's job is made even more difficult because even if a soldier is diagnosed with a combat-induced mental illness, he or she may still be deployed again for an additional tour. So the easiest way to replace a damaged soldier with a fresh body is to push for a discharge by virtue of a personality disorder.

Finally, administration officials in Washington have every reason to look the other way when lesser officials cheat servicemen and women out of their benefits. The cost of the war in Iraq has gone completely out of control. Already, Congress has appropriated more than $650 billion for the Iraq War—enough to pay for more than 64 million children to attend Head Start for a year (it's also more than five times the VA's annual budget).[11]

The long-term costs of the wars in Iraq and Afghanistan are equally astounding. A book published in March 2008 by Nobel Prize–winning economist Joseph Stiglitz and Harvard professor Linda Bilmes put the cost of the Iraq War alone at three trillion dollars. The economists note the $600 billion approved for the war ignores four other major costs of the conflict. "First, there are additional war-related costs buried in places such as the non-Iraq defense budget," Bilmes wrote, summarizing their analysis in the *Boston Globe*. "That budget has grown by $500 billion cumulatively since the beginning of the war. An estimated one-quarter of that growth is indirectly related to Iraq, including the increased costs of dealing with manpower shortages—recruiting and retaining soldiers and Marines."[12]

Second, there is the cost of rebuilding the military, which is withering under the weight of the war. "Partly this is due to deteriorating equipment; vehicles and weaponry are being used up at six to 10 times the peacetime rate, but not being replaced nearly as fast. Tactical aircraft are now 24 years old on average," Bilmes wrote, "the oldest since World War II."

Then, there is the cost of providing health care and disability benefits to wounded veterans—at the current rate, Bilmes reasoned, the VA can conservatively expect 700,000 new patients and disability claims from the Iraq and Afghanistan wars, with a projected cost of $683 billion.[13]

"On top of all this, the cost of the war will be multiplied because we are borrowing all the money needed to pay for it," she concluded in the *Globe*. "Instead of belt-tightening and sacrifice, this war has been accompanied by tax cuts for the rich and rising deficits. So we must add to the war cost all the interest we will be paying (much of it to foreign governments) to finance the borrowing binge."

Rising public consciousness of these costs is putting pressure on government officials to bring the cost of the Iraq War under control, but the only way they seem inclined to control it is to short-change the service members who have been sent to fight.

PART III

FIGHTING THE VA

9

MEET THE BUREAUCRACY

Even when a veteran gets discharged from the military with benefits intact, he or she is hardly free and clear. The veteran still needs to fight to get those benefits: and that means tangling with hostile and cumbersome bureaucracy at the Department of Veterans Affairs.

Twenty-five-year-old Specialist James Eggemeyer injured himself before he even set foot in Iraq—jumping out of a C-130 gunship during training at Fort Bragg, North Carolina. "I jumped out and the jumpmaster who was holding that line that was wrapped around my arm had to cut the line because I was pretty much being dragged behind the airplane," he told me. "I hit the side of the plane with my Kevlar. My parachute was twisted up like a cigarette roll and I hit real hard, and my ankle and my knee and my back and my shoulder [got hurt]. I tore my rotator cuff. I feel like a fifty-year-old man."

Military doctors prescribed several drugs: the painkillers Vicodin and Percoset and the steroid hydrocortisone. Then, in April 2003, they ordered him deployed to Iraq. For the next year, James Eggemeyer drove a Humvee running supply convoys all around the country. "I was everywhere," he said. "In Baghdad, al-Kut, Tikrit, Babylon. Every day, every other day going all the way up to Balad or down to Kuwait to get supplies."

Eggemeyer told me he never asked to be medically excused from the deployment. He was the only supply guy in his airborne unit, he told me, and besides, he wanted to reenlist when his term was up and become a sergeant, and after that maybe a higher-ranking noncommissioned officer. But his experience in Iraq was rough. His convoys were attacked twice. His worst day occurred early on, when the military truck in front of his Humvee hit a civilian vehicle.

"One of the cars in the oncoming traffic hit another car that was coming toward us and caused that car to swerve across the intersection and slam into the truck in front of me. The truck in front of me hit it pretty good and killed everyone inside," he said. He slammed on the breaks to avoid adding his Humvee to the pileup. Then he got out and loaded an entire family of dead Iraqis onto an American helicopter.

"A Blackhawk had come in when my first sergeant called the medics and they flew and the people got taken out," he said. "But they were already dead and so they just got transported: a little girl, two adult females, and a guy." After that, Eggemeyer's condition worsened. The longer he stayed in Iraq, the worse his body felt. He also started to take more of the painkillers and the steroids the military had given him. The more he took them, the more he needed to dull the pain.

But violence wasn't the only thing Eggemeyer had to deal with while deployed overseas. While he was in Iraq, he filed for divorce. His mother had called to tell him his wife was cheating on him with a man in a local hotel. Then Eggemeyer checked his bank account and found $7,000 had gone missing. So, for the duration of his time in Iraq, Eggemeyer's parents took custody of his son, Justin, who had been born just two months before his deployment.

Returning to Fort Bragg in April 2004, Eggemeyer was quickly discharged from the military. His experience in Iraq had changed his disposition. He started fighting with his captain and was given a "general discharge under honorable conditions," which allows him to use VA services, but denies him access to the GI Bill.

When his parents moved to Miami with Justin, Eggemeyer opted to stay on in his hometown of Port Saint Lucie on Florida's central coast, where he had secured part-time work detailing cars at Kare-Pro Car Wash for $8.00 an hour. "His job was to buff, wax, and shampoo the cars," manager Chris Askins explained. "Basically, just moving your hands around a lot to make the car look like new."

Kare-Pro had a decidedly upscale clientele. Located right outside the gates of the exclusive PGA Country Club and down the street from the private Legacy Golf and Tennis Club, it serviced Lexuses, BMWs, and large American SUVs. So less than a year after serving his country by driving a Humvee in a war zone, Eggemeyer was wiping down cars for the rich on Florida's central coast.

It did not go well. "He asked a lot of questions," Askins told me. "He didn't seem to get [detailing] down as quickly as some of our other workers. He had some difficulties, but we did the best we could to get the most out of him." Eggemeyer said his main problem was that the manual labor he engaged in at Kare-Pro was aggravating the injury he sustained in training at Fort Bragg. "My back started to get worse and worse, and I'd almost be crying from the pain in my back and the way my shoulder feels and my wrists. I was just having pains all over my body," he told me.

So Eggemeyer and Askins started to jaw back and forth, and on May 29, 2006, the Iraq War veteran quit his job. "He quit over not being able to get Memorial Day off," Askins explained. "We asked him to cover a shift on Memorial Day because a lot of other people were already on vacation. Nobody wanted to switch with him, so he had to work."

Eggemeyer remembers the exchange this way: "The president said on the TV that all veterans deserve to have Memorial Day off," he said. "And so I told him [his boss] I wasn't going to be there and that I needed the day off. And he said, 'If you don't show up you're fired.' And I said, 'You know what, I'm not making any money at this place anyway. I can't keep doing what I've been doing so just forget it.'"

In December 2006, when Eggemeyer filed a disability claim with the Veterans Benefits Administration, which is overseen by the Department of Veterans Affairs, he had already lost his apartment and had begun living out of his girlfriend's Ford Explorer. So when the VA responded to his claim with a letter to his old address requesting that he come in for a physical, he missed the appointment. It's a vicious cycle so familiar to homeless people across the country. They need help from the government because they don't have a home, but can't receive mail because they don't have an address.

Eggemeyer pawned everything he could: his girlfriend's ring, his guitar, his X-Box video game system, and his television. Then he went to get help, from Tony Reese, a veteran service representative working for Martin County, Florida. (Most local governments across the United States have one or two employees called "veteran service representatives" or "veteran service officers," who help former soldiers navigate the complicated, and often hostile, VA process. Veterans' organizations like the American Legion and Disabled Veterans of America also employ veteran service representatives, as does the VA itself.) Reese was familiar with the VA bureaucracy. He let James use his office as his address and made sure that James showed up at all his appointments. He made sure all of James's documents were in order and used the VA computer system to make sure his

Getting Help Filing a VA Claim

Having a veteran service officer greatly increases a veteran's chance of winning his or her claim with the VA. These representatives give free advice and guidance about filing a claim. You can find your local government's veteran service officer through the Web site of the National Association of County Veteran Service Officers (www.nacvso.org). National veterans' groups like Disabled American Veterans (www.dav.org, 202-554-3501) also employ veteran service officers.

claim was on the right bureaucrat's desk at the regional office in Saint Petersburg.

But even with that, the process dragged on. "We were just waiting for the VA," Reese told me. "I really don't know how the VA is processing these Operation Iraqi Freedom and Operation Enduring Freedom [Afghanistan] claims. Supposedly they're supposed to be separated and moving quicker but, you know, it doesn't seem like it to any veteran who files a claim. There's certainly room for improvement."

So Reese started to raise money from private organizations, just enough to keep Eggemeyer afloat until his claim was settled. In June 2007, Reese convinced the William J. Peterman Foundation for Disabled War Veterans to donate enough money to put James up in a cheap hotel for the month, with both Reese and the foundation believing Eggemeyer would surely be receiving a disability check by month's end. All the VA needed to do was have a claims adjuster stamp a decision on his file—and since Eggemeyer was homeless, his file theoretically should have been at the top of the stack.

But after thirty days passed, the VA still hadn't rendered a decision. The Peterman Foundation money ran out, and Eggemeyer had to go back to living in his car. Then, on July 21, 2007, Eggemeyer crashed his girlfriend's 1999 Ford Explorer, which was also his house. According to a report from the Stuart, Florida, police department, there were no other vehicles involved. Eggemeyer simply veered "onto the sidewalk and struck a utility pole" near a Winn Dixie grocery store on State Route 5.

The police report noted Eggemeyer wasn't drunk, and he was only cited for careless driving. "I was on so many painkillers that I thought I was getting in the turning lane, but it was actually the curb," he said. "So I wrecked [the car] and totaled it, and then I didn't have anywhere to live."

Tony Reese sprang into action again. He got the local Veterans Council, a membership organization of groups like the American Legion and the Veterans of Foreign Wars, to cough up enough money for Eggemeyer to buy a used truck to live in. Then they waited again. July passed, August passed, and Eggemeyer was still waiting, unemployed and homeless. On August 30, I called him on the telephone.

"A month ago I called the little 1-800 number for the claims hotline," he said.

> They said that I was at the rating board, that they had all the information and all the medical evidence that we need to proceed with my case. They said: "Now we're just waiting for a rater to rate it. You should have your decision in no time."
>
> Well about a week after that I called them again, and said: "What's the process? Have I been rated yet?" And they said: "Well, no you're missing these three forms. They're missing from your file. You need to send them in for your file in order for them to be rated." So I went in to see the veterans service officer [Tony Reese], and he helped me get the paperwork they said I missing and we faxed it over to them.
>
> Three days later, I called them and they said they had received it and I was back at the rating board. And they had everything they needed

and I would be rated and I would get my back pay for the months that I hadn't been rated and get my disability established. Well I called them up yesterday and it's back at the developmental stages and I'm not even at the rating board yet, and they told me they need to gather more medical information.

At that point, Reese went to work yet again. He called all the claims adjudicators he knew at the rating board in St. Petersburg. He reminded them of what they already knew from the forms he had faxed and mailed them multiple times: that Specialist James Eggemeyer had served his country in Iraq, but he had sustained both physical and mental injuries in the field of battle and was now homeless and suicidal.

On September 5, a claims official at the VA told Reese and Eggemeyer that the first check would come within the week. Eggemeyer had been given a 100 percent disability rating retroactive to the date he made his first claim, meaning he would get a lump sum of close to $30,000, plus about $2,700 a month for the rest of his life.

"It's a representative case," Reese told me. "The more you stay in contact with the VA, the more you stay on top of your claim, the more the chance of your claim getting processed as it should be. But sometimes weeks and months just pass by and before you know it the claim is sitting God knows where. [Eggemeyer], he's just your typical guy returning."

Indeed, the VA's own statistics reveal that Specialist James Eggemeyer received what could best be described as standard treatment. Since the start of the Iraq War, the backlog of unanswered disability claims has grown from 325,000 to more than 600,000. On average, a veteran must wait almost six months for a claim to be heard. If a veteran loses and appeals a case, it usually takes about three years.

The real question is why? Why does the VA make a young man or woman, who's just been injured in the line of duty, jump through so many hoops simply to receive the disability check?

"A veteran needs to see his relationship with the VA as an adversarial relationship," retired Air Force major John Roche told me when I put the question to him. "Imagine you are on one side of the street saying 'I am entitled to compensation benefits. I was injured in the service,'" Roche said. "And on the other side of the street, the VA is shouting back: 'Oh no! You have not proved to our satisfaction that your injury is service related.' This is the definition of an adversarial contest— someone who opposes somebody else in conflict, contest, or debate."

Roche should know. When he retired from the Air Force in 1969, he went to work for the VA as a claims specialist, where he decided which veterans should and should not receive benefits. He quit that job after three years, citing a toxic bureaucratic culture, and spent the next fifteen years working as a veteran service officer in Pinellas County, Florida, carrying out job duties similar to Tony Reese. Over the years, he's learned a lot about the VA and has written three books designed to help vets deal with the Department of Veterans Affairs: *The Veteran's Survival Guide, The Veteran's PTSD Handbook,* and, most recently, *Claim Denied! How to Appeal a VA Denial of Benefits.*

The whole claims process, Roche said, is designed to ferret out veterans trying to cheat the system, rather than compensate soldiers injured in the line of duty. To whit, the VA requires a veteran to prove all his or her injuries, complete with dates, times, and independent medical verification. For example, a veteran applying for compensation for post-traumatic stress disorder must submit a twenty-six-page form, the key to which is a detailed essay on the specific moments when he or she experienced a terrifying event or series of incidents that caused mental illness to develop.[1]

Further Reading on the VA Claims Process

Veterans for America (www.veteransforamerica.org, 202-483-9222) has published an online book called *The American Veterans and Servicemembers Survival Guide,* which is available as a free download from the group's Web site.

The book is the successor to *The Viet Vet Survival Guide,* a national best-seller that was published by Ballantine Books in 1985 and was endorsed by Dear Abby, Jack Anderson, and others. Like that original book, *The American Veterans Survival Guide* describes the problems facing current veterans and provides realistic, effective advice on how to grapple with those problems.

Topics include the military, the Department of Veterans Affairs, disability compensation, pensions, medical care, educational benefits, housing benefits, claims and appeals, discharge upgrading, the criminal justice system, employment, reemployment rights, benefits for family members, and special problems of women service members and veterans.

Two other excellent guides for navigating the VA claims process are *The Veteran's Survival Guide: How to File and Collect on VA Claims* and *The Veterans' PTSD Handbook: How to File and Collect on Claims for Post-Traumatic Stress Disorder.* Both are written by retired Air Force major and former VA claims adjudicator John D. Roche and are published by Potomac Books.

This is not easy, because one of the symptoms of PTSD is for a person to try to block out any memory of that event. According to the DSM-IV, the bible of psychiatric diagnoses, a person with PTSD often displays a "persistent avoidance of stimuli associated with the trauma and numbing of general responsiveness."[2] In other words, the last thing a person experiencing PTSD wants to do is sit down and write an essay on why, and exactly how, they've become mentally ill.

In addition, veterans must also back claims up with hard evidence that their PTSD is indeed "service connected"—in essence proving they were in the place they said they were and that the terrifying incidents did indeed occur. "They should go ahead and get copies of every single military record," Roche said, "and should not submit a claim until they got it all put together." This can be a long process, but experienced service officers like Roche have found that building a paper trail of war service and injury is absolutely essential to winning a claim. Roche recommends that every veteran file a Freedom of Information Act (FOIA) request for all their service records from both the Pentagon and the VA. "You can't argue a case if you don't know what they have in your records," he told me. The VA benefit claims process is essentially the same one that Vietnam-era veterans went through thirty years ago, and it's hard not to believe that the VA uses it to cheat those who've served their country out of the benefits they've earned. For decades, veterans' groups have tried to get the VA to streamline the process, but every effort has met with failure.

Since both the Pentagon and the VA often take months to respond to a FOIA request, Roche recommends going through a local congressperson's office. "Have them put in a request for your records and they'll come a lot quicker," he advised. "Congress controls the purse strings, so the last thing the Defense Department and the VA want to do is to get on some congressman's list."

But military record keeping isn't perfect. In a war zone, soldiers don't always fill out the proper forms after a battle, shooting, or IED explosion. Also, assault by a superior is a leading cause of PTSD and other psychological injuries, especially among military women—and many of those assaults go unreported until after the soldier leaves the service.

So in most cases, a veteran must also take the additional step of using their own money to hire a private doctor or psychologist to evaluate their medical claims. "Go to see an independent specialist and get an evaluation," Roche suggests, "and take a copy of the VA ratings manual that rates that condition so that the private physician can use that terminology to rate what he finds on the individual. That immediately alerts the VA that the veteran in this case has more than the normal amount of expertise and connections, and they'll pay more attention to your claim."

After all the forms and associated paperwork are submitted, it's time to wait while the VA sucks the vet's claim into one of its fifty-eight regional offices. If the bureaucrats who initially review the claim (they're called the Pre-Determination Team) don't see all necessary documents in order, they can send out a letter asking for more information. They can also reject a claim outright, setting the stage for an appeal that will likely drag on for years. (According to the VA, from October 1, 2007, to March 31, 2008, a total of 1,467 veterans died waiting to learn if their disability claims would be approved by the government. Veterans who appeal the VA's denial of their disability claims wait an average of 1,419 days, or nearly four years, for a response.)[3]

If, however, the Pre-Determination Team is satisfied with the veteran's initial paperwork, a letter is usually sent in a month or two requesting that the veteran come in for what's called a Compensation and Pension (C&P) medical examination. At that exam, a medical professional (sometimes a doctor, but more likely a physician's assistant or nurse practitioner) looks over the paperwork and checks to make sure the vet is indeed suffering from the illness or disability being claimed. This doctor (or physician's assistant or nurse practitioner) is different from the veteran's primary physician at the VA, has no background with the vet's medical history, and does not provide any health care. C&P examiners have only one job: to detect fraud.

The C&P examiner looks the vet over, writes down some notes, and sends those notes to the Rating Board, the next step in the VA bureaucracy. By now, months have been spent on paperwork and the veteran still has no idea if benefits will be granted or not.

If the veteran is lucky, the Rating Board will be the claim's last stop. Members of the Rating Board are the people who eventually decide whether a vet's claim is legitimate and how much disability and compensation the veteran deserves. But the term *Rating Board* is a bit of a misnomer: Despite what the name implies, a veteran's case is not heard by a panel of people, but is reviewed by a single claims adjudicator with no medical training.

There was a time when nearly every veteran's claim was heard by a skilled team, including a doctor and a lawyer, but those professionals were thrown out of the process by President Reagan in the 1980s as a way of saving money. Now, veterans' claims are heard by adjudicators who are just like any other civil servant. No degree is required, only the ability to follow steps listed in a government manual. All the adjudicator has to do is plug the information from the veteran and the C&P exam into a computer, which spits out a finding on the burden of the veteran's disability.

If the Rating Board approves the claim, the veteran will be in line to get regular disability checks totaling anywhere from $2,772 a month for a 100 percent disabled veteran living married with children, to just $117 a month for a single veteran rated at 10 percent disabled. The board can also reject the claim, ending the process or setting the stage for a lengthy appeal.

It's here that Roche and other veterans' advocates see the biggest problem. The VA promotes claims adjudicators based on how many cases they clear, not on whether they make the right decision. "A VA claims official is required to clear twelve claims a day," Roche noted.

"If they deny your claim, they can take an 'end product credit.' So as far as statistics go, they have cleared a claim. Denying twelve claims a day is an easy thing to do."

There is another way, of course. In her exhaustive study of the long-term costs of the wars in Iraq and Afghanistan, Harvard professor Linda Bilmes notes that almost all veterans tell the truth in their disability claims, with the VA ultimately approving nearly 90 percent of them. Given that, Bilmes suggests scrapping the lengthy process described above and replacing it with "something closer to the way the IRS deals with tax returns." A revamped "Veterans Benefits Administration," she writes, "could simply approve all veterans' claims as they are filed—at least to a certain minimum level—and then audit a sample of them to weed out and deter fraudulent claims. . . . VBA claims specialists could then be redeployed to assist veterans in making claims. This startlingly easy switch would ensure that the US no longer leaves disabled veterans to fend for themselves."[4]

Bilmes cautions, however, that such a switch would have a cost attached to it. If the process weren't so cumbersome, more disabled veterans would file claims. And if their claims were processed more quickly, more benefits would be dispersed: "The cost of any solution that reduced the backlog of claims is likely to be an increased number of claims, and a quicker pay-out," Bilmes writes. "If 88% of claims were paid within 90 days instead of the 6 months to 2 years currently required, the additional budgetary cost is likely to be in the range of $500m in 2007."

To me, that seems like a small price to pay. In 2007, Congress appropriated close to $200 billion for the wars in Iraq and Afghanistan. It would take just a drop in that bucket to ease the process for injured veterans after they come home.

10

DIDN'T PREPARE TO TREAT
THE WOUNDED

But the Bush administration was never seriously interested in helping veterans. The sorry state of care for Iraq and Afghanistan war veterans is not an accident. It's on purpose. After the invasion of Iraq in 2003, the Bush administration fought every effort to improve care for wounded and disabled veterans. At the root of that fight was its desire to hide the true costs of the war in order to boost public support.

Think back to 2002, before the invasion of Iraq, when leading neoconservative thinker and Donald Rumsfeld aide Ken Adelman predicted the war would be a "cakewalk."[1] On February 7, 2003, as American forces massed in Kuwait, Defense Secretary Rumsfeld got into the act himself, telling U.S. soldiers in Italy that the war "could last six days, six weeks. I doubt six months." Six weeks later, on March 16, Vice President Dick Cheney told NBC's Tim Russert the war would "go relatively quickly . . . [ending in] weeks rather than months."[2]

Months later, after the invasion had turned into a long-term occupation, members of Bush's team continued to present a rosy scenario. On September 22, 2003, Richard Perle, a member of the Pentagon's Defense Policy Board, told a gathering of the neoconservative

American Enterprise Institute that "a year from now, I'll be very surprised if there is not some grand square in Baghdad that is named after President Bush."[3]

That kind of optimistic thinking at the top was also present at the Department of Veterans Affairs, whose officials told Congress they didn't need any additional money to care for the war wounded. "The Department of Defense went to war in Iraq. They hired hundreds of thousands of extra soldiers from the Guard and Reserve to make the military larger so that they could do the invasion of Iraq," noted Paul Sullivan, a veteran of the first Gulf War who was a high-ranking civil servant at the VA when America invaded Iraq. "However," he told me, "the Department of Veterans Affairs didn't hire more doctors and they didn't hire more bureaucrats to help them with their paperwork."

Indeed, as the country prepared for war the Bush administration was actively involved in scaling back veterans' benefits. In January 2003, the VA announced that as a cost-cutting move it would start turning away middle-income veterans who applied for medical benefits. As a result, the number of uninsured veterans skyrocketed by more than 290,000. In October 2007, a team of researchers from Harvard found that 1.8 million veterans lacked health insurance, which meant that nearly 6 million of America's uninsured were veterans or their families.[4]

The Bush administration also proposed making the VA's prescription drug benefit less generous, increasing copayments for many veterans from $7 to $15 and requiring a $250 annual fee.[5] President Bush even moved to eliminate disability payments for veterans who abused drugs or alcohol—despite the fact that substance abuse has long been connected to psychological trauma caused by the death and destruction of combat.[6] All in all, the administration proposed cutting hundreds of jobs at the VA at precisely the time when programs should have been expanded to care for a tidal wave of Iraq and Afghanistan veterans.

President Bush also moved to politicize the Department of Veterans Affairs. In December 2004, he replaced the Secretary of Veterans Affairs Anthony Principi, who had spent his career in public service, with Jim Nicholson, a real-estate developer and former chair of the Republican National Committee who'd raised millions of dollars for Bush's 2000 presidential campaign.

In his resignation letter, Principi gave no specific reason for his departure, stating only that it was "time to move on to fresh opportunities and different challenges."[7] Months earlier, however, he had voiced his frustration, telling a House committee he had asked for an additional $1.2 billion dollars for veterans' care, but that his request had been denied.[8]

"Some people were disappointed when Principi abruptly left," Paul Sullivan remembered. "Nicholson came with no experience at all when the VA was mired in crises. The first crisis was a demand in health care and benefits by veterans. And the second crisis was a shortfall in appropriations from Congress because the VA failed to properly plan for the consequences of the Iraq and Afghanistan wars."

Unlike Principi, Nicholson made no requests for additional money, telling Congress his agency had all the resources it needed. As a result, between January 2000 and September 2004 the VA's patient to doctor ratio grew from 335 to 1, to 531 to 1.[9] The number of claims adjusters at the VA likewise dropped after the United States invaded Iraq in 2003. According to the American Federation of Government Employees, the VA employed 1,392 veteran service representatives in June 2007 compared to 1,516 in January 2003.[10]

President Bush was joined in his opposition to funding the VA by the Republican majority in Congress, which steadfastly agreed that two major wars in Iraq and Afghanistan did not require more money to be spent on veterans' health care or disability benefits. Among the most ardent adherents to this position was Vietnam veteran and former prisoner of war John McCain. Iraq and Afghanistan Veterans of America (IAVA) gave McCain a D+ when they scored his voting record for 2005 and 2006. He voted with the interests of Disabled American Veterans (DAV) only 20 percent of the time.[11]

In 2005 and 2006, McCain voted against measures to expand mental health care and readjustment counseling for service members returning from Iraq and Afghanistan, extend inpatient and outpatient treatment for injured veterans, and lower copayments and enrollment fees veterans must pay to obtain prescription drugs. "There was an effort to increase the budget for veterans' healthcare beyond what President [George W.] Bush had requested as part of his budget," DAV spokesperson Dave Autry explained. "The idea was to increase funding for veterans' health care by cutting back on tax breaks for the wealthy. The proposals were pushed by Democrats and opposed by Republicans in almost straight party-line votes." In other words, John McCain's votes indicate he would rather give tax cuts to the rich than care for wounded veterans. McCain also helped defeat a proposal by Democratic Sen. Debbie Stabenow that would have made veterans' health care an entitlement program like social security, so that medical care would not become a political football to be argued over in Congress each budget cycle.[12] What were George Bush and John McCain thinking? Perhaps they believed their own rhetoric about the invasion of Iraq going quickly and easily, and thought that somehow it would be a war that produced no wounded soldiers seeking health care or disability payments from the federal government. More likely, though, it seems the Bush administration was ignoring wounded veterans by design—because when injured soldiers actually started coming home from the war, the administration tried to implement policies to cut them off.

But the VA had to do something, because they were being flooded with hundreds of thousands of new disability claims—claims that came not only from newly returning veterans, but also from older, Vietnam vets whose mental trauma had been aggravated by the new wars in Iraq and Afghanistan. Between 2000 and 2006, the number of Vietnam vets seeking treatment for PTSD nearly doubled, from about 100,000 when President Bush took office, to 153,000 in 2003 at the time of the Iraq invasion, to 200,000 in 2006.[13]

"Clearly the current Iraq war, and their exposure to it, created significantly increased distress for them," explained John Wilson, a professor at Cleveland State University who has done extensive research on Vietnam veterans since the 1970s. "We found very high levels of intensification of their symptoms," Wilson told the *Washington Post.* "It's like a fever that has gone from 99 to 104."[14]After the launch of the Iraq War, Wilson performed a small study of Vietnam veterans at Cleveland State. Nearly 44 percent said they had fallen into a depression since the war began; 57 percent reported flashbacks after watching reports about the war on television; and almost 46 percent said their sleep was disrupted. Nearly 30 percent said they had sought counseling since combat started in Iraq.

Officials inside the Bush administration knew this was happening. In 2005, when Paul Sullivan was working as a project manager at the VA, he briefed political appointees and executives at VA headquarters about the sharply escalating mental health and PTSD disability claims among Iraq and Afghanistan war veterans. He advised them, in writing, that more claims processors would need be hired to meet the steeply rising demand.

Those briefings did not have the desired effect. Instead of requesting additional money to care for America's veterans, Sullivan said, the "VA launched a systematic effort to block, hinder, restrict, and otherwise prevent our newest generation of combat veterans from receiving the mental health care they need and that they earned." In 2005, VA brass ordered a reevaluation of seventy-two thousand previously approved PTSD claims to see if there had been any fraud—worsening a backlog of disability claims by shifting overworked adjudicators away from clearing a claims backlog that already stretched into the hundreds of thousands.[15]

The move also had the effect of opening old wounds. In October 25, 2005, the online magazine *Salon* published a report about the policy's effect on fifty-seven-year-old Vietnam veteran Greg Morris. "On October 8," journalist Mark Benjamin wrote, Morris "was found by his wife, Ginger, in their home in Chama, N.M., an old mining town of 1,250 in the Rocky Mountains. Lying at Morris' side were a gun and his Purple Heart medal." "For years," Benjamin continued, "Morris had been receiving monthly V.A. benefits in compensation for posttraumatic stress disorder. Next to his gun and Purple Heart was a folder of information on how the V.A. planned to review veterans who received PTSD checks to make sure those veterans really deserved the money."[16]

Benjamin also reported on the case of Vietnam veteran Ron Nestle, whose traumatic memories include a Claymore mine blasting a busload of civilians near his artillery base. He had been getting disability checks for PTSD for years. On August 11, 2005, Benjamin wrote, Nestle received a letter from the VA saying that his file was being reviewed. The letter warned that "confirmation" of his mental wounds "had not been established" and that his file at the VA "does not establish that the event described by you occurred nor does the evidence in the file establish that you were present when a stressful event occurred." Nestle told *Salon* that the letter left him shocked, angry, and afraid. The VA eventually confirmed that his claims were legitimate, and Congress stopped the agency's audits of approved PTSD claims after one thousand reviewed cases revealed no evidence of fraud.

The VA also instituted a "second signature" requirement for approving new PTSD claims at 100 percent—adding more paperwork and more delay to every claim. Again, Congress raised alarm and the VA suspended the policy.[17]

But the VA's politically appointed brass weren't done yet. They contracted with the federal Institute of Medicine (IOM) for the stated purpose of validating the diagnosis of PTSD.[18] "[The] VA's hidden purpose was to narrow the definition of PTSD so that fewer veterans would qualify for VA health care or VA disability benefits, thus blocking future claims and saving [the] VA money," Paul Sullivan said. "Luckily for our veterans, IOM validated the serious nature of PTSD."[19]

And yet, as the claims backlog grew, senior VA officials gave themselves bonuses. On May 3, 2007, the Associated Press (AP) acquired a list that revealed extra pay of more than $3.8 million, even as the financially strapped agency was, in the words of the AP, "straining to help care for thousands of injured veterans returning home from Iraq and Afghanistan."[20]

The AP reported that the VA bonuses were "the most lucrative in government." Three top officials received $33,000 bonuses, approximately 20 percent of the bureaucrats' annual salaries. The recipients were Rita Reed, the deputy assistant secretary for budget; William Feeley, a former VA network director who later became deputy undersecretary for health for operations and management; and Ronald

Aument, the deputy undersecretary for benefits, whose job included ensuring fast processing of claims.

By way of explanation, VA spokesperson Matt Burns told the AP that the bonuses were meant to prevent the high-ranking officials from bolting to the private sector. "Rewarding knowledgeable and professional career public servants is entirely appropriate," he said. "The importance of retaining committed career leaders in any government organization cannot be overstated." An alternative explanation is that the bonuses were meant to reward officials who kept costs down by denying care to veterans.

In July 2007, with close to 600,000 vets waiting to have their claims heard, a coalition of veterans' groups went to federal court to force the VA's hand. The lawsuit, originally known as *Veterans for Common Sense et al. v. Nicholson et al.,* was brought by Paul Sullivan's organization, Veterans for Common Sense, along with the California-based Veterans United for Truth. Their seventy-three-page complaint asked the federal bench for class-action status on behalf of the estimated 320,000 to 800,000 post-9/11 vets suffering from post-traumatic stress disorder.[21]

"The VA's motto, which is taken from Abraham Lincoln's second address, is to care for him who has borne the battle and for his woman and orphan," attorney Melissa Kasnitz told reporters at a press conference announcing the suit. "Instead of living up to this motto, the VA is abandoning disabled veterans and following a path that will lead to broken lives, homelessness and staggering social costs."[22]

What does the VA leadership have to say about all this? It's difficult to tell, because the contentious nature of the agency's relationship with veterans is perhaps only exceeded by its sour relationship with the media. When the lawsuit was launched, the VA's press office would only release a short statement: "The Department of Veterans Affairs

Veterans for Common Sense Class Action Lawsuit

If you are a U.S. veteran who has a pending disability claim based on post-traumatic stress disorder and you wish to join Veterans for Common Sense's class-action lawsuit against the VA, you can do so online at www.veteransptsdclassaction.org.

is committed to meeting the needs of our latest generation of heroes," the statement read. "Through outreach efforts, the VA ensures returning Global War on Terror service members have access to the widely recognized quality health care they have earned, including prosthetics and mental health care. VA has also given priority handling to their monetary disability benefits claims."[23]

It took the VA three months to disclose its true intentions. On September 25, 2007, government attorneys moved to dismiss the complaint "in its entirety." In its court filing, the VA ignored the litany of charges about defects in the VA system and argued that any claim of mistreatment must be "channeled" through a single veteran's appeal to the Board of Veterans Appeals. The VA belittled the veterans' lawsuit as "frustrations with political processes," and said the problems the veterans described could only be addressed to "representative branches of government" like Congress and the president.[24] In essence, the Bush administration's reaction to the veterans' lawsuit was to give them the finger.

When the case came to trial a few months later, VA lawyers were even more dismissive of the veterans' pain, calling the high rate of veterans' suicides "immaterial" and telling U.S. District Court judge Samuel Conti that "you cannot . . . expect to have a system where [disability] claims move expeditiously."[25] At the end of the trial, Conti, a conser-

vative judge appointed to the bench by President Nixon, ruled in favor
of the government on a technicality. The case is currently on appeal and
both sides are vowing to fight all the way to the Supreme Court.

There's one other wrinkle to this. While the VA's leadership sand-
bagged wounded veterans and the press, top officials *were* reaching out
to one group: Christian evangelicals. On September 4, 2007, Veterans
for Common Sense and the Military Religious Freedom Foundation
demanded an FBI investigation of Daniel Cooper, Bush's undersecretary for benefits at the VA. Their complaint stemmed from Cooper's
appearance in a fundraising video for the evangelical group Christian
Embassy, which carries out missionary work among the Washington
elite as part of the Campus Crusade for Christ. In the video, Cooper
said of his Bible study, "it's not really about carving out time, it really
is a matter of saying what is important. And since that's more important than doing the job—the job's going to be there, whether I'm
there or not."[26]

"He's prostituting his position," Mikey Weinstein, head of the Military Religious Freedom Foundation, told me. "This individual is
using his very high ranking position to promote this particular bibli-
cal worldview, which we refer to as the Weaponized Gospel of Jesus
Christ." A former aide to President Reagan and ten-year veteran of the
Air Force Judge Advocate General office, Weinstein summed up
Cooper's performance, saying, "We could have done just as poorly as
he's done by sticking a German shepherd or a cactus in that job."

Paul Sullivan of Veterans for Common Sense told me that when he
worked at the VA leaders sent clear signals that spreading Cooper's
evangelical faith was more important than helping veterans: "I was advised under repeated occasions that Cooper held prayer meetings, and
many VA employees sought to improve their chances of promotion by
attending these prayer meetings. That is highly unacceptable, highly

inappropriate, and illegal, for someone to be using religion as a litmus test for a government position. It's against our Constitution."

Cooper wasn't the only high-ranking official in the Christian Embassy video. It also featured Stephen Johnson of the Environmental Protection Agency and a slew of current and retired Pentagon officials, including Army brigadier generals Vincent Brooks and Robert Caslen, retired Army chaplain, Col. Ralph Benson, and Air Force major generals Peter Sutton and John Catton.

Long-time observers of the religious right say the controversy surrounding Daniel Cooper is part of a pattern. "Evangelicals have been working through the military and government agencies since the cold war as part of the fight against 'Godless Communism,' but they tried to follow certain boundaries," said Chip Berlet, a senior analyst at Political Research Associates in Boston. "With the Bush administration," he told me, "we've seen many egregious examples of officials stepping way out of line of any kind of boundary, of which this promotional video is a particularly notable example."

In another example, in 2005, the group Americans United for the Separation of Church and State accused officials at the U.S. Air Force Academy in Colorado Springs of religious discrimination.[27] Cadets were frequently pressured to attend chapel and take part in evangelical services, the group said, with prayer a part of mandatory events at the academy. In at least one case, a teacher ordered students to pray before beginning their final examination. Those who refused to comply were harassed and urged to drop out.

11

MORE BUREAUCRACY

In addition to fighting for disability benefits, veterans also encounter dismissive, overlapping bureaucracies in attempts to get health care from the Department of Veterans Affairs. Like the VA's Veterans Benefits Administration, the national network of VA hospitals and clinics seems to have been designed primarily to weed out fraud and save money.

It should come as no surprise, then, that the amount and extent of care a veteran is entitled to receive from a "service related" injury is derived from a series of complicated formulas. For example, VA policy requires that vets with "service connected" disability ratings of 50 percent, and all other veterans requiring care for injuries sustained in combat, be scheduled for care within thirty days of requesting an appointment. Veterans not sufficiently disabled, or disabled veterans seeking care for a non–service related injury (for example, a soldier with an injured leg going in for an eye appointment), can be put off for four months.

In a way, these policies seem fair. More severely injured veterans get priority over those with less debilitating disabilities. But a veteran's degree of disability is decided by the VA's own rating system, which, as we saw in previous chapters, is a three-ring bureaucratic circus.

Take the case of Durrell Michael, a twenty-nine-year-old Army veteran from York, Pennsylvania. Michael joined the military filled with patriotism after the 9/11 attacks, motivated by his mother's experience working as a legal secretary in lower Manhattan when the planes hit the Twin Towers. "I just thought it would be a good idea to go ahead and do my part," he told me. "So one day after work I went over and sat down with a recruiter and let him know what was going on with my situation. I figured it was the right thing to do."

Michael was also attracted by the job training and educational benefits the military touts to recruits. He had just become engaged to his now-wife Hope and dreamed of a life beyond his factory job at a printing press. By joining the Army, he reasoned, he could serve his country and get ahead in life at the same time.

After basic training, the Army sent Michael to South Korea, where he spent most of his days loading and unloading communications equipment like antennas, generators, and camouflage for vehicles. That's how he got hurt. "We were moving generators by hand when we really should have been moving them by Humvee, and as I was lifting one of the generators I noticed a problem in the lumbar area of my [lower] back," he told me. "I could barely walk. I couldn't stand erect. It was really painful. So I went to seek medical treatment, where I was given some Advils, some muscle relaxants, told to get some rest, and that's about it. I never received a scan or anything else so they never knew what was wrong."

By the time Michael returned to Fort Lewis, Washington, in October 2003, he was in excruciating pain. He still had no diagnosis, and the Army kept assigning him tasks that aggravated his condition: erecting more antennas, physical training that included sit-ups on concrete, and field exercises to prepare him for battle.

His commanders were pushing him hard in part because Michael's unit received orders to deploy to Iraq. Michael told them his back was in too much pain and argued he couldn't be sent to a war zone. His superiors told him he was lazy and a coward. "They thought I was just making up these conditions to get out of a deployment and it was a nightmare," he said. "A real nightmare. I was harassed on a regular basis. The worst was the badgering, the accusation of being a malingerer or lying about my condition. I had papers thrown at me, and was constantly forced to get vaccinations and make other preparations for going when I clearly couldn't even stand up for long periods of time." Michael's commanders even sent him to see a psychologist to see if he could be given a dishonorable discharge for "personality disorder."

Ultimately, however, Michael was able to see a military doctor who gave him a diagnosis: he had multiple herniated disks in the lumbar region of his lower back, which—because he had continued lifting heavy machinery and training for war—had blossomed into a degenerative disk disease that would get worse over time.

In September 2004, the Army gave Michael a medical discharge, freeing him of daily military duties and allowing him to access the VA's medical system. But the Army levied a parting shot on the way out. They gave Michael a 20 percent disability rating, below the amount that would give him medical retirement benefits.

The low disability score from the Army also forced Michael to go through the VA's complicated benefits application procedure. (The VA and Pentagon have different but parallel disability systems, and veterans often must navigate both of them. The Dole-Shalala Commission report that rose out of the Walter Reed scandal recommended merging these two systems under the VA to make the system less confusing. The two systems have since been merged somewhat, but the bureaucratic maze remains complicated.) After months of waiting, the VA declared Michael to be 40 percent disabled, which entitled him to a monthly cash payment of $518 and "Priority Two" access to the VA's health care services. It hasn't worked out.

Even with his wife Hope working two jobs—as a manager of a local bank branch and superintendent of their apartment building—Michael needed to find work. But he quickly found that he wasn't healthy enough to hold a job, and with Priority Two status at the VA, he couldn't manage to get healthy. "I was only given six chiropractic visits within a three-month period, which was not enough at all," he told me. "Instead of real care, they just give me pain killers and anti-depressants, and the side effects of those make it even more difficult for me to hold a job."

Durrell Michael has tried to work. Shortly after his discharge from the military, Michael landed a job as a private security guard for Tacoma-based Security Masters Corporation. "We sent him out to construction sites," manager Mike Batnik told me. "He was a great employee. I wish we could have kept him. But [Michael] kept calling in sick and that made it difficult for me because I had to keep shuffling people around to cover for him."

After four months at Security Masters, Michael quit and began to look for less strenuous work. "One day I'd bend down to pick up a quarter and be on my back for two or three days," Michael told me. "All that sitting, all that standing, I just couldn't do it. And if I had to manhandle somebody, it would definitely not be good." Michael tried to return to his old profession in manufacturing, landing a job similar to the one he had before he joined the Army, as a press operator at a stationery printer. But after a few weeks, he quit that job too.

Hope and Durrell would like to move back to their home state of Pennsylvania, where their families could help them through these difficult times. But right now Durrell Michael is appealing his disability percentage in the hopes of winning greater compensation, vocational training, and more frequent doctors' appointments. The couple is concerned that if they move, the VA will lose their paperwork. VA disability claims are handled at fifty-eight regional offices throughout the country. If a veteran like Michael moves from one part of the country, his files literally have to be mailed from one regional office to another—in Michael's case, from Seattle to Philadelphia. The VA claims adjudicators at the new office then start at the beginning, further lengthening the veteran's wait for a decision on health care and disability benefits.

To make matters worse, the VA doesn't always follow its own rules. In October 2007, the *Charlotte Observer* performed an audit of over 283,000 outpatient appointments at VA facilities around the country. Among their findings, 24 percent of veterans with traumatic brain injury had to wait more than thirty days for an appointment. At some hospitals, the wait times were simply abysmal. At the VA in Salisbury, North Carolina, 61 percent of appointments for the seriously wounded were scheduled for dates more than thirty days out. At the VA in Charleston, South Carolina, the paper reported "13 of 14 patients slated to be seen for brain injury waited more than a month. At 93 percent, that was the worst record nationwide."[1]

The *Observer* article appeared just a month after a similar audit by the VA's own Office of Inspector General. The Inspector General's report accused top VA bureaucrats of lying to Congress by telling America's elected leaders that 96 percent of veterans seeking primary medical care and 95 percent of veterans seeking specialty care were seen within thirty days of their "desired dates."[2]

The audit of 700 medical appointments at 14 VA facilities across the country found that 72 percent of the time there were "unexplained differences between the desired date of care documented in medical records" and the date the appointment actually occurred. In reality, the audit revealed that veterans seeking to use VA health care had to wait more than a month about 30 percent of the time.

Sometimes the waits were much longer. In one case, a veteran listed as 80 percent disabled was made to wait six months for an ear appointment—even though his "service connected" disability included damage to his ear. In another case, a veteran listed as 50 percent disabled waited almost a year for an eye appointment. According to the Inspector General, "on December 20, 2005, a veteran who was 50 percent service-connected was seen in the Eye Clinic. The provider wrote in the progress note that the veteran should return to the clinic in 6 weeks. However . . . the veteran actually waited 259 days for his appointment. The scheduling records did not contain any explanation for the delay. Medical facility personnel told us the reason this appointment took so long to schedule was because it 'fell through the cracks.'"

Pittsburgh, Pennsylvania, native Jonathan Millantz joined the Army at age twenty so he could become a health care specialist. When he got to boot camp, they assigned him for training as a combat medic. "It was deception from the very beginning," he told me.

In April 2003, Jonathan was deployed to Iraq with the Fourth Infantry Division. There, he ran more than two hundred combat missions and had several near misses with rockets and roadside bombs. One of those times, Millantz said, he was driving an unarmored Humvee along Route 1, the main highway that runs north-south across the length of Iraq.

"I was rolling down the road and the vehicle in front of me got hit by two 155 [mm] artillery rounds and three pounds of C-4 explosives,"

Storefront Help through the VA

Vet Centers (www.vetcenter.va.gov) are small storefront centers operated by the Department of Veterans Affairs that provide readjustment counseling and outreach services to all veterans who served in any combat zone. Services are also available for family members for military related issues. The Vet Center program operates 207 community-based counseling centers in all fifty states, the District of Columbia, Guam, Puerto Rico, and the U.S. Virgin Islands. Founded in 1979 by Vietnam veterans seeking an alternative to the traditional VA bureaucracy, it is separate and more informal than the VA hospital system. Vet Centers are staffed by small, multidisciplinary teams of providers, many of whom are combat veterans themselves. Vet Center staff are available toll-free during normal business hours at 800-905-4675 (Eastern) and 866-496-8838 (Pacific).

he said. "It pushed a thirty-five-ton tank five feet. I had a concussion. There was black smoke everywhere. Rocks hit off my helmet. It was just a complete mess. I came very close to being killed."

Millantz was also hit by numerous roadside bombs. "I know I had what they call shell shock," he told me. "The concussion of the bomb made me unaware of where I was and what time of day it was. It felt like getting punched in the face. It was a weird feeling. Your adrenaline's going crazy, but at the same time you're very spacey."

In November 2003, his unit named Millantz "Soldier of the Month." The recognition was small comfort, though. Inside, he was falling apart. "When I was on midtour leave I got a phone call that one of my soldiers had died in Iraq," he told me. "He was one of my soldiers. I was his medic and he died when I was at home. It was very hard for me to deal with that and I started drinking."

Millantz told me he was able to pull himself together and hold off drinking for the remainder of his tour in Iraq, and when he was discharged after finishing his Army contract in August 2005 he appeared to transition quite well. He started his own business, doing freelance small-scale landscape architecture on homes and gardens around Pittsburg. He also enrolled in courses at a community college, where he achieved a 4.0 GPA and was inducted into Phi Theta Kappa, the international honor society of two-year schools.

Initially, Millantz was saved a massive fight with the VA. His combat duty was well documented and easy to prove. The VA listed him as 100 percent disabled, with post-traumatic stress disorder and unrecoverable injuries to his back and foot. Millantz should have gone to the front of the line when it came to receiving treatment at VA hospitals. Despite that, he soon found himself doing battle with the VA's health care bureaucracy.

"At first when I got back the VA gave me Vicodin and Percocet," he said. "Then they took me off because I missed an appointment. So I had to find these painkillers on my own because I was in pain. I was in physical pain and emotional pain and I felt like I needed them to keep going to work and going to school." After some searching, he discovered the easiest drug to find was heroin. "I grew up in the inner city," he told me. "I knew where to get it and it was the easiest way for me to forget everything."

Millantz quickly realized he was making a mistake. His father was a Vietnam veteran who'd turned to booze after returning from the war zone, and he'd drunk himself to death when Millantz was fourteen years old. "I saw myself going down to the same fate he had, walking in the same footsteps," he told me. So two months later, with an addiction beginning to take hold, Millantz returned to the VA in search of substance abuse treatment. Doctors at the VA prescribed another pill, Suboxone, which is used to treat opium addiction. Millantz hoped to get additional appointments with counselors in the VA's well-regarded drug rehab program, but no matter how hard he tried he could not get in to see a specialist.

"I went to the VA three times for my scheduled appointments and the doctor wasn't even there," he told me. "I tried for a month to get into their program and gave up. I went through withdrawals by myself. I detoxed myself. I meditated and took vitamins and worked out and now I haven't touched the stuff in months."

Despite his recovery, Millantz is bitter. Like many other veterans, he feels betrayed by a system that promised education, adventure, and service to country but instead delivered an unpopular occupation of Iraq and an underfunded, unhelpful VA health care system. "The best advice I'd give to any veteran is to find programs or meetings in their community such as Narcotics Anonymous," Millantz said. "There are other ways to help you out. The VA isn't going to help you out of your problem. Trust me. I tried."

Rank-and-file VA workers react to stories like these with a mix of anger and regret. They argue (correctly) that the overwhelming percentage of VA doctors, nurses, and psychiatrists are both well-qualified and committed. They also argue that the VA's care is usually superior to the private sector's and that the bureaucracy, while certainly trying, isn't as bad as some veterans say.

"These vets have got to get a sense of perspective," a VA psychiatrist told me after we were introduced at a friend's dinner party. "They call me up and want an appointment that day. I try to get them in as soon as possible, but you can't go anywhere in America and get an appointment the same day. Anywhere you go, you'll have to wait a little while.

"I have Blue Cross," she continued. "I'm constantly arguing with them and fighting with their bureaucracy. If you have an HMO you're constantly told no or told you have to wait for an appointment. The problem isn't the VA. The problem is the war. Nobody goes to war and comes back the same. These kinds of problems will come out of any war. The president and Congress should have thought of the wounded before they started the war. The vets should have thought about that before they signed up. They just like to blame the VA because it's convenient. If they can blame the VA, then they don't have to blame the war itself."

I agree with many of those sentiments. The VA's care, when a veteran can access it, is often the best around. Politicians and veterans groups sometimes *do* beat up on the VA to distract them from the pain and suffering that flows from every war. But there's something very wrong with the comparison between private HMOs and the Department of Veterans Affairs. American servicemen and women made a bargain with their government when they signed up. They agreed to go and fight any enemy anywhere in the world so long as their Congress and commander in chief deemed it necessary for the sake of the nation. In return, the government agreed to take care of their wounds both on the battlefield and when they got home. Veterans have every right to feel a sense of entitlement when they approach the VA for the benefits they've earned.

Just because civilians have to battle private companies like Kaiser and Blue Cross to get their medical care approved and paid for doesn't mean that veterans should do the same. In fact, the whole VA system was set up precisely to ensure that those who've served their country don't have to depend on the vagaries of the market when they try to take care of their war wounds. This is a promise that the U.S. government makes to service members when they sign up for the military, and it is a promise that must be kept when they are injured in the line of duty. We should all have access to a smoother, more hassle-free health care system where doctors, not bean counters, decide what care we need and deserve. The Department of Veterans Affairs is controlled by the people through its elected representatives and we have the right to demand that it provide the services it was set up to provide.

PART IV

THE DOWNWARD SPIRAL

DRUGS, CRIME, HOMELESSNESS, AND SUICIDE

12

CRIME

Close to midnight on December 18, 1980, thirty-one-year-old
Manny Babbitt—high on marijuana and PCP—broke into the
Sacramento home of Leah Schendel, a seventy-eight-year-old
woman he did not know. He stripped the clothes off the lower half
of her body, took a hot iron to her vagina, beat her to death, and
robbed her house.

Then, less than twenty-four hours later, Babbitt struck again. He
grabbed a sixty-year-old woman out of her car on her way home. Babbitt dragged her into nearby bushes. He knocked her unconscious,
cracked her chest, stole her watch and wedding ring, and fled. The
woman, Mavis Wilson, survived.

In 1982, Manny Babbitt was sentenced to death for those crimes.
He was executed on May 4, 1999, at California's famed San Quentin
State Prison near the Golden Gate Bridge. A week later, he was buried
near his boyhood home in Wareham, Massachusetts.

Babbitt's case was one of the first stories I covered as a journalist,
and his death still haunts me today.[1] That's because Manny Babbitt
was a Vietnam veteran—and it seemed to me that his life and death

were a metaphor for the way the U.S. government treats its soldiers. Sign them up, teach them to kill, and then look the other way when they're less than perfect after they return home.

Manny Babbitt received a Purple Heart while in prison at San Quentin for his heroism at the battle of Khe Sanh, one of the bloodiest battles of the Vietnam War. During a seventy-seven-day North Vietnamese siege, 730 American soldiers died there, and more than 2,500 were wounded; 15,000 North Vietnamese died as well.

The battle turned out to have no strategic significance. The North Vietnamese attack on the remote village was just a diversion for the massive Tet Offensive that came immediately afterward. But for the soldiers who fought there, Khe Sanh made an indelible imprint. When Babbitt's case came before the State Board of Prison Terms, Vietnam veterans flew in from all over the country to testify at his clemency hearing. One was retired Detroit police officer Lynn Dornan, who said Babbitt saved his life when Viet Cong guerrillas attacked their roadside encampment.

"Instead of running across the road to the trench line, which would have been the smart thing to do, I started to run up the road along the trench line, parallel with it," he told the board. "Manny didn't just jump into the trench line. He followed me up the road. By this time, the next barrage was already on its way." Manny "jumped up and grabbed me by the flack jacket, pulled me up and started down the road," Dornan said. "Had Manny not found me fifty yards up the road, I'd still be laying on the road."

Manny Babbitt survived Khe Sanh despite being hit by shrapnel from a rocket that sliced his skull open. While going for help, he lost consciousness on the airstrip and was mistaken for dead; he was loaded onto a pile of dead bodies and body parts. Babbitt regained consciousness in the hull of a helicopter surrounded by severed limbs and heads and bloody bodies.[2]

Babbitt's supporters argued that he suffered from post-traumatic stress disorder and that he constantly relived the horrors of his wartime experience. They said the low valley fog that permeated Sacramento the night of Leah Schendel's killing made streetlights look like enemy helicopters. The situation was exacerbated, they said, because Schendel had been watching a Vietnam War movie.

Gary Dahlheimer was a mechanic in Babbitt's unit. A large man in a plaid buttoned-down shirt, he told the State Board of Prison Terms that PTSD was a disease that, if left untreated, could cause someone to kill. "I suffer 100 percent from severe and persistent post-traumatic stress disorder," he told the board, holding back tears. In the thirty-plus years since leaving Vietnam, Dahlheimer said his life had been "a horror."

"I'm unable to sleep," he said. "I'm unable to work. I'm unable to sleep with my wife. Because of my disassociative state I've nearly killed my wife on a number of occasions in my sleep." Dahlheimer spoke in a wavering, quaking voice—more emotional in his presentation than even the families of the condemned and the victims. It was clearly still difficult for him to talk about the war. It was a difficult thing to watch—a grown man and former Marine with tears welling up in his eyes in public. It was those tears, more than anything else at the hearing, that made me think Babbitt's life should be spared.

"I live every day listening to the screams in my head of the people who died at Khe Sanh," Dahlheimer said. "I smell the blood. I smell the live blood in my nose every day. I smell the cordite. I smell all the rotten, stinking smell of Khe Sanh daily."

Manny Babbitt's life went downhill after he came back from Vietnam. He developed strange habits like playing with the pull tabs from aluminum cans. He walked for hours by himself, playing with the tabs. He drank alcohol and used drugs. He had flashbacks and ended up in strange places without knowing how he got there. He went out all hours of the night and developed a criminal record: burglary, armed robbery, attempted rape, and indecent assault.

How many other people are there like Manny Babbitt, who have been damaged by war and then put to death by the state? More than you might think. The human rights group Amnesty International has documented at least eight cases of Vietnam veterans being put to death for crimes they committed while suffering from PTSD.[3] Two more vets diagnosed with PTSD are currently on death row after killing police officers in circumstances linked to their military service. These cases are likely only the tip of the iceberg, since they represent only the cases where PTSD was argued as a defense. It also doesn't represent cases originating before 1980, the year post-traumatic stress disorder became an official psychiatric diagnosis.

One of the veterans profiled by Amnesty International is George Page, a North Carolina man who served sixteen years in the military including a tour as a mechanic in Vietnam. On the morning of February 27, 1995, police officers were called to the scene of a shooting in Winston-Salem. When they arrived, they found that Page had fired several shots from the window of his apartment using a high-powered rifle. He fired more shots, one of which ricocheted through two car windows before striking Officer Stephen Amos in the chest, fatally wounding him.

Page received a stay of execution in 2004, after his ex-wife wrote an affidavit stating, "When George returned from Vietnam, he had completely changed. . . . When he got back, he was really standoffish and he just didn't get close to people again. After he returned from Vietnam, there were many times when I would wake up in the middle of the night and George wouldn't be in the bedroom. I would get up and would find him in the kitchen. He would usually be drinking. He would be sitting on the floor and crying. . . . The next morning, he would never remember what had happened. . . . Something traumatic must have happened to George while he was in Vietnam. He very rarely talked about his time in Vietnam but he seemed to be tortured by those experiences."[4]

Crime statistics for Vietnam veterans are truly frightening. By 1986, the National Vietnam Veterans Readjustment Survey reported that almost half of all male Vietnam veterans suffering from PTSD had been arrested or jailed least once—34.2 percent had been jailed more than once, 11.5 percent had been convicted of a felony.[5]

In his widely respected book *Odysseus in America,* psychiatrist Jonathan Shay argues that while PTSD certainly plays a role in the high crime statistics, prolonged combat itself can push a veteran toward criminal activity. Dr. Shay, who has spent the last twenty years counseling Vietnam veterans, writes of "the first way that combat soldiers lose their homecoming having left the war zone physically—they may simply remain in the combat mode, although not necessarily against the original enemy."[6]

For most veterans, Shay argues, combat experience provides little to no preparation for civilian employment. While former military pilots may find civilian employment at an airline, he writes, the picture is much grimmer for infantrymen who make up the majority of veterans of the wars in both Vietnam and Iraq. To prove his point, Shay lists off the "strengths, skills, and capacities acquired during prolonged combat":

• Control of fear
• Cunning, the arts of deception, the arts of the "mind-fuck"

Legal Help for Veterans Looking for a Fair Shake

The **National Lawyers Guild Military Task Force** (www.nlgmltf.org, 415-566-3732) assists those working on military law issues as well as military law counselors working directly with GIs.

- Control of violence against members of their own group
- The capacity to respond skillfully and *instantly* with violent, lethal force
- Vigilance, perpetual mobilization for danger
- Regarding fixed rules as possible threats to their own and their comrades' survival
- Regarding fixed "rules of war" as possible advantages to be gained over the enemy
- Suppression of compassion, horror, guilt, tenderness, grief, disgust
- The capacity to lie fluently and convincingly
- Physical strength, quickness, endurance, stealth
- Skill at locating and grabbing needed supplies, whether officially provided or not
- Skill in the use of a variety of lethal weapons
- Skill in adapting to harsh physical conditions

The list leads Shay to this chilling conclusion. "Combat service," he writes, "smoothes the way into criminal careers afterward in civilian life. . . . A criminal career allows a veteran to stay in combat mode, use his hard-earned skills, and even to relive aspects of his experience."

The house lights go down and the stage lights come up on *The Wolf,* the first production of VetStage, a nonprofit theater company run by

American veterans of wars in Iraq and Afghanistan. It opens with a funeral: a Roman Catholic priest preparing to deliver a eulogy for a U.S. soldier killed by a roadside bomb.

Quickly, the scene changes and we're transported to a group therapy session at a military mental institution, and we meet our two main characters. Both are members of the Marine Corps facing courts-martial. The first is a female soldier accused of killing a fellow Marine after he raped her. The second, a male Marine, is on trial for massacring an entire Iraqi family in their home.

The therapy session does not go well. "A lot of fucked-up shit happened in combat, that's what I think, supershrink," a third solider in the therapy session tells the military psychiatrist. "You know what? I'm tired, so why don't we move on."

The play's author and lead actor, Sean Huze, is also the founder of VetStage. He signed up for the Marine Corps on September 12, 2001—the day after the terrorist attacks in New York and Washington, D.C.—and served as an infantryman during the initial invasion and occupation of Iraq in March 2003.

The Louisiana native had acted in bit parts in commercials and on television before enlisting. Immediately after he returned, he wrote a play called *The Sand Storm*, a series of ten monologues describing the Iraq War from the soldiers' perspective. Huze said the play helped him work through psychological issues that surfaced after he came home from Iraq.

In Los Angeles, he founded VetStage, which seeks to present "one of the best opportunities for our nation's veterans to define their experience and how it is perceived by the public. In addition to that, it provides a positive, creative outlet for veterans to process their personal experience, enable them to make an artistic contribution to society, and ease the transition back into civilian life."[7]

The Wolf was VetStage's first production, in association with Iraq and Afghanistan Veterans of America. Huze told me he was drawn to write *The Wolf* when he saw how the U.S. government and the media reacted to a Marine Corps massacre of two dozen Iraqi civilians at Haditha in November 2005.

Time magazine first reported the killings four months after they happened, alleging that Marines "went on a rampage in the village after the attack, killing 15 unarmed Iraqis in their homes, including seven women and three children." Eman Walid, a nine-year-old survivor, told the magazine, "I couldn't see their faces very well—only their guns sticking into the doorway. I watched them shoot my grandfather, first in the chest and then in the head. Then they killed my granny." Then, Eman claimed, the troops started firing toward the corner of the room where she and her eight-year-old brother were hiding; the other adults shielded the children from the bullets, but died in the process. Eman told *Time* her leg was hit by a piece of metal and her brother was shot near his shoulder. "We were lying there, bleeding, and it hurt so much. Afterward, some Iraqi soldiers came. They carried us in their arms. I was crying, shouting, 'Why did you do this to our family?' And one Iraqi soldier tells me: 'We didn't do it. The Americans did.'"[8]

The victim's account was backed up by video footage, which prompted politicians in Washington to do what they usually do: condemn the people shown in the video and demand an investigation.

"There are two tracks," White House press secretary Tony Snow said. "What happened with reporting the incident, and what happened, and the Marines are taking this very seriously and they're proceeding aggressively."[9] Soon, a group of enlisted soldiers and low-ranking officers were court-martialed at Camp Pendleton.

Once on trial, the accused Marines presented their defense, arguing that they were following rules of engagement that had been drilled

Arts Programs by and for Veterans

VetStage (www.vetstage.org, 818-308-6296) is not the only arts troupe in the country dedicated to helping veterans express themselves.

The **National Vietnam Veterans Art Museum** in Chicago (www.nvvam.org, 312-326-0270) houses over fifteen hundred works of art, including paintings, photography, sculpture, poetry, and music created by more than one hundred artists who chronicled their individual experiences from the Vietnam War. The museum is increasingly featuring works by veterans of Iraq and Afghanistan.

Iraq Veterans Against the War (www.ivaw.org, 215-241-7123) holds regular workshops for returning veterans as part of its Warrior Writers Project. The writing from the workshops is compiled into books, performances, and exhibits that provide a lens into the hearts of people who have a deep and intimate relationship with the Iraq War.

into them even before their deployment. One soldier testified that under the Marine Corps' rules of engagement, which are taught to infantry Marines at Camp Pendleton and in Iraq, it is permissible to shoot and kill persons running away from a roadside bomb attack, even if they are unarmed and there is no proof that they were involved in the attack.[10]

Accused Marines mounted a similar defense in another case. In April 2006, seven Marines and a Navy Corpsman dragged an unarmed Iraqi civilian from his house, fatally shot him, and then planted an AK-47 assault rifle near the body to make it look like he had been killed in a shootout.

"We were told to crank up the violence level," Corporal Saul Lopezromo testified at the court-martial of his buddy, Corporal Trent Thomas. Lopezromo told the military jury that after that order came down, his unit became much rougher during daily patrols. Asked by a juror to explain, he said, "We beat people, sir."[11]

Lopezromo, who was not part of the late-night mission, said he saw nothing wrong in what Thomas and the others did. "I don't see it as an execution, sir," he told the judge. "I see it as killing the enemy." He added that Marines, in effect, consider all Iraqi men as part of the insurgency. "Because of the way they live, the clans, they're all in it together," he said.[12]

Watching these trials unfold in nearby Los Angeles, Marine Corps veteran Sean Huze felt a kinship with the killers. "I watched this strong condemnation [that came from the media and politicians in Washington], but while I felt a lot of things, condemnation wasn't one of them," Huze told me. "Some lance corporal is going to do ten years in the brig or longer, and in the meantime the people who train Marines to do it, that condition Marines to do this, basically get off. They hang the individuals out to dry when really they're doing what they're trained and conditioned to do. That's why I took this kind of route with this play."

In the first act of *The Wolf*, the two soldiers break out of a military mental institution, but they can't lie low. Violence follows them wherever they go. At one point, the male protagonist points a gun at his own mother and then ties her up to prevent her from calling the cops. Later, he shoots a liquor store clerk who happens to be from an Arab country. Eventually, the main character runs to his church where he confesses killing the Iraqi family to a local priest: "They were sheep," he says, "and I am a wolf and I did what wolves do and that's what I told 'em and that's why they keep me locked up."

"And what about now—you're still a wolf?" the priest asks.

"You can't turn someone from a sheep into a wolf and then back again, so where does that leave me now?"

Among the actors in the play was Karl Risinger, an Army veteran who trained soldiers before their deployments to Iraq and Afghanistan. He believes the war in Iraq is a just cause, but like Huze links the military training and the experience of war with crime back on the home front.

"I like the production," Risinger said. "I think it's a story that needs to be told. [Veterans] have been programmed and trained and they're soldiers, and suddenly they get out of the military and they're home to normal life and they don't have to go through the normal regimens they have to go through in the military." He added, "They're dealing with the stuff they've done during their military careers. Nobody really knows how to deprogram a soldier."

Now a new generation of veterans is returning home from a war that—like Vietnam—gives soldiers morally suspect rules of engagement. This lack of ethics, psychiatrist Jonathan Shay writes, is a leading contributor to the development of PTSD and a possible life of crime.

"Every atrocity strengthens the enemy and potentially disables the service member who commits it," Shay argues. "The overwhelming majority of people who join our armed services are not psychopaths; they are good people who will be seared by knowing themselves to be murderers." Calling out politicians who say we need to support the troops by bending the rules of international law, Shay says, "You do not 'support our service men' by mocking the law of land warfare and calling it a joke."[13]

Instead, veterans groups argue, supporting service men and women means listening to them when they get home. Therapist and Vietnam veteran Shad Meshad, who founded the National Veterans Foundation, told me the current atmosphere in America reminds him of the national mood thirty years ago. "When I go through airports I see soldiers just sitting up against a wall—you may see hundreds of them in a large airport—just by themselves. No one goes up to them, that positive energy toward them is faded," Meshad said. "No one is spitting or shouting, but they're still left with the fact that they're responsible for what they did or didn't do and they're supposed to think about that alone."

Given the experience of Vietnam vets, Meshad believes the American people ignore veterans at their own peril. "These are the goal pieces of the future," he said. "I don't need to tell you the stories of the Vietnam vets, of the percentages in prison and on the streets homeless. We're going to repeat that same thing, I can sense it, if we don't take action and Congress doesn't create services to help these folks over the next ten or fifteen years." Unfortunately, with 1.7 million Americans having served in Iraq and Afghanistan, there are already echoes of Vietnam in the types and rising number of crimes returning service members have committed.

In August 2005, the *Seattle Weekly* reported that in the first two years after the Bush administration sent U.S. troops to Iraq, there were seven homicides and three suicides in western Washington alone involving active-duty troops or Iraq War veterans. Five wives, a girlfriend, and one child were slain; four other children lost one or both parents to death or imprisonment. Three servicemen committed suicide—two of them after killing their wife or girlfriend. Four soldiers were sent to prison. One awaited trial.[14]

Are we providing better care and counseling to Iraq war veterans than we gave to Vietnam vets, or are we, again, ignoring the problems that inevitably develop when a war comes home? On May 21, 2006, a military court-martial at Fort Lewis, Washington, sentenced twenty-year-old Specialist Brandon Bare to life in prison for killing his eighteen-year-old wife, Nabila, with a meat cleaver after returning home from Iraq. Bare turned himself in the day of the killing and signed a confession with Army detectives. His lawyers hoped his combat experience could be used as part of his defense: Bare served as a machine gunner in some of the most dangerous parts of Iraq and received a Purple Heart after being wounded in a grenade attack in Mosul in March 2005. He was sent home to recover from internal ear injuries and later was enrolled in an intensive psychiatric group therapy program. But at his court-martial at Fort Lewis, the judge ruled Bare's lawyers could not try to link the killing with psychological or emotional problems he might have suffered as a result of his combat service and injuries in Iraq. The judge said that might confuse the jury about the question he said was at issue in the trial: whether Bare had formed a plan to kill his wife.

This was the same answer Manny Babbitt got when his lawyers argued that his combat experience should be taken into account in his drive for clemency back in 1999. At the time, California governor Gray Davis told me he would consider only one factor in his deliberations: "Is there evidence of innocence that has not been presented to a court? That is what I think my job is," he said. "I'm not going to relitigate the issue or question the wisdom of a jury or the many appellate courts that have heard this case."

But, like so many recently returned Iraq war veterans, Manny Babbitt never argued that he was innocent. And so, early one May morning, he was strapped to a gurney and given the three injections that ended his life.

13

HOMELESS ON THE STREETS
OF AMERICA

The U.S. Vets Westside Residence Hall is a hulking eight-story structure a few blocks from Los Angeles International Airport. The building is an imposing peach-colored concrete and steal behemoth, bringing to mind a Soviet apartment block. The only concession to aesthetics is a small, grass courtyard in the center. On each floor, the small rooms open up onto a walkway overlooking the courtyard. With 525 dormitories, it's the largest transitional housing and employment center for homeless veterans in the country.

The center's outreach director, Ivan Mason, met me at the front door. A large black man with a crew cut and a white buttoned-down shirt, Mason served in the Army from 1979 until 1982. He spent the next fifteen years homeless or in prison before entering the U.S. Vets residential treatment program in 1997. "I needed to learn how to live again," he told me as we began our tour of the facility. "That's the typical cry of a lot of the vets that go through our system. They cry out a new way of living their lives. This is the first time I've been living life on life's terms and I'm fortysomething. And it's only when I got in my midthirties that the light went on and said, 'Hey, you gotta do something with your life or it will get away from you.' That's pretty much the story for a lot of vets here."

One of the first residents we met was thirty-one-year-old Michael Hall. He wore wire-rimmed glasses and a black T-shirt and jeans, and had a shaved head and a neatly trimmed goatee. An Army staff sergeant, he enlisted shortly after high school and served ten years as a heavy-equipment mechanic and technical weapons specialist in Bosnia, Cuba, Kuwait, and Afghanistan before being severely injured in Iraq in 2003.

"I was hit by a rocket-propelled grenade," Hall told me as he limped into a recreation room on the building's ground floor. "I suffer from compression of the spine. I used to be six foot four. Now I'm six two and a half." He added, almost as an afterthought, "I got knocked through a wall. I just deal with it on a day to day basis. I can't ever run again."

The Department of Veterans Affairs considers Hall to be 100 percent disabled. He has difficulty walking, dragging his feet with each step he takes. Sometimes, he uses a cane. He also suffers from mental injuries—bipolar disorder and post-traumatic stress disorder—conditions he did not exhibit before he went to Iraq.

Hall said his problems really started when he got back to the States and started "hanging out with an old group of friends" from before he joined the military. One of them introduced him to methamphetamines, which he started using to dull the pain. "I knew a lot of people who were killed in Iraq," he explained, "so the pain of losing loved ones on the battlefield, the pain of not being there for my children, of not knowing how to live in this civilian society after so many years in the military—I stuffed these things down deep inside because I considered myself a hard-core guy. But after the effects of the methamphetamine went away, I still felt the same. No matter how much I could do or how much I could smoke, the results were the same. It was the insanity of it all."

Hall has four children, ages seven, four, two, and one. But his be-havior since being released from the military has kept him away from them. In addition to using drugs, he started dealing as well. Since leav-ing the military in 2003, he has served time in federal prison in Okla-homa for felony home invasion and has had numerous other run-ins with the law. "I tried to be stronger than the drug," he said. "I used to tell my customers 'do the drug, don't let the drug do you,' but then I found myself in that same predicament. The drugs took over my life."

Within three years, Hall hit rock bottom—one of twenty-seven thousand homeless vets on the streets of Los Angeles.[1] He lived on the streets for six months before his step-father, who served in Vietnam, told him about the U.S. Vets transitional housing and drug treatment program. Hall now attends regular Narcotics Anonymous meetings and receives regular treatment from the VA health system. U.S. Vets also helped him win back custody of his four children, though until he can find stable housing and employment they'll live with Hall's parents.

Dwight Radcliff, the chief operating officer of U.S. Vets, told me the organization is increasingly coming into contact with relatively young homeless veterans involved in custody disputes over their chil-dren. "It's a sign of the times," he said. "It's a lot freer now than even in the 1970s. So it's not surprising to see a veteran who is twenty-three years old who has children, who cannot get along with the custodial parent, who needs support and help to navigate that system."

Radcliff added that the presence of those children can also be a mo-tivator to get the veteran off the streets and clean from drugs. U.S. Vets now offers a Father's Program, a special four-phase track to help non-custodial fathers become emotionally and financially involved in their children's lives. The program uses intensive case management to assist the veteran in obtaining and maintaining full-time employment,

Help for Homeless Veterans

The **National Coalition for Homeless Veterans** (www.nchv.org, 800-VET-HELP) is a clearinghouse of community-based service providers and local, state, and federal agencies that provide emergency and supportive housing, food, health services, job training and placement assistance, legal aid, and case-management support for hundreds of thousands of homeless veterans each year.

U.S. Vets Inc. (www.usvetsinc.org, 310-348-7600) is the nation's largest provider of transitional housing for homeless veterans, with programs in Southern California, Nevada, Hawaii, Arizona, Texas, and Washington, D.C.

Swords to Plowshares (www.swords-to-plowshares.org, 415-252-4788) provides transitional housing, drug treatment, and psychiatric counseling in the San Francisco Bay Area.

Black Veterans for Social Justice (www.bvsj.org, 718-852-6004) provides housing and mental health care for homeless vets in New York City.

transitioning into stable permanent housing, maintaining sobriety, and completing a course of parenting classes.

On any given night, the VA estimates that nearly 200,000 veterans sleep on the streets of America. Nearly 400,000 experience homelessness over the course of a year. Conservatively, the National Council for Homeless Veterans estimates one out of three homeless men sleeping in a doorway, alley, or box in our cities and rural communities has put on a uniform and served this country.[2]

About half of the estimated 400,000 homeless veterans served during the Vietnam years, but those who provide care to veterans note they did not usually become homeless until nine to twelve years after their discharge. By contrast, some Iraq War veterans are becoming homeless almost immediately after returning home. "These are guys who are pretty much going straight from deployment to the streets," said Rachel Feldstein, associate director of New Directions, a residential care center for homeless veterans inside the VA complex in West Los Angeles. Already, she said, Iraq War vets are living on the streets, getting seriously addicted to drugs, and falling into criminal behavior.

Firm estimates of the number of homeless Iraq War veterans are hard to come by. By the end of 2006, the number of Iraq and Afghanistan veterans seeking homeless services from the VA had exceeded six hundred. Because veterans, particularly recent veterans, are loath to seek help, the real number is undoubtedly much higher.

According a to report by the San Francisco–based services agency Swords to Plowshares, the reasons Iraq War veterans are becoming homeless faster than Vietnam vets are closely related to the way the war is being fought. The fact that soldiers and Marines are forced to serve so many tours in Iraq is putting service members under unprecedented strain. In addition, the stop-loss program, which some call a "backdoor draft" forces some members of the country's volunteer armed forces to remain in service beyond their contractually agreed-upon term. "Servicemembers are enduring repeated, extended deployments, combat exposure and continual family disruptions, all risk factors for homelessness," according to the report.[3]

More than that, though, the type of combat soldiers are exposed to in Iraq is not like that of any other war America has fought. There is no rear detachment in this war. Even those in support operations can easily end up homeless.

Twenty-three-year-old Jason Kelley grew up in Tomahawk, Wisconsin, a small town of just 3,700 in the state's great Northwoods near the Canadian border. A strong man with a sharp face, he spent a year in the Army guarding convoys on their fourteen-hour drive between Kuwait and Camp Anaconda in Balad, north of Baghdad.

His convoys regularly came under attack, and after a few months in Iraq he had a mental breakdown. Medically evacuated back to the States and given full veterans' benefits, he returned to Tomahawk but didn't fit in. "I was bored," he deadpans. "There's not much to do there." Three months later, he picked up and drove to Los Angeles. Almost immediately, he ended up on the streets.

"I got stuck in a little predicament where I couldn't get a job because I didn't have an apartment and I couldn't get an apartment because I didn't have a job," he told me. "The money I saved up in Iraq ran down and I was living on the street." Kelley brought himself to the U.S. Vets Westside Residence Hall, where he's trying to stabilize his life and find a job. He has no plans to return to Wisconsin.

"What's unique about the men and women coming back from Iraq and Afghanistan is that they're not able to integrate with their family," New Direction's Rachel Feldstein said. "They've seen horrible things. They've been in horrible places and their family can't relate. And so you become homeless in the last place you lived."

Sixteen Iraq War veterans have entered residential drug rehab at New Directions over the last four years. Most have been referred to the program as an alternative sentence after being convicted of a crime. Very few have come in on their own. "One young gentleman has been here seven times. It's difficult for him to know that at age twenty-three he needs help, so he comes and he leaves and he comes and he leaves. Being twenty-three and saying 'I'm going to dedicate some time to dealing with my addiction' is pretty difficult when he sees that everyone else who's twenty-three is drinking and using and partying," Feldstein said.

On a tour of New Directions, most of the formerly homeless veterans I saw were older, in their fifties or sixties. In the detox center, where new entrants try to rest away their withdrawal symptoms, almost all the vets had white hair. One man pushed himself with a walker. The center provides veterans with healthy meals and hooks them up with twelve-step programs, but the atmosphere was tired and it was hard for me to imagine any of the Iraq War veterans I know feeling comfortable there.

Downstairs, as I left, New Direction's director, Toni Reinis, told me her agency is brainstorming about how to make the social service more palatable to the younger generation. Ideas include stepped-up family counseling to keep veterans from burning their bridges and becoming homeless in the first place.

"We've realized over the last year that we really have two totally different client populations," she said. "We have the older, chronically mentally ill homeless veteran who's been in and out of prison for a very long period of his life, and then we have this young twenty-two-year-old who doesn't feel like he fits into this client population."

Compounding the problem is that the federal government appears afraid to spend money to help homeless veterans. On July 17, 2007, a self-congratulatory VA press release announced that homeless veterans in "37 states will get more assistance, thanks to the Department of Veterans Affairs (VA) selection of 92 community organizations to receive funds for transitional housing this year. 'Only through a dedicated partnership with community and faith-based organizations can we hope to reduce homelessness among veterans,' said Secretary of Veterans Affairs Jim Nicholson in the release. 'These partnerships provide safe, comfortable housing in caring communities for veterans who need a helping hand.' "[4]

But the amounts of money doled out were so low as to be humorous. In the entire country, the VA announced it would be spending just $24 million to expand services for homeless veterans. Los Angeles, with its 27,000 homeless veterans, would be given just over a million dollars to pay for community service organizations to construct fifty-nine beds of transitional housing. Chicago, with an estimated 18,000 homeless veterans, got no money at all. New York, where the VA estimates that there are 12,000 homeless vets, was slated to receive enough money to build sixty-seven beds.

What this means is most veterans are left to fend for themselves when they come home, a situation made difficult not only by physical and mental wounds, but also by the disproportionately poor backgrounds of soldiers, many of whom look to the military for a leg out of the ghetto. These difficulties are vividly chronicled in the documentary film, *When I Came Home,* the story of Pvt. Herold Noel, who returned to New York after the serving in "the tip of the spear" of the Iraq invasion completely incapable of relating to his wife and three children.

"When I first seen my wife when she walked toward the bus, she looked like an Iraqi lady walking toward me," Herold tells the camera. "I couldn't hold her. I couldn't hold my kids because I'd seen kids die over there. I just wanted to be away from everybody."[5]

"He'd get upset easily," his wife Tamara remembered. "We were arguing all the time. One time we got in an argument and he put me in the car and drove me to some bushes and he said he would kill me if I kept arguing with him. I was really scared. He was never like that before."[6]

Herold tried to get help, but the VA denied his disability claim. Everywhere he went doors closed in front of him. When he tried to apply for public housing, he was told there was a freeze on new applications. When he stayed at a city shelter for the homeless, all his clothes, and his military medals, were stolen.[7]

Unable to cope, Herold moved into his red 1994 Jeep. His wife started temping as a clerk at a local hospital and moved in with her sister. One son crashed with family and friends. His other two children, six-year-old twins, moved to Florida to stay with their grandmother.[8]

"Herold represents what typically happens to adults that go into the military at seventeen or eighteen," the late Ricky Singh of Black Veterans for Social Justice says in the film. "When they return home, the same kind of economic conditions that force them toward the military still exist or have gotten worse. Herold returned to New York City, a town where the unemployment rate for African American males and Hispanic males was 48 percent. This may seem like an extreme comparison, but it's relevant."

Relevant also because soldiers discharged from the military often leave without skills that are transferable to the working world. Herold Noel joined the military straight out of high school, and while he had experience hauling fuel tankers through Baghdad and Fallujah, that experience didn't translate into job prospects in Brooklyn or Manhattan.

In many ways, Singh argues in the film, society does more to help former prisoners succeed than it does for veterans who have served their country. "Every person released from prison in this country is given a discharge plan and part of that discharge plan is a housing plan," Singh says. "It should happen for soldiers too. If a soldier is returning to a difficult housing situation, the soldier should have in his hand a Section 8 [federal] housing voucher."

But Herold didn't have that kind of help. So, with everyone from the City of New York to the VA turning their back, Herold turned to the press. With the help of Iraq and Afghanistan Veterans of America and Black Veterans for Social Justice, Herold was able to attract the attention of the *New York Post, Air America,* the *CBS Evening News,* the *Christian Science Monitor,* and Pacifica Radio. And yet, all of those interviews and favorable articles failed to move a single politician or part of the U.S. government to step in and help Herold Noel obtain housing.

It was a crushing blow. Herold told filmmaker Dan Lohaus that after going to the press he "thought everyone would give me a helping hand and help me and my family get stable and help me help other people come out and get stable. But people don't give a fuck."

"It was incredible to watch," Lohaus told me. "Herold really got his hopes up and then they were completely dashed. He started cutting everyone off. I got so worried about him I let him sleep on my couch for a while because I was worried he would do something drastic."

Desperate for a way to get back on his feet, Herold even thought about rejoining the military, visiting a recruiter who told him he could have him back with his "old unit by the end of next week if I want, and I told him that's what I want."

A veterans' advocate talked him out of it. "You want to go to a place where you're going to hold a weapon and get shot at! You can't deal with the subway right now," Paul Rieckhoff, founder of Iraq and Afghanistan Veterans of America, yells at him onscreen. "You're going to sit in a C-130 for seventeen hours? You're gonna sit in the back of a Chinook with all your gear on? You're gonna have some NCO screaming at you every day when you've got nowhere to go, you can't walk out, you can't decompress for a year?"

Fortunately for Herold, his story had a happy ending. On February 1, 2005, the *New York Post* announced an "anonymous angel" had "swooped down" and given the Brooklyn-born vet "the gift of a lifetime—an apartment for the decorated military man and his family."[9] After seeing Herold's story in the *Post,* the anonymous donor had contacted Iraq and Afghanistan Veterans of America (at the time it was called Operation Truth) and donated a three-bedroom apartment in the Mott Haven section of the Bronx.

When Herold moved into the apartment in March 2005, he did so with the press in tow. Cameras flashed everywhere as he lay down in the center of one of the rooms' clean floors. "I'm happy for whoever reached out to me, I'm happy for that," Herold told the assembled reporters. "I just want to give them a big hug and a kiss right now, but I'm not totally happy because the government and the Congress who are sitting in their lavish homes right now could have reached out, but that wasn't the case. It was just a regular Joe with a heart who said 'I'm going to help this guy.'"[10]

Herold's happiness was mixed with outrage, because even as his family moved into their new apartment, the lack of political attention to the issues he faced meant hundreds of thousands of other veterans would sleep homeless on the street.

"I just want to say 'thank you' to that congressman who never called me back," he said. "If you all know a councilman, he still has yet to return my call, but right now it's not about me no more 'cause I still got to go out there and get the rest of my family. Because the other soldiers are my family. Because I went to war with them so I gotta go out there and find the rest of my family."

14

SUICIDE

Dane and April Somdahl own the Alien Art tattoo parlor on Camp Lejeune Boulevard, just outside the sprawling Marine Corps base of the same name in Jacksonville, North Carolina. In an interview from the back of her shop, April told me how her customers' tastes have changed since George W. Bush ordered the invasion of Iraq in March 2003.

As the war approached, she said, "the most popular tattoos were eagles and United States flags. Those were coming in so often and, you know, everybody was like 'I gotta get my flag.'"

Then, a year into the war, the Somdahls noticed a new wave of Marines coming in to get information from their military dog tags tattooed onto their bodies. Most said they wanted so-called meat tags so their bodies could be identified when they die.

"We went through over a year of meat tags, but then that passed too," April said. "Now we are seeing a lot of memorial tattoos. Even the wives are getting memorial tattoos—moms and dads in their fifties too. And in a lot of cases they're getting their first tattoos. And they're saying, 'We didn't think we would ever get a tattoo, but this one is to remember my son.'"

Because of the changing needs of their clientele, the Somdahls no longer blast rock-and-roll music inside the shop. Instead, the artists work in silence. "The mood has died," April told me. "For our employees to do tattoos of photos of fallen heroes, fallen friends, it plays hard on them. It makes it so our artists are depressed. The tattoo isn't done just for decoration or just for fun anymore. The tattoo has become a solid symbol of their [the clients'] feelings, and a lot of it dealing with the war."

The mood is particularly heavy because the Somdahls have had a death in their own family. On February 20, 2007, April's younger brother, Sgt. Brian Jason Rand, shot himself under the Cumberland River Center pavilion in Clarksville outside Fort Campbell, Kentucky.

Brian Jason Rand was born on December 9, 1980, into a military family on base at Camp Lejeune. Throughout his life, he had always been in and around the military. He deployed twice to Iraq, returning for the final time on January 2, 2007.

It was during his first tour that April first noticed a change. She chatted with him every evening over the internet. In the afternoon, while it was nighttime in Baghdad, she would sit in front of her computer in North Carolina, hook up a microphone, and talk with her brother, trying to keep his spirits up. But she could tell her brother was having an emotional meltdown. "He would say, 'April, I'm having terrible nightmares,'" she said. "He told me about nightmares about dead Iraqis, their souls and spirits haunting him, following him, telling him to do stuff and it got scarier and scarier."

April said she talked Brian to sleep nearly every night during his deployment—trying to keep him alive by giving him something to live for. "I would talk to him in a very quiet voice and make sure not to make any sudden noises," she said. "I would tell him the grass is still green over here. The sky is still blue. Just close your eyes and picture the lawn that we laid on staring up at that sky. And it's still there. When you get back, when your job is done, when you do everything that they ask you to do, come back to me and we'll lay on the grass and we'll stare at the sky and we don't have to talk about anything."

But Brian's return home from Iraq wasn't the end of his nightmares. He was emotionally unstable. He knew he had problems, his family said, and he sought help from the military. He filled out a post-deployment health assessment form, admitting to combat-related nightmares, that he felt down or hopeless and had mood swings.

"When someone checks 'yes' to these types of things, clearly they should be evaluated for mental help," his widow Dena Rand told Clarksville's *Leaf Chronicle* newspaper, "but according to them, he never requested help."[1] Brian Rand never had a chance to see a psychiatrist. Instead of giving him the help he needed, the Army deployed him to Iraq a second time.

"We didn't have very many phone conversations at all during his last deployment," his sister April told me. "The phone calls only came when he was spiraling out of control, so it was very difficult to figure out what he was trying to communicate."

When he returned to Fort Campbell for the final time in January 2007, his family said he had completely changed. "He'd flip on a dime," his wife, Dena, told the *Leaf Chronicle,* describing scenarios, in public and private, that made him paranoid and agitated. The newspaper reported Dena said her husband "was either intensely happy or desperately sad; there was no middle ground, which was nothing like the man she married, whom she described as a gentle person who would 'drop anything he was doing to help anyone.'"

On February 8, 2007, Dena called the police when Jason started screaming at his stepdaughter, Cheyanne. "Mrs. Rand stated that her husband was yelling at her daughter," Officer Mathew Campbell wrote in his report for the Clarksville Police Department. "Mrs. Rand went upstairs to make him stop and she stated that he turned and smacked her in the face. Mr. Rand was gone upon arrival."

About the same time, Jason called his sister, April. "He said, 'Oh, I can see everything April. It all makes perfect sense now. I know what I have to do and it makes so much sense. I have to die. I have to leave the physical realm and leave earth and go up in heaven and be part of the Army of God and I've got to stop this war and save my guys here. And the best way I can do that is to do it up in heaven 'cause I can't do anything while I'm down here.' "

April told me she tried to talk her brother out of suicide. She mentioned that Dena was pregnant with their first child together. That child was going to need a father, she argued.

But Brian wouldn't listen. "He said the baby will be fine," April told me. "The baby will be taken care of . . . and then he started talking about his favorite music and then from his favorite music he goes to saying, 'You're going to have to know this. You're going to have to know my favorite movie. When I am gone you're going to want to watch my favorite movie, April. My favorite movie is *Mousetrap*.' "

Less than two weeks later, on February 20, 2007, the Clarksville police received a call about a body lying facedown under the entertainment pavilion on the banks of the Cumberland River. In their report, Officers Heather Hill and Jeff Derico wrote that "2 citizens called the police and said there was apparently a male person laying on the ground with a gun beside him. We arrived on the scene, made contact with body. The male was obviously deceased from apparent gun shot wound. Shotgun was lying next to the body. Crime scene was established. . . . Suspect's vehicle was towed to major crimes. EMS arrived on the scene and removed the body."

Officials at Fort Campbell refused to comment on Brian Rand's suicide, saying they don't comment on any individual soldier's death. But military brass have been investigating what seems like an increasing trend of soldiers taking their own lives. In August 2007, the Army issued a document called the *Army Suicide Event Report,* which showed suicides to be at their highest point in twenty-six years.[2]

"There was a significant relationship between suicide attempts and number of days deployed" in Iraq, Afghanistan, or nearby countries where troops were participating in the war effort, the report said. The same pattern seemed to hold true for those who not only attempted, but succeeded in killing themselves.

The Army confirmed ninety-nine suicides among active duty soldiers during 2006, up from eighty-eight the year before. But those numbers are undoubtedly an underestimate in part because they only include *confirmed* suicides. Many suicides are simply called accidents.

"We had one woman in my unit who died when she shot herself in the chest with her M-16," explained Garrett Reppenhagen, a former Army sniper who served in Iraq from February 2004 to February 2005. "The Army said it was an accident, but you can't accidentally shoot yourself in the chest with an M-16. It's a huge weapon. Imagine the logistics of that. . . . They must have thought they were doing her family a favor by saying it was an accident." A favor, because the families of soldiers who commit suicide are not eligible for survivor benefits.

Also ignored in the Army report are soldiers and reservists who commit "suicide by cop"—where a soldier or veteran deliberately provokes a confrontation with law enforcement as a way of killing themselves. No one keeps records on the number of people who die this way, but their stories can be found on the crime pages of local newspapers around the country.

"In Colorado, there was a woman that I had for Vets4Vets counseling sessions named Jessica Rich," Reppenhagen told me. A twenty-four-year-old Army Reservist, Rich served a tour in Iraq and was diagnosed with post-traumatic stress disorder in 2004. She received a medical discharge in 2005.

Her friend, Makayla Crenshaw, who served with Rich in Iraq, told the *Denver Post* that Rich couldn't shake some of her memories from the war, including witnessing the suicide of a fellow soldier in Iraq. "She was having nightmares still, up until this point—flashbacks and anxiety and everything, the whole bucket of fun," Crenshaw said. "She said it was really hard to get over it because she couldn't get any help from anybody."[3]

Rich died on February 8, 2007, after a high-speed auto accident on I-25 through El Paso County, Colorado. The coroner's report put her blood-alcohol level at twice the legal limit. "She got tanked up and was speeding down the wrong side of the interstate with no seatbelt and slammed head-on into a Suburban [SUV] that killed her instantly," Reppenhagen said. "So, these things are happening and there's not a lot being done to treat these soldiers. It's common. Really common."

Take the case of Brian William Skold, a twenty-eight-year-old National Guard veteran of the Iraq War from Sauk Rapids, a small community in central Minnesota one mile outside of Saint Cloud. According to an Associated Press account, Skold served with distinction in Baghdad from November 2004 until December 2005. When he returned from Iraq, he was a Guard member in good standing. But back home, his family said, he became suicidal.[4]

At 4:00 a.m. on the morning of Sunday, May 27, 2007, Skold's family called the police and told them he was driving his truck drunk with a loaded 12-gauge shotgun. A half hour later, Douglas County Sheriff deputies spotted him as he traveled west of I-94. According to the *Minneapolis Star-Tribune,* they followed him to a rest area outside Alexandria seventy miles from home.[5]

When Skold left the rest area and drove into the city, members of a city-county SWAT team took up the chase. Skold then got back on I-94 and drove east toward his home until officers used "stop sticks" to disable his pickup just beyond the exit at Osakis, Minnesota, about 120 miles northwest of Minneapolis.

"As a deputy continued to negotiate with him, Skold left his truck several times, brandishing his shotgun," the *Star-Tribune* reported. "The second or third time he fired the weapon, officers returned fire. A doctor at the scene pronounced him dead."

Officials at the Minnesota National Guard refused to comment on Brian Skold's death. Was the tragic shooting linked to the guardsman's service in Iraq? They wouldn't say. "In a tragedy such as this, our thoughts and prayers are with the loved ones of Specialist Skold," Lt. Col. Kevin Olson told the Associated Press. "This is an active police investigation," he added. "It would be inappropriate for me to speculate on the cause of the incident."[6]

Sometimes the police are clearly out of line—like in the case of Sgt. James E. Dean, who was shot by Maryland State troopers while sitting alone in his father's farmhouse on Christmas night, 2006.

Jamie Dean grew up in rural Maryland on the banks of the Chesapeake Bay, a big guy with a broad smile, who loved hunting and fishing. In the summer of 2001, Jamie shocked his family when, at age twenty-three, he decided to join the Army. He told them he wanted to experience life beyond installing air conditioners in confining St. Mary's County. His younger sister, an Air Force medic, had been talking up the military.

At the time of his death, Jamie had already served an eighteen-month tour in Afghanistan, where he was a sergeant, leading a small infantry unit. He received a number of awards: for service in defense of the nation, for good conduct, and for outstanding marksmanship with rifles and grenades.

But he didn't return home the same as he left, and when he went to the VA hospital, they diagnosed him with post-traumatic stress disorder. "The patient states he feels very nervous, has a hard time sleeping, feels nauseous in the a.m., and loses his temper a lot, 'real bad,'" reads a VA evaluation from December 2005. "Was nearby an explosion that destroyed a Humvee with four G.I.'s killed in front of his eyes. . . . The patient is tired of feeling bad."[7]

After his diagnosis, Jamie started regular therapy and took his medication, but he also drank. "Jamie wasn't one to open up anyway," his widow Muriel Dean told me. "The only thing he would ever say is, 'Nobody understands unless they've been there. You just don't understand.'"

"He told me that I didn't want to know what he had to do over there," Muriel added. "That I didn't want to know about the things he'd seen and the things that had gone on, and I never asked why." Then, a few days after Thanksgiving, a FedEx truck delivered an envelope to the Dean farm just as Jamie was about to go hunting. It was a form letter ordering him redeployed, effective January 14.

Muriel said her husband started pulling away from her as the deployment date grew closer. Then, at 9:10 P.M. on Christmas Day, Jamie barricaded himself inside his father's farmhouse in rural Maryland. He called his sister and told her he "just couldn't do it anymore" and fired a gunshot. Jamie's sister called the emergency services hotline and the police showed up in force. They cordoned off the house and fired tear gas inside. They brought in armored vehicles and blew a hole in the right side of the house. Just past midnight on December 26, a state police sharpshooter shot Jamie Dean dead.

"He was on a family farm," Muriel said. "There were no neighbors. There was nobody there with him, so if he was going to hurt anybody it was going to be himself. Time was on their side. If they had left him alone, he would have calmed down. He would have gone to sleep," she said. "He would have been fine."

In May 2007, the Maryland State's Attorney's office released a report on the incident. It called law enforcement's response "progressively assaultive and militaristic." The report largely agreed with the Dean family's assessment. "It is difficult to understand the necessity of an aggressive paramilitary operation, vis-à-vis a containment operation, directed at an individual down at the end of a dark road, holed up in his father's house with no hostages," the report reads.[8]

The Dean family hired a lawyer to look into their legal options. Their main interest, Muriel Dean said, was to force law enforcement authorities to think twice before laying into a veteran. "God forbid this situation happens again, it needs to be handled differently," she told me. "It happens everywhere that law enforcement goes into these situations all gung ho, and it's not good for them because these guys are trained just like the cops are. They're trained to kill as well when they're attacked like that. When they're already in their minds in a war zone, you don't put them back in there."

On January 2, 2007, James Emerick Dean was buried at Charles Memorial Gardens in Leonardtown, Maryland. The epitaph on his tombstone reads: "A Country Boy Can Survive."

15

SUICIDE AFTER THE WAR

Military documents like the *Army Suicide Event Report* do not address the number of veterans who commit suicide after leaving the service—a number that already appears to be exceeding the tally of soldiers who kill themselves while in uniform.

A November 2007 *CBS News* investigation found that 120 veterans kill themselves every week; over 5,000 per year. CBS asked all fifty states for their suicide data, based on death records for veterans and nonveterans, and found that veterans were twice as likely to commit suicide. In 2005, CBS found a total of at least 6,256 suicides among those who served in the armed forces.[1]

CBS's findings seemed in line with earlier estimates by scientists and advocacy groups who've argued that suicide among veterans has been high for decades. Internal VA documents show that high-ranking government officials also agree with this assessment. "There are about eighteen suicides per day among America's twenty-five million veterans," said the VA's chief of mental health Ira Katz after the story broke. "VA's own data demonstrate four to five suicides per day among those who receive care from us."[2] Over the last thirty years, most observers believe more Vietnam veterans have committed suicide than the fifty-seven thousand who died fighting the war.

No number is definite, however, because over the years the Department of Veterans Affairs has stubbornly refused to track the number of veterans who commit suicide. "We have had a 'see no evil, hear no evil' approach to examining post-deployment psychological reintegration issues such as suicide," writer Ilona Meagher told a Congressional hearing on suicide. "After all we have learned from the struggles of the Vietnam War generation—and the ensuing controversy over how many of its veterans did or did not commit suicide in its wake—why is there today no known national registry where Afghanistan and Iraq veteran suicide data is being collected? How can we ascertain reintegration problems—if any exist—if we are not proactive in seeking them out?"[3]

A study published in the June 2007 edition of the *Journal of Epidemiology and Community Health* found male veterans twice as likely to commit suicide as men with no military experience. The researchers, who followed the lives and deaths of more than 320,000 people over twelve years, found that veterans of World War II, Korea, Vietnam, and the Gulf War were all significantly more likely to kill themselves than those with no military experience.[4]

Portland State University professor Mark Kaplan, the lead author of the study, told me he was concerned that the suicide rate for Iraq and Afghanistan war veterans may be even higher than in previous wars, owing to the large number of wounded. "More and more soldiers are surviving this war with severe psychological trauma," he said. "There are also painful, debilitating injuries that people would have died from in previous wars—brain injuries or very disfiguring disabilities with third degree burns throughout the body. In our study we found that disability was an important risk factor [for suicide] among vets from all wars. . . . The vets that we found that had committed suicide were more likely to have a disability."

Another reason for concern, Kaplan said, is that with the all-volunteer nature of today's Army, only certain parts of society have had to fight this war—a factor that may make Iraq and Afghanistan veterans "more likely to feel socially isolated and depressed."

But suicide statistics are not inevitable. Suicide can be prevented. So it is especially troubling that even vets who seek out care through the Department of Veterans Affairs often end up taking their own lives. Of the 5,000 veterans the VA estimates commit suicide every year, 1,000 kill themselves while receiving treatment from the government.[5]

As with the deaths of active-duty soldiers, the reasons and the blame for suicides of Iraq War veterans are clear when you look at the headlines that have begun popping up in daily newspapers across the country—headlines telling the stories of people like twenty-seven-year-old Derek Henderson, a native of Louisville, Kentucky, who had been deployed to both Iraq and Afghanistan. After his discharge from the Army in October 2003, Henderson's family told the *Louisville Courier-Journal,* Derek became edgy and quick-tempered, began to carry a foot-long knife in his car, and carried a gun, "for protection."[6]

"One night," the *Courier-Journal* reported, "when his mother stopped at his apartment, he seemed agitated as he took her hand, forcefully pulled her to her knees and demanded she pray. 'Derek,' she told him, 'you've got to get help.'"

In November 2006, Derek's mother went to court and petitioned to have her son committed to the VA medical center, and the judge agreed, calling for a sixty-day involuntary hospitalization. But despite the judge's recommendation, VA doctors released him after a week. His only ongoing treatment: an antianxiety medication called BuSpar.

A few minutes after midnight June 22, 2007, Derek jumped off a bridge into the Ohio River and died. Derek Henderson's suicide is hardly unique. Stories of Iraq veterans' suicides, while varying in their intimate details, have one theme in common: a VA bureaucracy that either turns suicidal vets away or limits treatment to the prescription of psychotropic medication—rather than providing personalized care that could save their lives.

On January 11, 2007, Marianne Schulze drove her stepson Jonathan seventy-five miles from their family farm to the VA facility in Saint Cloud, Minnesota. In 2004, Jonathan had returned from Ramadi with two Purple Hearts and a severe case of post-traumatic stress disorder. Everyone knew something was wrong. Jonathan turned to drugs and alcohol and was prone to violent outbursts. The antianxiety drugs he'd been prescribed weren't helping. He talked openly of suicide.

But in January 2007, the Schulze family saw a way to recovery. Jonathan told his parents he wanted to be checked into the VA's mental health ward. When they arrived, they were met by an intake counselor: "She asked, 'Why do you want to be seen?' " Marianne Schulze told *CBS News*. "I was standing behind him and he was sitting in a chair, his shoulders were slumped and (his father) Jim was standing in the doorway and he said, 'I feel suicidal.'"[7]

But Jonathan wasn't admitted to the VA hospital that day. The intake counselor told the Schulze family that the clinician who pre-screened cases like Jonathan's was unavailable. Jonathan would need to go home, she said, and call back tomorrow. The next day, when Jonathan called, the VA told him he was number twenty-six on a waiting list. The hospital didn't have a bed for him.[8] Four days later, on January 16, he wrapped a household extension cord around his neck, tied it to a beam in the basement, and hung himself.[9]

Corporal Jeffrey Lucey of Belchertown, Massachusetts also hung himself after being turned away from the VA. His parents, Joyce and Kevin Lucey, have filed a lawsuit alleging "wrongful death, medical malpractice, pain and suffering, and other damages" caused by the VA's "negligence, carelessness, and lack of skill" in treating their son.[10]

Jeffrey's family remembers him as a happy-go-lucky kid who joined the Marine Corps Reserves shortly after graduating from high school in 1999. "Jeffrey said something about needing money for college," his mother Joyce told me. "But we had already put his sister through school and I told him it wouldn't be a problem. I think he really wanted to prove something to himself; that he could go through Marine Corps boot camp."

After the 9/11 attacks, the Marine Corps activated Jeffrey, and in 2003 they sent him to Iraq as part of the initial invasion of the country. Jeffrey's job was to drive convoys—screaming down Iraq's highways at top speeds in the dark of night with his headlights off, guided only by the shadow image of the vehicle in front of him.

It was dangerous work, but in July 2003, Jeffrey returned to the States uninjured and seemingly psychologically unharmed. He threw himself back into life at home, helping plan his sister's wedding and assisting his mother in recovering from a stroke. He reenrolled in school at a local community college and spent most nights at his girlfriend's house. A few weeks after returning, though, Jeff's girlfriend Julie began to notice some odd behaviors.

"They went to Cape Cod to spend a weekend alone and Jeff wouldn't leave the hotel," his father Kevin said. "Of course Julie wanted to walk to the beach because that's what they used to do. And Jeff made a side comment that he had enough sand to last a lifetime. That kind of isolation or reclusiveness was the only sign we saw that anything might be wrong."

Jeffrey's family let that incident pass, because the Marine Corps had told them it was normal for veterans to need some time to adjust after their return from the war zone. "We were told, 'Whatever you do, don't pressure them,'" Jeff's father Kevin Lucey told me. "It echoed in our head. 'Whatever you do, don't force them or pressure them to do something they don't feel comfortable doing.'"

As time passed, however, the Luceys began to think that something might be seriously wrong with Jeffrey. He vomited every day and started to drink. He even kept dog tags around his neck of Iraqi soldiers he said he'd shot at close range. On Christmas Eve 2003, he got drunk, took off the dog tags, and threw them at his sister Debbie, shouting, "Your brother is a murderer."

Debbie shouted back, "No, you're my big brother."[11]

Then, on Christmas Day, Jeffrey was back to normal. He continued to drink and occasionally screamed out from nightmares that woke him, but in other ways he continued to be functional. He was completing his classes at school and on Valentines Day he cooked his girlfriend an elaborate lobster dinner.

"He kicked us out of the house," Joyce Lucey said, laughing. "We went and got a hotel room for the night in Connecticut so Jeffrey and Julie could have their romantic dinner for two."

Then, on his twenty-third birthday, March 18, 2004, Jeffrey started to descend into a depression that ended in his suicide only a few months later. "He just stared into the fire," Joyce told me. "From that point on, it was a downward slide. He was skipping classes and not going. He was sleeping at his girlfriend's family's house, and his girlfriend would go to school but he wouldn't. He'd just stay at home, drink, and watch TV."

When he did go to school, Jeffrey had trouble staying in class. He experienced a hypervigilance so common among veterans suffering from PTSD. He thought the other kids were always staring at him. One day, a student slammed a door and Jeffrey dropped to the floor with his books.

At his parent's urging, Jeffrey went to go see a local doctor, who prescribed the antianxiety drug Klonopin and the antidepressant Prozac, and sent him home. "Jeff didn't want to go to the VA or to anywhere that the Marines would find out that he was having problems," Kevin Lucey told me. "Jeff was so concerned that he would let the other guys down in the unit, and he was also concerned that it would be the end of his military career and would also destroy any chance he had to become a police officer or a nurse, which were the two careers he was trying to pick between."

In May 2004, Jeffrey agreed to see a private therapist in nearby Amherst, Massachusetts. At the conclusion of their first session, however, the therapist told the Lucey family Jeffrey needed to go to the VA immediately where he could get more intensive, specialized care than the therapist could provide.

By then, Jeffrey had taken a turn for the worse. He drank constantly but wouldn't eat. He hallucinated, didn't sleep, and kept a flashlight close at hand, which he used to "check for camel spiders" at night. He told his sister he had a rope and a tree picked out where he intended to kill himself near a brook that ran by the family home.

On Friday, May 28, 2004, his family decided they had to step in. At 3:00 P.M. Kevin Lucey drove his son, who was almost too drunk to stand, forty miles to the VA medical center in Leeds, Massachusetts, where they had him involuntarily committed to the psychiatric ward.

Once inside the VA, however, Jeffrey received almost no mental health care. "There was no psychiatrist who saw Jeff either Saturday,

Sunday, or Monday," his father said. "Jeff told me he felt like a prisoner there. He didn't feel like a veteran. He just felt like he was being warehoused."

Then, on Tuesday, three and a half days after being admitted to the psych ward, the VA released Jeffrey saying they could not treat him for PTSD until he had been clean and sober for several months. "Joyce and I were under the impression that our son was going to be assessed for PTSD while he was there, and all the sudden we hear this archaic policy," Kevin said. "We were also advised to kick Jeff out of the house if there were any problems after he got home. Let him hit rock bottom, they said, and when he hits rock bottom he's going to realize that he's got to get help."

Two days after being discharged from the VA, Jeffrey crashed the family car while on a trip to Dunkin' Donuts. No other vehicles were involved in the accident, and Jeffrey tested negative for alcohol. Brought home in a police car, he handed his mother the two cups of coffee he bought on the trip and went up to his room.

The next day, June 5, 2004, was graduation day. Jeffrey's sister Debbie was graduating from Holyoke Community College. Jeffrey was supposed to be walking too, but he was so drunk and self-destructive that he wasn't able to take his finals. As it was, he barely arrived at the ceremony; and when he did he was lit up on German beer and Goldschlager schnapps. He had to be escorted to his seat by the fire marshal. After that, he didn't stay in his chair.

"He went running up to Debbie while she was going up on stage to get her diploma and gave her a hug," Joyce Lucey told me. "Right after he did that he came back to us and we got him out of there, brought him home, and we tried to have some kind of celebration for Debbie. We were supposed to have a cookout, but mostly we were just very sober and worried about Jeffrey."

What happened next is described in detail in the VA Office of Inspector General report compiled after Jeffrey Lucey's death at the request of Senator John Kerry:

> The patient's father and sister telephoned a psychiatric staff nurse at the VAMC [Veterans Administration Medical Center] who had developed some rapport with the patient during the patient's hospitalization. The patient's father stated that the patient was "out of control" and drinking large amounts of alcohol with clonazepam [Klonopin]. The family reported that the patient voiced thoughts of suicide. The patient's sister informed the triage nurse in this telephone call that the patient showed her a rope with which he planned to hang himself. His family also reported that the patient was threatening to "beat family members up." The patient's father got back on the phone with the staff nurse who could hear the patient screaming in the background. His father stated that he was going to call the police. The patient subsequently agreed to go with his sister to speak with someone at the medical center. Although the patient's family indicated that they told the patient that they just wanted him to go to the medical center to talk to someone and that they did not want to commit him, they reported that they did, in fact, hope that he would be committed or that he would agree to come into the hospital.[12]

When the Luceys got to the medical center, however, Jeffrey refused to enter the building. At first, he wouldn't even get out of the car. He wouldn't speak with a doctor. Then a nurse who was a Marine Corps veteran came out to talk with him and the two of them sat on a brick wall outside of the hospital. Other nurses came out and attempted to get Jeffrey to agree to be admitted to the VA's psych ward, but he continued to refuse. He told the psychiatric nurses that he had no intention of killing himself or anyone else and didn't want any treatment from the VA.

"The nursing clinical coordinator noted that the patient 'offered no grounds to seek a commitment or placement under protective custody by the VA police.'" the Inspector General reported, and the Lucey's were sent home, "advised to call 911 or the police if the veteran acted out at home, became aggressive, or threatened harm to self or to others."[13]

Back at the Lucey's house in Belchertown, a sense of dread set in. The family now believed they were only marking time before Jeffrey's inevitable suicide, although they did everything they could think of to keep him alive. "All of the sudden, we felt totally abandoned just like Jeff did," his father told me. "We were left watching this happen to our son. I was angry at Jeff. I was angry at everyone."

The Luceys disabled Jeffrey's car and rummaged through his room, taking away all his bottles of liquor, his knives, and anything he had taken to Iraq. They hid the family step-stool, their dog chains, and searched their home for anything else that Jeffrey might use to kill himself.

Everyone was on a short fuse. "Jeff wasn't sleeping that much, and we weren't sleeping that much because we were waiting to listen for Jeff going outside or Jeff walking around," Kevin said.

One day Joyce came home with her daughter Debbie and Jeffrey was in his room and the door was locked. "Both Debbie and I were scared," Joyce said. "We knocked on the door, nobody was answering. We walked around the house to the window and got something to stand on so we could look in, but we were both scared to look in. Then Debbie heard him snoring and she said, 'It's okay, he's in there.' It was a nightmare."

Another time Jeff snuck out with his friends. When he returned, his father said, he was dressed in his full camouflage uniform with a modified .38 caliber pistol in one hand and a six-pack of beer in the other.

"I just broke down and I can remember hurling bottle after bottle against the tree," Kevin Lucey told me, "and Joyce took two of the bottles and she started walking away, and Jeff in a very polite way, pleaded with her to give him just one bottle of beer so he could pass out."

Shortly before his death, Jeffrey went on a walk with his mother, where he asked her to listen to the song "45" by the heavy-metal band Shinedown. He had taken to listening to the song again and again in his room with the door closed. The song begins:

> In these times of doing what you're told
> You keep these feelings, no one knows
>
> What ever happened to the young man's heart
> Swallowed by pain, as he slowly fell apart
>
> No real reason to accept the way things have changed
> Staring down the barrel of a 45[14]

On June 22, 2004, sixteen days after Jeffrey was turned away from the VA, Kevin Lucey found his son hanging dead from a garden hose tied to a beam in the cellar of the family home. Before descending into the basement, Jeffrey had taken the dog tags of the Iraqi soldiers he killed off of his neck and placed them as a memorial on his bed in his room.

"Dear Mom and Dad," he wrote in a suicide note. "I cannot express my apologies in words for the pain I have caused you but I beg for your forgiveness. I want you to know that I loved you both and still do but the pain of life was too much for me to deal with.

"I thought long and hard about how this would affect the family," he added, "but I had a happy childhood and I want you to remember me when I was happy, young, and proud."

Jeffrey Lucey was twenty-three years old when he died.

Even as the Luceys grieved, they got active. They filed a Freedom of Information Act request for their son's medical records and called their representatives in Washington demanding an investigation. One of those representatives, Senator John Kerry, obliged asking the VA's Office of Inspector General to look into Jeffrey's death.

Ultimately, the Inspector General said the Leeds VA Medical Center was right to deny Jeffrey PTSD treatment while he was intoxicated. The Inspector General also said the VA was right to refuse to hospitalize Jeffrey against his wishes the day of his sister's graduation. But that conclusion had a qualifier on it: "The patient was not formally examined by a physician, psychiatric nurse mental health clinical specialist, or a qualified psychologist."[15] Such a medical professional would have been able to commit Jeffrey against his will and possibly save his life.

The Lucey family could take heart from another finding of the Inspector General—that since Jeffrey's death, the VA in Leeds had made a number of changes designed to help mentally wounded veterans of Iraq and Afghanistan. The psychiatrist of the day was to be called regarding all admissions, and clinicians are instructed to make a follow-up phone call to patients who are not admitted to the hospital. A specially trained social worker is also assigned to help returning Iraq and Afghanistan war veterans.[16] In addition, veterans admitted to the psych ward are now guaranteed treatment every day—weekends and holidays included. The medical center has also promised to make its specialized PTSD programs more accessible to veterans, though veterans still might be turned away if they are too drunk. The VA also made other improvements, launching a twenty-four-hour suicide prevention hotline at 1-800-273-TALK and increasing the number of medical centers with mental health professionals on-site round the clock, seven days a week.

This is not everything that the Luceys hoped for, but the changes represented some progress. So the family sat back and watched to see

24-Hour Suicide Helpline

The **National Suicide Prevention Lifeline** (www.suicidepreventionlifeline.org) has a new feature for veterans. Call for yourself or someone you care about: 800-273-TALK and press 1 to be connected to VA suicide prevention and mental health professionals. Calls are free and confidential.

what would happen next. What they saw was more veterans dying. "We've heard from families who have gone since," Joyce Lucey said, "and it doesn't seem like those improvements have really been initiated. They're promises that only exist on paper."

In January 2006, thirty-five-year-old Army Reservist Douglas Barber stepped onto his porch in eastern Alabama and fired a shot into his skull. After returning from Iraq after taking part in the initial invasion, Barber had kept a blog that chronicled his two-year fight to get treatment for PTSD and disability compensation from the VA. Just days before he shot himself, Barber wrote, "We cannot stand the memories and decide death is better. We kill ourselves because we are haunted by seeing children killed and families wiped out."[17]

In an August 2007 interview from their Massachusetts home, Joyce and Kevin Lucey told me they were particularly distressed by the suicide of Minnesota Marine Corps veteran Jonathan Schulze. Like Jeffrey, Schulze had killed himself a few days after being denied admission to a VA hospital.

"That was two and a half years after Jeff died," Kevin said. "When we saw that we said, 'This administration is not doing a thing to really support our troops after they get home.' The past Congresses have done absolutely nothing to help our troops after they come home.

The Joshua Omvig Suicide Prevention Act

On November 5, 2007, President Bush signed the Joshua Omvig Suicide Prevention Act. Named for an Iowa soldier who deployed to Iraq and killed himself when he returned, the legislation requires mandatory psychological screening of veterans returning home. Those at higher risk of committing suicide would be referred for counseling. The bill was pushed through Congress by Joshua Omvig's parents, Veterans and Military Families for Progress (www .vmfp.org, 202-841-1687), Iraq and Afghanistan Veterans of America (www.iava.org, 212-982-9699), and Veterans for Common Sense (www.veteransforcommonsense.org).

This Congress we hope to God they will, but right now I have my doubts."

In July 2007, the Lucey family filed a wrongful death lawsuit against the VA, demanding compensation for their pain and suffering, the costs of Jeffrey's funeral, and lost wages from the fifty-seven additional years they said their son would have lived had he received proper treatment from the VA.

"Right now, if it's only going to take the family of Jeff to at least start something, we're here to start it," Kevin said. "I'm telling you. I have lost faith in so much, and that's the tragedy of all this."

PART V

FIGHTING BACK

16

A HISTORY OF NEGLECT

In some ways, the government's neglect of soldiers after they've served and sacrificed is nothing new. Over the last fifty years, a series of presidents have fought successive generations of veterans as they've tried to get their rightful benefits. The entire approach of government has not been to help veterans, but to make the benefits of service *seem* attractive to soldiers when they enlist, while extracting as little money as possible from the federal treasury.

Just ask veterans of the Vietnam War, who had to fight tooth and nail to receive treatment and compensation for cancer, Hodgkin's disease, brain damage, diabetes, and birth defects in their children brought on by wartime exposure to the toxic defoliant Agent Orange.

For decades, official Washington maintained the spraying of more than twenty million gallons of dioxin-laced herbicide was linked to only one ailment: chloracne, a relatively mild skin disease that causes blackheads and cysts to erupt in a person's armpits, groin, and on the cheeks. This denial despite a mountain of scientific evidence proving dioxin's deadly effects. As early as 1966, a report by the National Cancer Institute found Agent Orange to cause birth defects in mice and rats. Other studies conducted during the war showed that even "vanishingly small" amounts of dioxin in an animal's diet could cause cancer. Researchers also found that lower concentrations of dioxin produced the same effects as higher concentrations, but merely took longer to do so.[1]

By 1969, South Vietnamese doctors reported an increase in miscarriages and deformed infants. The doctors told the Saigon press the problem started in 1967—the same year that Agent Orange spraying accelerated.[2] All signs pointed toward devastating consequences down the line for American servicemen and Vietnamese people who'd served, and lived, in the war zone. But the Department of Veterans Affairs and the Pentagon didn't look into what those consequences might be. Instead, they averted their eyes.

For close to ten years, the U.S. government stood by silently as a growing number of Vietnam veterans died prematurely or reported severe illnesses or birth defects in their children, but in 1978 two things happened: a courageous VA employee stepped forward, and a vet called a lawyer.

In 1977, Maude DeVictor, a former U.S. Navy nurse and a benefits counselor in the VA's Chicago office, received a call from the wife of a career Air Force vet, who said her husband was dying of cancer because he had been sprayed with a defoliant in Vietnam. In 1978, when DeVictor learned that the vet had died and that the VA had refused his widow's claim for benefits, she began to research the health effects of exposure to Agent Orange.[3]

In addition to her work as a benefits counselor, DeVictor started volunteering at the Chicago VA hospital interviewing many Vietnam vets, especially those listed "Diagnoses Undetermined," and found that many of them had been in areas where defoliants were used. She began gathering statistics on exposure to Agent Orange by questioning veterans who visited her office for benefits, as well as asking widows and wives of veterans about the health of their husbands and children.

When her bosses at the VA told her to "cease these additional inquiries and concentrate on her assigned duties," DeVictor took her findings to Bill Kurtis, a reporter at Chicago's CBS affiliate, WBBM.[4] On March 23, 1978, WBBM aired Kurtis's documentary: *Agent Orange, the Deadly Fog*.

The broadcast caused a firestorm. Forced for the first time to respond to allegations of neglect and worse, VA spokesman Vern Rogers told reporters there was "absolutely no evidence" that Agent Orange could cause deaths.[5] VA officials in Washington issued a memorandum stating that all neurological symptoms associated with the herbicide were "fully reversible." It also instructed VA personnel not to make any file entries suggesting a "relationship between a veteran's illness and defoliant exposure" unless that case had been referred to VA headquarters. VA employees were also told not to initiate any examinations for dioxin "poisoning" or make any public statements about Agent Orange without clearing them with headquarters.[6]

The head of the VA, triple amputee and Vietnam vet Max Cleland, even wrote a personal memo telling his workers there could be no certainty about Agent Orange's harmful effects "for another decade," even though there were already piles of government and university studies documenting the harmful effects of dioxin. Maude DeVictor was forced to resign.[7]

But DeVictor wasn't the only one clanging an alarm bell. Early in 1978, Paul Reutershan, a former helicopter crew chief responsible for transporting supplies to the Twentieth Engineering Brigade, appeared on NBC's *Today* show and shocked many of the show's viewers by announcing: "I died in Vietnam, but I didn't even know it."[8]

He told the national television audience how he flew almost daily through clouds of herbicides being discharged from C-123 cargo planes, and how he observed the dark swaths cut in the jungle by the spraying and watched the mangrove forest turn brown and die. When he returned home from Vietnam, Reutershan, who neither smoked nor drank and considered himself a heath nut, was diagnosed with a virulent, terminal form of abdominal cancer.

Until Maude DeVictor came forward, however, Reutershan didn't think there was much he could do about his illness. But one day the Long Island resident read an article in the *New York Daily News* describing how DeVictor's data showed a correlation between health problems and exposure to Agent Orange.[9] Convinced he had identified the cause of his cancer, Reutershan wrote a letter to President Jimmy Carter asking him to intervene to help him gain admission to a VA hospital.

The answer came in a form letter from a White House aide, who conveyed Carter's "thanks" and assured Reutershan that "careful concern is given to all suggestions from those who share his [Carter's] concern for the well being of the nation."[10]

On December 14, 1978, at the age of twenty-eight, Reutershan died from cancer of the liver, colon, and abdomen, deeply in debt for medical expenses and for his efforts to inform other veterans about Agent Orange.[11]

Before he died, however, Reutershan started a movement. He called a lawyer who started what would eventually be a national class-action lawsuit against Dow, Monsanto, and three other chemical companies that manufactured Agent Orange. Just as importantly, he drew other vets around him who vowed to continue his work.

Among those who agreed to fight was Frank McCarthy, a staff sergeant from the First Infantry Division who received a Bronze Star and Purple Heart for his service in Vietnam. Like Reutershan, he had returned from war only to fight a battle with the VA. When he'd gone to the VA to receive relief for shrapnel that was still lodged in his body, he was told he couldn't see a doctor for three months. "I threw my papers at them and walked out feeling hopeless," he told writer Peter Schuck, "until I looked at the rows of guys sitting in wheelchairs who would never walk again."[12]

In 1973, the VA's long delays in sending his disability and educational assistance checks caused McCarthy to be evicted from his apartment; his belongings were strewn on the sidewalk and stolen by thieves. "That was the worst day of my life," he said, "worse even than Vietnam. I felt that my country had forsaken me." For several weeks, McCarthy had no place to sleep and lived on the streets.

But McCarthy didn't give up. In 1975 he won his battle with the VA and received a retroactive compensation check of $5,000. Then he started helping other veterans. In 1978, when McCarthy saw a newspaper article about Vietnam veterans dying of cancer, he traveled to Paul Reutershan's hospital bed. There, he decided to devote his energies to a new organization called Agent Orange Victims International, which was dedicated to winning treatment and compensation for Agent Orange victims and their children.

McCarthy worked hard on the class-action lawsuit and started doing everything he could to pressure the VA. On May 30, 1979, he was on hand in the East Room of the White House when President Carter unveiled a new postage stamp for Vietnam veterans.

"What about Agent Orange, Mr. President?" McCarthy screamed as President Carter was giving his prepared remarks. An Associated Press report describes Carter as "obviously stunned."[13]

"What? What?" Carter asked.

McCarthy continued: "Twice as many men are dying here in the United States as died in the war. Agent Orange contains dioxin, the most toxic substance known to mankind. Dow Chemical company lied to this country, lied to the government, when it said it wasn't toxic."

"I understand," Carter said.

"We need an epidemiological study done on the Vietnam Veteran," McCarthy continued.

Carter's rejoinder was timid. "Max and I both agree," the president said, referring to VA chief Max Cleland, who had previously ruled out such a study. Soon after McCarthy's altercation in the White House, however, Carter authorized the first VA study of Agent Orange.[14]

But that study only proved to be a first small step in a struggle that would continue for more than two decades. Congressional hearings opened in Washington, but didn't lead to treatment or compensation. When Carter left office in 1980, not a single Vietnam veteran had been treated or compensated for health complications resulting from the spraying.

A better day seemed to come with the election of President Reagan in 1980. On the campaign trail, the former California governor and actor had called Carter out on the issue of Agent Orange and pledged to give medical care and "adequate compensation for veterans who were harmed" by the chemical.[15]

Within two months of taking office, veterans saw a different president. In their book, *The Wages of War: When America's Soldiers Came Home: From Valley Forge to Vietnam*, *New York Times* reporter Richard Severo and attorney Lewis Milford write that "the VA provided the Reagan transition team with a position that effectively would reduce Government responsibility—a move that the Reagan Administration embraced. The VA's Agent Orange Advisory Committee informed Reagan's people in the last week of January 1981 that 'excessive workloads [for the VA's workers] and anxiety would be created if President Reagan went on television inviting any Vietnam veteran who is worried about Agent Orange to report to a VA hospital for an examination.'"[16]

Reagan also received pressure from his budget director, David Stockman, a supporter of "supply-side" economics. According to Severo and Milford, Stockman warned Reagan that payouts to victims of Agent Orange poisoning could jeopardize the president's much vaunted defense buildup.

Stockman's Office of Management and Budget (OMB) also worried that if Vietnam veterans were successful they might set a precedent, making it easier for other groups of people poisoned by government and industry to seek compensation. An internal OMB memo warned that an "incipient movement towards federally financed toxic substances compensation [poses] political difficulties of the highest order—because it involves the political cost of resisting popular proposals now in order to avoid potentially heavy costs in the more distant future."[17]

"The Reagan Administration," Severo and Milford write, "which had courted veterans as one of its ploys to obtain power, was now quietly undermining one of its own publicly announced approaches to social policy."[18]

In 1984, the veterans settled their suit with Dow for a lump sum of $180 million dollars. It sounded like a lot, but because it was divided among so many claimants each sick veteran only received about $3,800.

Vietnam veterans still looked to their government for medical care and disability payments, but when Ronald Reagan left office in 1988, only five veterans had been recognized by the VA as suffering from the skin disease chloracne. None of them had received compensation. Out of 150,000 Agent Orange disability claims, not one had been approved.[19]

Vietnam veterans were still fighting for benefits and health care when Reagan's successor, President George Bush Sr., deployed

700,000 American servicemen and women to the Persian Gulf. Saddam Hussein had invaded Kuwait. Unlike the Vietnam War, the 1991 invasion of Iraq was quick and successful. In just four days, a U.S.-led international military coalition drove Saddam's vaunted Iraqi Army out of Kuwait and back to Baghdad. Just as importantly, it appeared that Iraq was unable to use any of its dangerous chemical or biological weapons. Only 147 American soldiers had been killed in combat.

The surge of patriotism around the Gulf War was so great that Congress—which had previously taken only baby steps on the issue of Agent Orange—unanimously passed a bill guaranteeing compensation for veterans who were victims of two types of cancer caused by the toxic herbicide: non-Hodgkin's lymphoma and soft-tissue sarcoma.

On February 6, 1991, George Bush Sr. signed the bill into law. "A grateful nation salutes our veterans," Bush said as bombs rained down on Baghdad. The Senate sponsor of the bill, Senator Bob Graham of Florida, told the *Chicago Tribune,* "Fairness demands that we treat disabled veterans at home with respect. While we are supporting our troops in the Persian Gulf, we must not forget those disabled in past wars."[20]

After a twenty-year fight, the U.S. government had finally given in and had begun to grapple with the toxic legacy of the Vietnam War. Today, the VA recognizes dozens of types of cancer as being caused by wartime defoliants, including Hodgkin's disease, multiple myeloma, non-Hodgkin's lymphoma, porphyria cutanea tarda, respiratory cancers, soft-tissue sarcoma, peripheral neuropathy, brain cancer, and prostate cancer. The VA will also provide health care and disability payments to children of Vietnam veterans who suffer from the birth defect spina bifida. The VA also gives compensation to Vietnam vets suffering from diabetes, and still acknowledges Agent Orange causes the skin disease chloracne.[21]

Helping Vietnamese Agent Orange Victims

After nearly four decades of fighting, American veterans of the war in Vietnam have finally won compensation for cancers, birth defects, and other disabilities brought on by exposure to Agent Orange. But the U.S. government and the companies who made the defoliant continue to refuse to help Vietnamese people poisoned by the chemical. The **Vietnam Agent Orange Relief and Responsibility Campaign** (www.vn-agentorange.org) is an initiative of U.S. veterans working to change that. The group is supporting a lawsuit by the Vietnamese government in U.S. courts that seeks the same compensation for disabled Vietnamese people from Dow and Monsanto that American veterans got. "With this campaign," the group says, "we seek to fulfill our responsibility by insisting that our government honor its moral and legal responsibility to compensate the Vietnamese victims of Agent Orange."

But even as Vietnam vets won compensation and the Gulf War ended in victory, new health maladies began to emerge. As with Vietnam, thousands of soldiers who had deployed to the Persian Gulf in peak condition came back complaining about a strange series of unexplained ailments, which would come to be called Gulf War syndrome: rashes, stomach distress, brain legions, chronic fatigue, severely swollen muscles, and memory loss.

The Pentagon wanted to bask in its victory. The last thing officials in Washington wanted to do was think about the pain of wounded soldiers and the costs of properly caring for them. "The GIs turned to the military doctors and Veterans Administration hospitals for help," wrote journalist Seymour Hersh. "However, the initial response of the military medical system was to turn away, characterizing the illness as having nothing to do with service in the Gulf. Word filtered down the chain of command suggesting that those who complained were . . . malingerers and malcontents—men and women who could not handle the stress of combat."[22]

One of those soldiers was 1st Lt. James Bunker of Topeka, Kansas. While he was in Iraq, the First Infantry Division blew up a large ammunition storage area. "At the time of this demolition, I became ill," he told a congressional committee. "I was treated for all the classic symptoms of nerve agent poisoning, including convulsions. Then, I was given the antidote for the nerve agent and medically evacuated. Over time, I completely lost the use of my arms and hands. . . . I [also] deal with headaches and cognitive dysfunction during the day."[23]

When he returned home, Bunker told Congress the Army gave him a medical discharge, but refused to give him any treatment. "No one seemed to care what was making us sick," he said. "The Army told me the VA would help me. The VA told me it was all in my head."

In September 1992, George Bush Sr.'s Office of Management and Budget instructed the VA to bill veterans claiming to be victims of Gulf War syndrome for all medical treatment, unless their illnesses were deemed "service connected." At the same time, the VA was denying most claims, saying there was no evidence that the illnesses resulted from the war. Almost as soon as it had ended, the fight over Vietnam veterans' health care and compensation was repeating itself in the lives of veterans of the Persian Gulf.[24]

Eventually, more than 100,000 Gulf War veterans would step forward with symptoms like James Bunker's. Yet throughout the 1990s, the Pentagon and VA would continue to turn a blind eye to the wounded—even as evidence mounted revealing the reasons for the illnesses.

In mid-1991, for example, United Nations weapons inspectors began to pore over Iraq to find and destroy its stockpiles of weapons of mass

The National Gulf War Resource Center

The **National Gulf War Resource Center** (www.ngwrc.org, 866-531-7183) was organized by veterans of the 1991 Gulf War who began to experience an unexplained illness after coming home. The group advocates for health care and self-help for the estimated 150,000 Gulf War veterans who fell ill as a result of their service and for those who have served the United States and its allies since the Gulf War. The group has expanded its focus from Gulf War Illness to also include other toxin-induced illnesses, traumatic brain injury, and post-traumatic stress disorder.

destruction. Among the places they looked was Khamisiyah, a huge weapons depot the Americans had blown up as they withdrew from the country. Poking through the wreckage of the depot, the UN inspectors found more than three hundred leaking and partially destroyed rockets, which had previously been filled with sarin gas and cyclosarin.[25]

Chemical weapons weren't the only possible reason for the symptoms of Gulf War syndrome. Other causes included the massive numbers of vaccines given to soldiers before their deployments and exposure to giant oil-well fires lit by Saddam's army as it retreated from Kuwait. The use of depleted-uranium (DU) munitions also emerged as a cause. Made from the by-products of nuclear fission, DU is significantly denser than lead, so much so that artillery rounds made with DU could easily penetrate a tank and cause it to burst into flames.

During the Gulf War, over 1,400 Iraqi tanks were destroyed by an estimated 860,000 rounds of DU munitions. The weapon was one reason the war was such a rout. But as the years went by, the chemical's costs began to emerge. Iraqi children began to develop leukemia and other cancers at an alarming rate.[26] In the United States, veterans began to wonder if the low-level radioactive weapon could be the cause of their ailments.

Yet even as this information came to light, the Pentagon and VA continued to stonewall veterans, arguing that symptoms like chronic fatigue and memory loss were caused by stress. Other symptoms, like kidney stones and cancer, were deemed to be "not service connected," meaning veterans were not eligible for treatment or compensation.

When Capt. Julia Dyckman was deployed to the Gulf in 1991, she had already served more than twenty years as a nurse in the U.S. Navy and the Naval Reserve. During the Vietnam War, she had been stationed in theater on the Hospital Ship Sanctuary, which treated tens of thousands of wounded soldiers while stationed off the coast of South Vietnam. In 1991, Capt. Dyckman was assigned to the Saudi Arabian desert, where she helped build a five-hundred-bed military hospital and then, when the hospital was constructed, she served as its chief nurse for the emergency room and out-patient clinics.

As a manger of nurses in a combat hospital, Dyckman expected to see soldiers with wounds from bullets and shrapnel. Instead, she saw black skies overhead and rain that included oil droplets. She smelled ammonia. Soldiers started coming in with respiratory problems, unexplained fevers and rashes and stomach pain, diarrhea, and heart problems.

Dyckman also started to experience problems herself. Before her deployment, she was in excellent health (she had just received a physical). While in Saudi Arabia, she started to develop open sores and legions, high blood pressure, and an irregular heartbeat. Doctors at the hospital had to perform surgery on her to remove "black gunk" from her foot.

When she returned to America, however, she was given the runaround. "You go back and forth and it takes years to get approval on a lot of stuff that's already been decided," she told me. "It's not that

you want money. It's that you want a better life, and dealing with the
VA wears you out. You're worn out to begin with because chronic fatigue and joint pain are symptoms of Gulf War syndrome, and now
you're dealing with a system that's very upsetting and takes a long
time, and still after all that may not recognize that you're sick."

Like Vietnam veterans before them, veterans of the Gulf War
turned to Congress for support. In 1992, Congress passed a law requiring the Pentagon and the VA to create health registries. Further
legislation in 1994 permitted the VA to provide benefits for unexplained symptoms. And in 1998, President Bill Clinton signed a bill
ordering the VA to presume that Gulf War vets with a certain set of
symptoms had a service-connected illness.

As with the battle over Agent Orange, congressional action was
only somewhat helpful. Gulf War veterans were frustrated and getting
sicker without needed care or compensation.

As he campaigned for president, Texas governor George W. Bush
seized on that frustration. In a series of speeches in the crucial primary
state of South Carolina, Bush accused the Clinton administration of
providing inadequate health care for veterans and being slow to process compensation claims to those who served in the military. "Soldiers once ordered to stand in the line of fire should not be asked to
stand in line at the nearest federal bureaucracy waiting with hat in
hand," Bush said as he began a November 1999 bus trip.[27]

"This applies to veterans of the Gulf War," he added. "They should
not have to go to elaborate lengths to prove that they are ill, just because their malady has yet to be fully explained. All that is going to
end. In the military, when you are called to account for a mistake you
are expected to give one simple answer: 'No excuses sir.'"

Shortly after Bush took office, an official apology came from
Washington. When a government scientific panel released a report

demonstrating Gulf War veterans suffer from numerous types of neurological damage, the VA made a public about-face and acknowledged that strong evidence exists linking brain damage to exposure to toxins. The Bush-appointed deputy VA secretary, Leo Mackay, admitted in an address to the scientific panel that, in the past, the U.S. government had "a tin ear, cold heart and a closed mind" about toxic chemical exposure and drug-chemical interactions as possible causes of Gulf War syndrome.[28] He pledged things would change.

But, once again, things didn't change. In 2004, the Government Accountability Office reported that funding for research into Gulf War syndrome peaked in the year 2000 (the last year of Clinton's presidency) and declined precipitously every year the Bush administration stayed in office. As a result, doctors at the VA weren't making any progress in learning how to treat the syndrome.

The VA bureaucracy also continued to strike a hostile posture toward veterans who reported what had by then become the illness's signature symptoms. In May 2007, the VA reported that it had denied 75 percent of disability claims for Gulf War syndrome (officially known as "Undiagnosed Illness"). Of the more than 100,000 vets believed to suffer from the illness, only 3,384 had been approved for compensation.[29]

After nine years of fighting, Julia Dyckman finally won her claim for disability compensation. In 2000, the government listed her as 80 percent disabled, 100 percent unemployable, which entitles her to about $2,700 a month. The victory was mostly an emotional one, however, because Dyckman's disability pay is deducted from her military retirement.

It also didn't solve the underlying problem of her affliction with Gulf War syndrome: getting compensation because "you can't work doesn't do anything for treating your illnesses," she said. Sixteen years after the Iraqi Army was driven out of Kuwait, the VA still doesn't have a regular procedure for treating Gulf War syndrome, which it still calls "undiagnosed illnesses."

So Dyckman goes to the private sector for most of her care, where she's forced to pay out of pocket. Her private doctor has diagnosed her with a battery of service-related afflictions, including autonomic nervous system damage, which causes an irregular heart rate, high blood pressure, and blood clotting. She also has regular migraines and suffers from osteoarthritis.

"If you don't have an official title for the illness, you aren't even trying to find a way to treat it," she argues. "If you don't have something called Persian Gulf syndrome, you can't have statistics of how many people died from it."

On September 11, 2001, members of the terrorist group al-Qaeda crashed airplanes into the World Trade Center and the Pentagon, and a new war was on. In October 2001, the United States invaded Afghanistan. Less than two years later, we invaded Iraq. Once again, veterans of America's previous wars were pushed into the background, their needs still unmet, the government's promises still unfulfilled.

Julia Dyckman thinks of her three sons, who have all decided to become fighter pilots. "They wanted to fly Hornets," she told me. "Two of them went to the naval academies. My youngest is in the ROTC in Villanova. One of them is working on projects for NASA. It's exciting for them."

"I don't hate the military," she added, "but I've seen how many people are medically injured. I think they should take care of people who they damage and try to prevent the same things from happening in the future. The government isn't learning from its mistakes."

17

WINNING THE BATTLE AT HOME

This leads up to the question, "Why?" Why is it that, generation after generation, Americans who've risked their lives for their country return to do battle with their own government? In virtually every generation, politicians repeat again and again that they "support the troops" even as their policies and budget conditions ensure a difficult homecoming.

Part of the answer seems to be that Washington officials, like Americans in general, prefer to see war as a series of lines and arrows on a map rather than something with consequences for human beings. That's because when the American public comes face-to-face with the true cost of war, war itself becomes less popular. A modern illustration of this can be seen in the Bush administration's ban on photography of flag-draped coffins of dead American soldiers returning from Iraq and Afghanistan. Officially, the ban was put in place to provide privacy for the families of those lost on the battlefield. Many commentators noted, however, that it was photos of body bags coming home from Vietnam that turned many Americans against that war.

Usually (as is the case with the Iraq War) the shortchanging of veterans starts while a war is just beginning. The aim: keeping the public's eye off the true cost of war. In 1966, for example, President Lyndon Johnson threatened to veto any bill that made the GI Bill more generous, even though at the time, the GI Bill paid vets $10 a month less than what Korean War veterans had gotten. In his book *Home to War: A History of the Vietnam Veterans Movement,* Gerald Nicosia noted LBJ made his threat for "purely political reasons."

"A big GI Bill," Nicosia wrote, "would have forced him [Johnson] to acknowledge that a major war was in progress, which he was trying to play down; and it would have added substantially to the cost of a war that was already beginning to bankrupt the Great Society. The problem Johnson created for veterans was never overcome, for their benefits began from such a small base that even what the VA considered 'large increases' meant little, and failed to catch them up to World War II levels."[1]

When the war in Vietnam ended, veterans faced a different problem. Successive presidents from both parties, Richard Nixon, Gerald Ford, Jimmy Carter, and Ronald Reagan, all sought to avoid paying for the human costs of the war launched by President Johnson. They each had their own priorities and projects. Funding health care and disability for Vietnam veterans would have meant less money available for their own goals.

"People try to put the war behind them," explained retired *New York Times* reporter Richard Severo, who coauthored *The Wages of War.* "They feel guilty," he told me. "They want to close the door to it and move on. Americans like to say 'We're moving on.' They like to put unpleasantness behind them. Wounded veterans are not a pleasant thing to think about."

Perhaps most importantly, Severo told me, veterans lack the political power to force politicians to bend to their will. "Getting money for veterans doesn't win you votes in this country," he said, "so politicians know they can get away with shortchanging veterans. Veterans have no real advocates, at least in the way that other interest groups do. I think if you asked a decent politician in Washington if he supports veterans he would say yes, but nobody is pushing him, and in this country if you don't push hard, you don't get anything."

That analysis may seem odd given there are more than 24 million veterans in America and all of them are eligible to vote. When you add in immediate family members of veterans (widows, children, etc.) who are eligible to receive benefits through the VA, that number grows to 74.5 million people—surely enough to swing an election one way or the other.[2]

But unlike members of the National Rifle Association, AARP, or organized labor, veterans do not make up an effective interest group or voting block. Veterans in America join different organizations depending on their politics and the war they fought in. Groups like the American Legion and the Veterans of Foreign Wars have gained a reputation as being extremely conservative, and they primarily represent the interest of World War II–era veterans. Vietnam veterans and Gulf War veterans have their own groups, as do veterans of the current wars. All of these groups cooperate, but they do so in an ad hoc fashion, and none of them spend the kind of money on politics or politicians that's necessary to win in Washington.

"In order to be an effective lobby, you need to have a lot of money or a lot of members, but if you have neither your voice tends to be drowned out by better funded, better organized interests," explains Massie Rich of the Washington-based nonprofit Center for Responsive Politics.

The group's Web site, OpenSecrets.org, tracks the influence of money in politics. The site shows veterans groups to be underfunded and disorganized compared to other "single-issue groups." In 2006, for example, the American Legion spent just $83,000 lobbying Congress, while the Veterans of Foreign Wars spent $26,000. Vietnam Veterans of America spent $120,000. Disabled American Veterans and the Paralyzed Veterans of America weighed in with more, at $500,000 and $342,648 respectively. By contrast, that same year the National Rifle Association spent $1.6 million lobbying Congress—more than all veterans groups *combined*. And the NRA wasn't even close to the biggest spender in Washington. Defense contractors shelled out $124 million on lobbying, organized labor spent $31 million, AARP shelled out $23 million, and environmental groups about $10 million.[3]

The result was that as Democrats and Republicans crisscrossed the country campaigning in 2006, they talked a good game about helping veterans, each accusing the other of not providing for "America's heroes." When they got to Washington, however, they spent most of their time meeting with the paid lobbyists who brought them to office—very few of whom talk to them about the treatment of America's veterans.

Part of the problem is that members of the armed forces have—since World War II—primarily come from the poorer side of the economic scale. During the Vietnam and Korean wars, university students (including Bill Clinton, George W. Bush, and Dick Cheney) grabbed deferments to avoid service. After that, the dismantling of the draft and the creation of an all-volunteer Army led to what some call a "poverty draft." While some wealthier Americans undoubtedly join the military to serve their country, the services today are disproportionately made up of inner-city kids and the children of rural America: people who see the Army and Marine Corps at least partially as a way to escape to a different environment.

When these enlisted men and women become veterans, some coping with physical disabilities and post-traumatic stress disorder, they initially have to focus on caring for themselves and their families. Those lucky enough to return without being injured have to focus on getting a job or preparing for school. As a result, veterans are in an especially bad position to make their case to Congress and must depend on the general public for support. These days the general public is at the mall. Most Americans sympathize with veterans, but for the most part they're more concerned with the daily pressures of their own lives. So when they go to the polls, they choose primarily on the issues they see as affecting them: education, child care, taxes, health care, their own personal security, and the safety of the country.

When a scandal breaks, like the one about substandard care at Walter Reed Medical Center, most Americans are outraged. But they don't pay close attention. They assume that since politicians appear on television *saying* action will be taken, that action has in fact been taken. They assume, when they don't hear any follow-up reporting, that the problem has been solved.

In this atmosphere, it is incumbent on veterans to band together and fight for their rights just as they fought the enemy in battle. Members of Congress and bureaucrats at the Pentagon and the Department of Veterans Affairs may not be attacking vets with mortars and IEDs, but they are literally killing them with indifference.

At this point, one story told earlier in this book bears repeating: the creation of the GI Bill. In 1943, injured soldiers returning home during the middle of World War II met some of the same indifference and substandard care that face veterans today. The people that helped those veterans the most turned out to be veterans of World War I, who had returned three decades earlier to found the American Legion. World War I vets (who themselves had to march on Washington, twenty-five thousand strong, in order to receive a bonus when they lived homeless during the depths of the Depression) worried the same thing would happen to their sons when they returned home from fighting Hitler and Hirohito.

So the American Legion put everything it had into lobbying Congress for something different and unique in American history: a GI Bill that included not only education, but also access to low-interest zero-down loans to buy homes and start small businesses. Officers of the American Legion wrote the bill and walked it through the halls of Congress, eventually winning the biggest victory for veterans since the Civil War.

At first, the legion was told some of the same things vets are told today. FDR favored a more limited program that would provide returning veterans up to one year's vocational training, but not college. Some congressional leaders said the plan was too expensive, others opposed it simply as a matter of procedure, arguing the larger GI Bill should be split into a series of smaller bills that could be passed (or discarded) individually: one for education, one for business, one for farming, and so on. Deans and presidents of colleges and universities lobbied against the larger GI Bill, worried that a flood of scruffy veterans would poison their elite collegiate atmosphere.[4]

These opponents were joined by less ambitious veterans' groups like the Veterans of Foreign Wars, the Disabled American Veterans, and the Order of the Purple Heart, who worried that the GI Bill was "so broad in scope and potential cost, that its enactment . . . would probably not only prevent any consideration of several more equitable proposals to solve such problems, but might also jeopardize the entire structure of veterans' benefits." Those groups presented their own, more limited plan, which simply paid returning veterans a cash bonus upon their return home.[5]

But the American Legion decided to press forward. More than a million signatures were gathered on petitions around the country.

Ultimately, the GI Bill succeeded with a helping hand from the media. The most powerful media mogul in America, William Randolph Hearst, ordered his newspapers to begin printing editorials and articles in favor of the measure. Reporters for Hearst papers around the country placed calls to undecided congresspeople at the start of each day, asking them where they stood. Some papers printed petitions that ordinary citizens could fill out and mail back to their members of Congress. Small-town newspapers were provided with prewritten editorials. Across the country, support for the GI Bill was made a litmus test for politicians. If they "supported the troops," they would have to support the GI Bill too.

"The techniques of mass media and ward politics were blended," wrote journalist Michael Bennett in his book *When Dreams Came True.* "The campaign was in many ways a precursor to every 'beyond the beltway' political campaign since."[6] In short, the benefits of the GI Bill were not given to veterans as a reward for their service, they were taken, by veterans and their allies. Politicians in 1940s Washington, might have liked the idea of supporting the troops, but they weren't going to do it unless they got a healthy push.

Ultimately, the GI Bill passed both houses of Congress unanimously. FDR signed it into law on June 22, 1944, as Americans fought in Europe to capture Cherbourg, and in the Pacific in the Philippines.

The world has changed a lot since the GI Bill's passage. More than sixty years and four major wars have come and gone, but the formula of advocacy that worked for World War II veterans in 1944 also worked for Iraq and Afghanistan veterans in 2008. President Bush didn't want to sign an expanded GI Bill and many in Congress said the plan was too expensive, but veterans from previous generations stepped up and supported the young men and women returning from Iraq and Afghanistan. The American Legion and Veterans of Foreign Wars both

lobbied hard for the bill providing some of the muscle needed to
to make progress on Capital Hill. "I noticed a window of opportunity," Iraq and Afghanistan Veterans of America's Patrick Campbell
told me after the bill's passage. "I realized that even though the veterans community as a whole seems to be fractured and talking about
different GI Bills, we weren't all that far from each other and we just
sat down and started having conversations, small conversations at first
and then a little bigger and a little bigger and then we developed a con-
sensus. So when people tried to pick us off and get us to support
smaller, less ambitious bills, we stuck together because we knew we
could do this."

Veterans also walked the halls of Congress, meeting with hundreds
of lawmakers and showing representatives how a new GI Bill would
help returning soldiers in their own districts. Major newspapers like
the *New York Times, Los Angeles Times,* and *Washington Post* wrote editorials in favor of the measure and it ended up passing overwhelm-
ingly. "The way this bill came into being is the way government
should work," Campbell said.

The successful fight for a new GI Bill isn't the only example of veterans across generations working together for progress. After the 2003
invasion of Iraq, for example, the Vietnam Veterans of America Foundation changed its name to Veterans for America and launched a campaign to ensure that service members and veterans who have served in
Iraq and Afghanistan get the care they need. Staff at Veterans for
America led an investigation into terrible conditions at Fort Carson,
Colorado, which helped spur reforms at the facility itself and a
broader discussion about post-traumatic stress disorder and traumatic
brain injury nationwide.

Another example of this cross-generational advocacy can be seen in
the class-action lawsuit launched against the VA in July 2007. The two

veterans' groups filing suit, Veterans for Common Sense and Veterans United for Truth, are both made up primarily of veterans of earlier wars. Veterans for Common Sense is headed by Paul Sullivan, a veteran of the 1991 Gulf War. Veterans United for Truth is headed by Bob Handy, a retired Navy man who served in Vietnam.

One of the lawsuit's lead attorneys, Gordon Erspamer of the law firm Morrison and Forrester, is an experienced hand at fighting the VA. He took the veterans class-action case for free because it reminded him of the suffering of his own family. Erspamer's father Ernest was exposed to extensive radiation during atomic bomb tests on the Pacific's Bikini Atoll in 1946 and later developed leukemia, which took his life in 1980. Even with her son's help, it then took Erspamer's mother more than ten years to obtain disability and death benefits from the VA.

"This isn't a case about isolated problems or the type of normal delays and administrative hassles we all occasionally experience with bureaucracies," Erspamer said at a press conference announcing the lawsuit. "This case is founded on the virtual meltdown of the VA's capacity to care for men and women who served their country bravely and honorably, were severely injured, and are now being treated like second-class citizens."[7]

The media has helped a little to publicize these actions. When it was launched, the veterans' class-action lawsuit garnered coverage in newspapers across the country, from the *Los Angeles Times* to the *New York Times* to *USA Today*. But the next day the news coverage was gone, and when the Bush administration moved to dismiss the suit two months later none of the big media outlets covered the story.

It reminded me of the media's response to Herold Noel's story. A man returning from the war zone in Iraq and becoming homeless became front-page news in the *New York Post* and was featured on the

CBS Evening News and in the *Christian Science Monitor.* None of these publications bothered to follow up, however. None of them returned a few weeks later to file a story describing how Herold was doing: to see if the indignity of a homeless Iraq War veteran was continuing or if the problem had been solved. The media covered the case of Herold Noel, but no news outlet used his story to launch a campaign of coverage about homeless veterans. If an anonymous donor hadn't stepped forward and donated an apartment in the Bronx, Herold might still be homeless today.

"How many reporters are employed full time covering the VA?" Veterans for Common Sense's Paul Sullivan asked reporters rhetorically at the launch of his organization's class-action lawsuit. "Zero. There is not a single reporter at a large American news organization who works full time covering the VA. We have daily updates on news from the Pentagon because there are dozens of reporters whose jobs are covering the Pentagon. The same is true for the State Department, the Energy Department and even the Department of Agriculture."[8]

Without public information, Sullivan argued, there can be no public outcry. If we are to take care of Iraq and Afghanistan war veterans, the media must lead the way in educating the public. If Lou Dobbs can rant every night on CNN about the horrors of illegal immigration, and FOX's Greta Van Sustren can spend hours on Britney Spears's antics, there must be some space in the media for a campaign of stories about Americans who've put on a uniform and served their country. Where is today's William Randolph Hearst, a wealthy media mogul willing to give pages and pages of ink and hours of screen time to the scandal of today's neglected veterans? Until that mogul emerges, veterans themselves will have to push especially hard.

THE WAR INSIDE

This book was not easy for me to write. It wasn't that the journalism was hard. On the contrary, the scandal that is America's treatment of its veterans is one of the most tragically obvious scandals of our times. Finding the veterans interviewed in this book was easy. Most of them were eager to tell their stories. I'm only sorry that I can't give them a bigger megaphone.

No, the difficulties I had writing this book were more personal. It was not easy to face this war on a regular basis, especially when my wife, parents, and most of my friends could not relate to the pain I felt as I did this work. Indeed, this book was actually more difficult than reporting in Iraq itself.

In Iraq, it seemed perfectly normal to get up each morning, eat a simple breakfast of yogurt and dates, meet up with my translator, and then head out for a harried day in Baqouba or Sadr City. If we ran into a checkpoint, we simply went around it. If a particular location proved too much of a security risk, we would go somewhere else that day. The Iraqi police station across the street from our building was regularly bombed by those opposed to the American presence, but I could live with that. I rationalized that since I wasn't a member of the U.S. military or Iraqi police, those fighters would never come for me.

I lived in a furnished apartment building where almost all the other residents were independent journalists. Every night we would get together and commiserate about our experiences. We were all going through the same thing, and if one of us was acting a little bit crazy or withdrawn, we cut the person slack. We knew what he or she was going through because we were living the same thing ourselves.

Writing this book was different. There is no similar community of journalists who regularly cover veterans' issues back home in San Francisco. There are only a handful of us in the entire country. To my knowledge, none of them has spent a considerable amount of time interviewing Iraqi civilians.

When I was in Iraq, my typical interview went something like this: My translator and I would arrive at the home of a "regular Iraqi" with no security in tow. We carried no weapons and were invited in and given warm hospitality. Then we heard stories of killings, beatings, and arrests that had been carried out by American soldiers.

In the middle-class Baghdad neighborhood Mustansuriye, for example, I met a mechanic named Salhadul Kareem. He told me he was sitting in his home with his family when the U.S. Army swept through the neighborhood on one of their patrols. There were dozens of Humvees. "They arrested everyone," he said, every man at least. Kareem told me he was taken away along with his older brother and his fourteen-year-old brother, who suffers from severe mental retardation. Most of his neighbors were also taken away and incarcerated in the nearby U.S. base, where they were kept for questioning.

"They were looking for someone who had been attacking their base," Kareem recalled. "His name was Mazen. So they kept asking us 'Are you Mazen!? Who is Mazen!?' " Kareem said his family was held for two days before authorities located Mazen and they were released. Kareem was comparatively lucky. He wasn't taken to Abu Ghraib, where he would have been held for months. But he hardly felt secure in his home.

Back here in the United States, I am coming face-to-face with the soldiers' side of that story—a perspective I could not get as an unembedded journalist in Iraq. Getting that side of the story is important to me. As a journalist, I want to expose all the human costs of war, not only those on the Iraqi side. Too often, the media covers war like it's a simple exercise in politics or a Nintendo game. Other times, the media glorifies soldiers without ever asking them about their condition or what they think about the war they've fought. This is not a service to the soldier, but simple propaganda for the Pentagon and the president.

I am glad I've written *The War Comes Home,* but the process has reopened wounds I thought I'd closed after my return from Iraq. Sometimes, when I met a particular soldier, it brought on a flashback. At the beginning of the book, I told the story of Specialist Patrick Resta, who returned from Iraq with a case of post-traumatic stress disorder. You'll recall that on his last day in Iraq, Patrick posed for a picture with a group of Iraqi children. After the Restas shared that picture with me in May 2007, I had trouble sleeping for days.

You see, Patrick looked exactly like an American soldier who'd pointed his machine gun at me at a checkpoint during my first day in Iraq. That soldier mistook me for an Iraqi. When I reached for my passport, he reached for his weapon. The only thing that saved me was the appearance of a blond journalist whose very existence calmed the soldier's nerves. It was the only time during my entire stay in Iraq that I truly feared for my life.

Suddenly, four years after the incident, I was looking at someone remarkably similar. The two soldiers were both white men of about the same height and build, and they both wore helmets that were clearly too large for their heads. They both spoke with a pronounced southern accent. Even though they were different people (Patrick was stationed in Baqouba while I was reporting in Baghdad), the image nevertheless set me on edge. It took two months of brooding for me to feel comfortable telling anyone else about the reasons behind my funk, though my wife could tell my mood wasn't what it should be.

I wanted to tell someone who already knew, for whom I wouldn't have to start at the beginning. Finally, while I was at the Veterans for Peace/Iraq Veterans Against the War convention in Saint Louis two months later, I told a reporter friend over bad, fast-food Sushi.

"That man could have shot me in Iraq," I said, "and now I'm writing a book where I'm supposed to be sympathetic to him. Intellectually I understand that's the whole reason I'm writing this book—to show that war makes regular people do terrible things and that it's not their fault, but that it's the fault of the leaders who start the fight. It's just that personally, emotionally, that's a really big step to take."

That veterans' convention proved to be a turning point for me. The presence of so many Iraq War veterans in the same place threw me for a loop. I spent an unreasonably large amount of time in my hotel room, did few formal interviews, and barely slept. I sat in on a Warrior Writers' workshop designed to help veterans cope with their war trauma. When one of the veterans read his poem aloud, I wrote down some reflections of my own.

"Why am I here?" I wrote.

Why do I keep coming back to this war again and again. Why can't I just leave it behind, move on to the next thing. . . .
   Why can't I just get a job, a normal job covering City Hall, producing a Morning Show, or something less stressful?

Why do I care so much about this war? And what does it mean that it will go on forever? Will I wander for years allowing this war to stalk me from behind?

I'm very happy I'm here, but only in a certain way. When I heard [one of the veterans] read his poem it sent me back. Back to Iraq but not in a good way.

I want to end this war, but I don't want to think about Iraq anymore. I don't want to think about the dead and the injured.

I remember walking through the hospital in Sadr City and snapping a photo. It was easier for me to write that story because there was an urgency, but now it's just a slow grind and the soldiers make me cry.

When the convention ended, I decided to scrap a plan to drive to Kentucky and report a story at Fort Campbell. I needed to get home right away. So I paid an extra $200 to change my ticket and flew back to California.

One veteran, a National Guardsman I'd met in my normal, relaxed state in Washington, D.C., a few months earlier, wrote me an e-mail that I read on my return to California. "I have been doing a lot better," he wrote. "I feel stronger as I understand more and more what I can do to help things now. I was wondering how you were doing though. I was not sure, as we did not have much time to talk, but I did get the sense that you were stressed. Was it because you were surrounded by all these vets? I would have to imagine that things are difficult working [with] the veterans and at the same time knowing the Iraqi people."

It was. Even now, nearly four years after my last trip to Iraq, I cannot look at a veteran without imagining the faces of the Iraqis they may have killed. I recoil reflexively at any mention of soldiers as "heroes," because much of me sees nothing heroic about traveling to occupy another person's country on the orders of a misguided president and compliant Congress.

To me, veterans are simply fellow members of the human race. They are my neighbors. They are American citizens who've undertaken difficult tasks and incredible risks to their own safety. In return, they simply expected the government to keep its promises. If we can't even keep our promises to American veterans, how can we possibly do anything good for the people of Iraq or Afghanistan?

Looked at in this light, the current public mood in this country concerns me greatly. Most Americans now see the invasion of Iraq as a mistake and want to put the war behind them. This feeling is based not on a coherent critique but on a kind of collective exhaustion. The American people are tired of this war and are tuning it out. A March 2008 survey by the Pew Research Center found that only 28 percent of Americans knew that approximately 4,000 U.S. soldiers had died in the war. Most thought the number was closer to 2,000 to 3,000. According to the same survey, media coverage of the war dropped from an average of 15 percent of stories in July 2007 to just 3 percent in February 2008.[1]

The implications of these findings could be disastrous for people affected by the war, American and Iraqi alike. In many ways, we as a country find ourselves in a mood like the one we were in toward the end of the Vietnam War: we are tired and simply want to move on and forget the conflict ever happened. But those of us who experienced this war firsthand cannot forget. The war remains inside us. Nearly four years after my last trip to Iraq, I am beginning to realize that I may never fully heal from my own experience overseas. I do not suffer from disabling post-traumatic stress disorder or traumatic brain injury, but in my mind I am still regularly transported back to Baghdad, Diyala, and Fallujah. These feelings and images come suddenly and are sometimes so visceral that I lose my connection to the peaceful reality that surrounds me here in America.

For example, one day in April 2008, I suddenly felt a powerful need to escape my apartment. I rode my bicycle along the San Francisco Bay for hours, and then hopped on a train to Sacramento, a hundred miles away. Why I felt in danger sitting in my living room I cannot say, but I can tell you when I finally sat on the Amtrak train as it rolled north I was able to breathe a sigh of relief. It was the same feeling I had when I got into a taxi to Kurdistan and left Baghdad for the last time.

A few weeks later, the disassociation hit again. I was attending a journalism conference in Silicon Valley, when suddenly I saw a Bradley Fighting Vehicle burning right before my eyes. I did my best to keep my attention on the speaker at the front of the room, but I could not do it. Other times I start crying for no reason, because I am finally experiencing the emotional pain of something I witnessed in the past.

As I mentioned before, my problems are relatively small compared to those of the veterans featured in this book. If these veterans cannot heal their wounds, we as a nation will not be able to move on. There will continue to be stories of veterans killing themselves, killing their spouses, and being shot by police. There will be broken marriages and stories of war veterans sleeping on the street. What we need are proactive solutions that prevent the sad history of America's Vietnam veterans from repeating itself.

Consider the April 2008 RAND Corporation study mentioned earlier in this book, which found that at least 300,000 Iraq and Afghanistan war veterans suffer from post-traumatic stress disorder or major depression, while another 320,000 suffer from traumatic brain injury. The same study also found that a majority of the injured are not receiving help from the Pentagon and VA, which, as I've shown, are oftentimes more concerned with concealing unpleasant facts than with providing care.

The RAND Corporation also noted that the federal government fails to care for war veterans at its own peril—noting that post-traumatic stress disorder and traumatic brain injury "can have far reaching and damaging consequences."

"Individuals afflicted with these conditions face higher risks for other psychological problems and for attempting suicide. They have higher rates of unhealthy behaviors—such as smoking, overeating, and unsafe sex—and higher rates of physical health problems and mortality. Individuals with these conditions also tend to miss more work or report being less productive," the report said. "These conditions can impair relationships, disrupt marriages, aggravate the difficulties of parenting, and cause problems in children that may extend the consequences of combat trauma across generations.

"These consequences can have a high economic toll," the RAND report concluded. "However, most attempts to measure the costs of these conditions focus only on medical costs to the government. Yet, direct costs of treatment are only a fraction of the total costs related to mental health and cognitive conditions. Far higher are the long-term individual and societal costs stemming from lost productivity, reduced quality of life, homelessness, domestic violence, the strain on families, and suicide. Delivering effective care and restoring veterans to full mental health have the potential to reduce these longer-term costs significantly."[2]

By the time you read this, a new president will be taking office. That president and the Congress will have the power to stop this problem before it gets worse. It's not too late to extend needed mental health care to our returning Iraq and Afghanistan war veterans; it's not too late to begin properly screening and treating returning servicemen and women who've experienced traumatic brain injuries; and it is not too late to simplify the disability claims process so that wounded veterans do not die or become homeless while waiting for their checks. This isn't just in the best interest of veterans; it's in the best interest of our country in the long run.

A NOTE ON SOURCES

This book is based primarily on hundreds of interviews and my own coverage of events reported from Iraq itself, Washington, D.C., and across the United States. This first-person coverage is buttressed by an increasing number of government documents and official reports on the experience of veterans coming home from Iraq and Afghanistan. These documents come primarily from the Department of Veterans Affairs (VA), the Pentagon, and the nonpartisan Government Accountability Office (GAO). Much has also come to light in congressional hearings and through the independent Dole-Shalala Commission formed in the aftermath of the scandal at Walter Reed Army Medical Center.

I have also relied on the reporting of other fine journalists. Often, I was able to interview parties to a particular veteran's story, but not all of them, and so I have cited another journalist's work to fill out my account. I've also relied to a lesser extent on books about the history of veterans' struggle for justice, especially in my explanation of the 1944 passage of the GI Bill and of the trials and tribulations of Vietnam veterans. Readers interested in the government reports, books, and articles cited can find necessary details in the endnotes. Wherever possible, I have included Web links for easier access.

NOTES

PREFACE

1. All of Andrew's observations are from *The Blood of My Brother*, DVD, directed by Andrew Berends (Parsippany, NJ: Lifesize Entertainment, 2006), www .lifesizeentertainment.com.

2. Antony Feinstein, John Owen, and Nancy Blair, "A Hazardous Profession: War, Journalists, and Psychopathology," *American Journal of Psychiatry* 159.9 (2002): 1570–75, http://ajp.psychiatryonline.org/cgi/content/abstract/159/9/1570.

1 A SOLDIER COMES HOME

1. Charles Hoge, C. Castro, S. Messer, Cotting D. McGurk, and R. Koffman, "Combat Duty in Iraq and Afghanistan, Mental Health Problems, and Barriers to Care," *New England Journal of Medicine* 351.1 (2004), http://content.nejm .org/cgi/reprint/351/1/13.pdf.

2. Department of Veterans Affairs, "Analysis of VA Health Care Utilization among U.S. Global War on Terror (GWOT) Veterans," March 25, 2008.

3. The 15 percent figure is from ibid. The 50 percent figure is from the Department of Defense Task Force on Mental Health, *An Achievable Vision: Report of the Department of Defense Task Force on Mental Health* (Falls Church, VA: Defense Health Board, 2007), www.ha.osd.mil/dhb/mhtf/MHTF-Report-Final.pdf.

4. Associated Press, "18 Percent of Deployed Fort Carson Troops Suffered Brain Injury," April 11, 2007.

5. Steven L. Sayers, Victoria Farrow, Jennifer Ross, Christine Beswick, Lauren Sippel, Vince Kane, and David W. Oslin, "Family Problems among Recently Returning Military Veterans" (paper presented at the American Psychological Association 115th Annual Convention, San Francisco, August 17, 2007).

6. International Committee of the Red Cross, *Report of the International Committee of the Red Cross (ICRC) on the Treatment by the Coalition Forces of Prisoners of War and Other Protected Persons by the Geneva Conventions in Iraq during Arrest, Internment and Interrogation* (International Committee of the Red Cross, 2004), available at Truthout.org, www.truthout.org/mm_01/4.rcr.iraq.pdf.

7. Zogby International, "U.S. Troops in Iraq: 72% Say End War in 2006," February 28, 2006, http://zogby.com/news/ReadNews.dbm?ID=1075.

8. Herbert Hendin and Ann Pollinger Haas, *Wounds of War: The Psychological Aftermath of Combat in Vietnam* (New York: Basic Books, 1984).

9. Joshua Casteel, "Returns: A Meditation in Post-trauma" (unpublished play, Iowa City, IA).

2 TRYING TO ADJUST

1. Lisa Burgess, "Divorce Rate among Active-Duty Army Officers, Enlisted Has Risen Dramatically," *Stars and Stripes,* July 9, 2005, www.estripes.com/article.asp?section=104&article=28797&archive=true.

2. President's Commission on Mental Health, *Mental Health Problems of Vietnam Era Veterans,* vol. 3 (Washington, D.C.: Government Printing Office, 1978).

3. R. A. Kulka, W. E. Schlenger, J. A. Fairbank, R. L. Hough, B. K. Jordan, C. R. Marmar et al., *Trauma and the Vietnam War Generation: Report of findings from the National Vietnam Veterans Readjustment Study* (New York: Brunno/Mazel, 1990).

4. David Hackworth, "Other Priorities," Military.com, September 24, 2004, www.military.com/Resources/ResourceFileView?file=Hackworth_092404.htm.

5. This and subsequent quotations from Brig. Gen. Karpinski are from ibid. unless otherwise noted.

6. Sara Corbett, "The Women's War," *New York Times,* March 18, 2007, www.nytimes.com/2007/03/18/magazine/18cover.html?pagewanted=1&ei=5070&em&en=a87c0d108c311ae7&ex=1174536000.

7. Government Accountability Office, "Military Personnel: Preliminary Observations Related to Income, Benefits, and Employer Support for Reservists

During Mobilizations," testimony submitted to the House Committee on Armed Services, Subcommittee on Total Force, Washington, D.C., March 19, 2003, www.gao.gov/new.items/d03549t.pdf.

8. Brendan Koerner, "The Winner of the War on Terrorism is . . . US Industry," *Mother Jones,* September 1, 2002.

3 A DIFFERENT KIND OF CASUALTY

1. Amy Fairweather, *Risk and Protective Factors for Homelessness among OIF/OEF Veterans* (San Francisco: Swords to Plowshares, 2006).

2. Robert Burns, "Pentagon Abandons Active-Duty Time Limit," Associated Press, January 12, 2007, available at Truthout.org, www.truthout.org/docs _2006/011207M.shtml.

3. Mental Health Advisory Team (MHAT) IV Operation Iraqi Freedom 05-07, Final Report; Office of the Surgeon Multinational Forces Iraq and United States Army Medical Command, November 17, 2006. Available at www .armymedicine.army.mil/news/mhat/mhat_iv/mhat-iv.cfm.

4. Trin Yarborough, *Surviving Twice: Amerasian Children of the Vietnam War,* (Washington, D.C.: Potomac Books, 2005), 16–19.

5. Allison Batdorff, "Human Trafficking Training Mandatory for Overseas Troops," *Stars and Stripes,* October 22, 2006, http://stripes.com/article.asp ?section=104&article=39956&archive=true.

6. This exchange with Donald Rumsfeld is reported in William Branigin, "Bush, Rumsfeld Pledge to Protect Troops," *Washington Post,* December 9, 2004, www .washingtonpost.com/wp-dyn/articles/A51481-2004Dec9.html. A full transcript of Rumsfeld's comments is available at the Department of Defense Web site, www.defenselink.mil/transcripts/transcript.aspx?transcriptid=1980.

7. Lisa Hoffman, "Humvees Linked to 1 in 5 U.S. Deaths in Iraq," Scripps Howard News Service, December 30, 2004, http://shns.abc15.com/shns/story .cfm?pk=HUMVEES-12–30–04&cat=II.

8. U.S. Department of Defense, *Measuring Stability and Security in Iraq: September 2007 Report to Congress; In Accordance with the Department of Defense Appropriations Act 2007 (Section 9010, Public Law 109–289)* (U.S. Department of Defense, September 14, 2007), www.defenselink.mil/home/pdf/9010_March _2007_Final_Signed.pdf.

9. Brooks Jackson and Justin Bank, "False Claims about Body Armor," Factcheck .org, September 26, 2006, http://factcheck.org/article438.html.

10. Joseph Stiglitz and Linda Bilmes, *The Three Trillion Dollar War* (New York: Norton, 2008), 60.

11. Department of Defense: Afghanistan War (Operation Enduring Freedom, OEF), Casualties from October 7, 2001, through August 2, 2008; Iraq War (Operation Iraqi Freedom, OIF), Casualties from March 19, 2003, through August 2, 2008; DoD Contingency Tracking System, through March 31, 2008. The Pentagon's Defense Manpower Data Center updates statistics every month at http://siadapp.dmdc.osd.mil/personnel/CASUALTY/WOTSUM.pdf (Afghanistan); and http://siadapp.dmsdc.osd.mil/personnel/CASUALTY/OIF-Total.pdf (Iraq). Department of Veterans Affairs, "Analysis of VA Health Care Utilization Among US Global War on Terrorism (GWOT) Veterans," March 25, 2008. Department of Veterans Affairs, "VA Benefits Activity: Veterans Deployed to the Global War on Terror," April 16, 2008.

12. Terri Tanielian and Lisa H. Jaycox, *Invisible Wounds of War: Psychological and Cognitive Injuries, Their Consequences, and Services to Assist Recovery* (Santa Monica, Calif.: RAND Corporation, MG-720-CCF, 2008), 492 pp.; available at http://veterans.rand.org.

13. Associated Press, "18 Percent of Deployed Fort Carson Troops Suffered Brain Injury," April 11, 2007.

14. Erin Emery, "Nearly 2 in 10 Carson GIs Got Brain Injuries in Iraq," *Denver Post,* April 11, 2007, final edition, A1.

15. Associated Press, "18 Percent of Deployed Fort Carson Troops Suffered Brain Injury," April 11, 2007.

16. U.S. Department of Veterans Affairs, Veterans Health Administration, "Screening and Evaluation of Possible Traumatic Brain Injury in Operation Enduring Freedom (OEF) and Operation Iraqi Freedom (OIF) Veterans," VHA Directive 2007-013, April 13, 2007, www.iava.org/documents/VHADirective.pdf.

4 THE SCANDAL AT WALTER REED

1. This and subsequent quotations are from the *Post*'s first Walter Reed article, Dana Priest and Ann Hull, "Soldiers Face Neglect, Frustration at Army's Top Medical Facility," *Washington Post,* February 18, 2007, A01, www.washingtonpost .com/wp-dyn/content/article/2007/02/17/AR2007021701172.html.

2. Michael Abramowitz and Steve Vogel, "Apologies, Anger at Walter Reed Hearing," *Washington Post,* March 6, 2007, A01, www.washingtonpost.com/wp -dyn/content/article/2007/03/05/AR2007030500676_pf.html.

3. Ibid.

4. "President Bush Discusses Care for America's Returning Wounded Warriors, War on Terror at American Legion," transcript of speech to American Legion, Washington, D.C., March 2, 2007, www.whitehouse.gov/news/releases/2007/ 03/20070306-1.html.

5. "President Bush Visits Troops at Walter Reed Army Medical Center," transcript of address to Walter Reed staff, Washington, D.C., March 30, 2007, www .whitehouse.gov/news/releases/2007/03/20070330-6.html.

6. Mark Benjamin, "Behind the Walls of Ward 54," *Salon,* February 18, 2005. http://dir.salon.com/story/news/feature/2005/02/18/walter_reed.

7. Greg Jaffe, "As Benefits for Veterans Climb, Military Spending Feels Squeeze," *Wall Street Journal,* January 25, 2005, p.1, http://webreprints.djreprints.com/ 1156160669825.html.

8. Scott Shane and Eric Lipton, "Stumbling Storm-Aid Effort Put Tons of Ice on Trips to Nowhere," *New York Times,* October 2, 2005, www.nytimes.com/2005/ 10/02/national/nationalspecial/02ice.html?_r=1&adxnnl=1&oref=slogin& adxnnlx=1195070480-2Rp1w8LdaZDxzmdUmP+g+g.

9. Ashley Gibson, "Crosland Preps for Uptown Move; Neffgen Moves On," *Charlotte Business Journal,* March 12, 2004, www.bizjournals.com/charlotte/ stories/2004/03/15/tidbits1.html?page=1.

10. Kelly Kennedy, "Committee Subpoenas Former Walter Reed Chief," *Army Times,* March 3, 2007, www.armytimes.com/news/2007/03/ Weightmansubpoena/.

11. Garrison Cdr. Peter Garibaldi to Maj. Gen. George Weightman, "Challenges Concerning the Base Operations A-76 Study and Resulting Reduction in Force (RIF) at Walter Reed Army Medical Center," September 12, 2006, available from the House Committee on Oversight and Government Reform, http:// oversight.house.gov/Documents/20070302140159-96391.pdf.

12. Government Accountability Office, "Preliminary Observations on Efforts to Improve Health Care and Disability Evaluations for Returning Servicemembers," testimony submitted to the House Committee on Oversight and Government Reform, Subcommittee on National Security and

Foreign Affairs, Washington, D.C., September 26, 2007, www.politico.com/static/PPM41_gaowoundedwarrior.html.

13. Mike Cassidy's comments are reported in Will Higgins, "Hoosier Soldier Honored for Service," *Indianapolis Star,* October 2, 2007, www.culver.org/news/News_Articles/Articles_0708/Summer_grad_succumbs.htm.

14. GlobalSecurity.org, "CSC Scania/Convoy Support Center Scania/Camp Scania," www.globalsecurity.org/military/world/iraq/nippur.htm.

15. Associated Press, "Family Raising Questions about Soldier's Death, Care," October 5, 2007.

16. "Indiana National Guard Soldier Dies," WISH-TV (Indianapolis), September 26, 2007.

17. Mary McDermott, "Community Honors Soldier Who Died after Serving in Iraq," WISH-TV (Indianapolis), October 2, 2007.

18. Senator Evan Bayh to Secretary of the Army Preston Geren, letter demanding investigation into Sgt. Gerald Cassidy's death at Fort Knox, October 10, 2007, http://bayh.senate.gov/Geren-Cassidy%20Letter.pdf.

5 COMING TOGETHER

1. President's Commission on Care for America's Returning Wounded Warriors [Dole-Shalala Commission], *Serve, Support, Simplify: Report of the President's Commission on Care for America's Returning Wounded Warriors* (President's Commission on Care for America's Returning Wounded Warriors, July 2007), www.pccww.gov/docs/Kit/Main_Book_CC%5BJULY26%5D.pdf.

2. Deborah Sontag and Lizette Alvarez, "For War's Gravely Injured, Challenge to Find Care," *New York Times,* March 12, 2007, www.nytimes.com/2007/03/12/us/12trauma.html?pagewanted=1.

3. Debbie Reynolds, "Person of the Week; Sgt. Eric Edmundson," *ABC News,* June 29, 2007.

4. John Gonsalves's recollections are reported in Matt Tessnear, "Non-profit Group Gives Home to Injured Sergeant," *New Bern Sun Journal,* October 7, 2007, State and Regional News section.

6 **EDUCATION**

1. Quoted in Michael J. Bennett, *When Dreams Came True: The GI Bill and the Making of Modern America* (1996; Washington, D.C.: Brassey's, 1999), 94.

2. Quoted in ibid., 94–95.

3. Quoted in ibid., 96.

4. Ibid., 95.

5. Roosevelt's and the subsequent comments from congressional representatives are quoted in ibid., 129.

6. Quoted in ibid., 243.

7. Bennett, *When Dreams Came True.*

8. Aaron Glantz, "Vets Tough March from Military to College," *San Francisco Chronicle,* July 1, 2007, A-15, www.sfgate.com/cgi-bin/article.cgi?f=/c/a/2007/07/01/MNGGIQP8011.DTL&hw=Aaron+Glantz&sn=001&sc=1000.

9. Quoted in Aaron Glantz, "Bill Would Ease U.S. Vets' Return to School," OneWorld.net, July 2, 2007, http://us.oneworld.net/article/view/150880/1.

10. U.S. Senate, "Statements on Introduced Bills and Joint Resolutions," remarks by Senator James Webb in favor of S.22, *Congressional Record* (January 4, 2007): S56–57, http://thomas.loc.gov/cgi-bin/query/F?r110:95:./temp/~r110oz4scc:e156898:.

11. Congressional Budget Office, *Quality Soldiers: Costs of Manning the Active Duty Army,* June 1986, www.cbo.gov/ftpdocs/59xx/doc5936/doc17b-Entire.pdf.

12. Senator James Webb testimony at the "Hearing on Pending Benefits Legislation," Senate Committee on Veterans Affairs, Washington, D.C., May 9, 2007, http://veterans.senate.gov/public/index.cfm?pageid=16&release_id=11110&sub_release_id=11125&view=all.

13. David Lerman, "Tuition Bill for War Vets Wilts: The Likely Cost of Sen. Webb's Veteran Education Plan Made It Hard to Attract Bipartisan Support," *Newport News (VA) Daily Press,* June 18, 2007.

14. Editorial, "Mr. Bush and the GI Bill," *New York Times,* May 26, 2008; available at www.nytimes.com/2008/05/26/opinion/26mon1.html?ref=opinion.

15. White House press release, "President Bush Signs H.R. 2462, The Supplemental Appropriations Act, 2008," June 30, 2008. Available at http://www.whitehouse.gov/news/releases/2008/06/20080630.html.

16. Ben Feller, "Bush Signs $162 Billion War Spending Bill," Associated Press, June 30, 2008.

7   DRUGS, CRIME, AND LOSING YOUR BENEFITS

1. I obtained this Pentagon data from the Defense Manpower Data Center in response to my Freedom of Information Act request for discharge data broken down by U.S. Military SPN Code.

2. Department of Defense Task Force on Mental Health, *An Achievable Vision: Report of the Department of Defense Task Force on Mental Health* (Falls Church, VA: Defense Health Board, 2007), www.ha.osd.mil/dhb/mhtf/MHTF-Report -Final.pdf.

3. Gregg Zoroya, "Battle Stress May Lead to Misconduct," *USA Today*, July 1, 2007, www.usatoday.com/news/washington/2007-07-01-marine-stress_N.htm.

4. Leo Shane, "New Guidelines Allow Troops Who've Recovered from Traumatic Stress Disorders to Redeploy," *Stars and Stripes,* December 22, 2006, mideastern edition, www.stripes.com/article.asp?section=104&article=41293&archive=true.

8   LOSING YOUR BENEFITS

1. Department of Defense Task Force on Mental Health, *An Achievable Vision: Report of the Department of Defense Task Force on Mental Health* (Falls Church, VA: Defense Health Board, 2007), www.ha.osd.mil/dhb/mhtf/MHTF-Report -Final.pdf. All task force quotations are from this document.

2. Steven L. Sayers, Victoria Farrow, Jennifer Ross, Christine Beswick, Lauren Sippel, Vince Kane, and David W. Oslin, "Family Problems among Recently Returning Military Veterans" (paper presented at the American Psychological Association 115th Annual Convention, San Francisco, August 17, 2007).

3. Lisa Chedekel, "Most Stress Cases Missed; Army Admits Disorder Is Under-Reported," *Hartford Courant,* August 6, 2007, A1.

4. Ibid.

5. According to data provided to me by the Defense Manpower Data Center under the Freedom of Information Act, 23,275 active-duty personnel had been discharged by the Department of Defense as of September 30, 2007.

6. U.S. Army, *Personnel Separations: Active Duty Enlisted Administrative Separations,* Army Regulation 635–200, June 6, 2005.

7. Joshua Kors, "How Specialist Town Lost His Benefits," *The Nation,* April 9, 2007, www.thenation.com/doc/20070409/kors.

8. Specialist Town's testimony is from "Post Traumatic Stress Disorder (PTSD) and Personality Disorders: Challenges for the U.S. Department of Veterans Affairs," hearing of the House Committee on Veterans Affairs, Washington, D.C., July 25, 2007, http://veterans.house.gov/hearings/hearing.aspx ?NewsID=45.

9. Kors, "How Specialist Town Lost His Benefits."

10. Jason Forrester's testimony is from "Post Traumatic Stress Disorder (PTSD) and Personality Disorders: Challenges for the U.S. Department of Veterans Affairs," hearing of the House Committee on Veterans Affairs.

11. These figures were taken from data prepared by the National Priorities Project, which has developed an online calculator (www.costofwar.com).

12. Linda Bilmes's summary is from her "Another Year, Another $300 Billion," *Boston Globe,* March 16, 2008, E9.

13. Joseph Stiglitz and Linda Bilmes, *The Three Trillion Dollar War* (New York: Norton, 2008), 41. See also Linda Bilmes, "Soldiers Returning from Iraq and Afghanistan: The Long-Term Costs of Providing Veterans Medical Care and Disability Benefits," Faculty Research Working Paper RWP07-001, Harvard University, January 2007, http://ksgnotes1.harvard.edu/Research/wpaper.nsf/ rwp/RWP07-001.

9 MEET THE BUREAUCRACY

1. Department of Veterans Affairs, "VA Form 21–526, Parts A, B, C, &D," www .vba.va.gov/pubs/forms/21–526.pdf.

2. American Psychiatric Association, "309.81 Posttraumatic Stress Disorder," *Diagnostic and Statistical Manual of Mental Disorders,* 4th ed. (Arlington, VA: American Psychiatric Publishing, 2000), www.psychiatryonline.com/content .aspx?aID=3357&searchStr=post-traumatic+stress+disorder.

3. *Veterans for Common Sense vs. Peake,* Case No. C-07-3758, U.S.D.C. (N.D. Cal. 2007), final transcript, pp. 1369, 1372.

4. All Linda Bilmes quotations are from her "Soldiers Returning from Iraq and Afghanistan: The Long-Term Costs of Providing Veterans Medical Care and Disability Benefits," Faculty Research Working Paper RWP07-001, Harvard

University, January 2007, http://ksgnotes1.harvard.edu/Research/wpaper.nsf/
rwp/RWP07-001.

10 DIDN'T PREPARE TO TREAT THE WOUNDED

1. Kenneth Adelman, "Cakewalk in Iraq," *Washington Post,* February 13, 2002, A27.

2. Both of these quotations are from Susan Page, "Prewar Predictions Coming
    Back to Bite," *USA Today,* March 31, 2003, www.usatoday.com/news/world/
    iraq/2003–03–31-then-and-now-usat_x.htm.

3. Richard Perle, "Turkey at the Crossroads," speech given to members of the
    American Enterprise Institute, September 22, 2003.

4. David U. Himmelstein, Karen E. Lasser, Danny McCormick, David H. Bor, J.
    Wesley Boyd, and Steffie Woolhandler, "Lack of Health Coverage among US
    Veterans from 1987 to 2004," *American Journal of Public Health* 97.12 (2007),
    www.pnhp.org/veterans_study/APHA_Veterans_galley.pdf.

5. "Statement of the Honorable Anthony J. Principi, Secretary of Veterans
    Affairs," testimony before the Senate Committee on Veterans Affairs,
    Washington, D.C., February 26, 2003, available at the Department of Veterans
    Affairs, www.va.gov/OCA/testimony/svac/03fe26TP.asp.

6. "Statement of Daniel L. Cooper, Undersecretary of Benefits," testimony before
    the House Committee on Veterans Affairs, Subcommittee on Benefits,
    Washington, D.C., April 10, 2003, available at the Department of Veterans
    Affairs, www.va.gov/OCA/testimony/hvac/03ap10DC.asp.

7. Dana Bash, "Snow Staying at Treasury, Principi Leaving VA," CNN.com,
    December 9, 2004, http://edition.cnn.com/2004/ALLPOLITICS/12/08/snow
    .principi/index.html.

8. Suzanne Gamboa, "Principi Wanted $1.2B More for VA Budget," Associated
    Press, February 4, 2004, www.washingtonpost.com/wp-dyn/articles/A13666
    -2004Feb4.html.

9. Anne C. Mulkern, "VA Not Ready for Casualties from 2 Fronts, Critics Say,"
    Denver Post, July 4, 2005, A01.

10. Author interview with Michael Victorian, American Federation of Government
    Employees, August 21, 2007.

12. For a full listing of how veterans' groups ranked John McCain's record in the
    Senate, visit www.votesmart.org/issue_rating_category.php?can_id=53270&
    type=category&category=66&go.x=4&go.y=11.

12. Disabled American Veterans' listing of Senator John McCain's votes is available at http://capwiz.com/dav/bio/?id=192.

13. Libby Lewis, "Iraq War Stirs Memories for Vietnam Vets," National Public Radio, September 25, 2007, www.npr.org/templates/story/story.php?storyId=14529768.

14. Donna St. George, "Iraq War May Add Stress for Past Vets," *Washington Post,* June 20, 2006, A01, www.washingtonpost.com/wp-dyn/content/article/2006/06/19/AR2006061901400.html.

15. "Post Traumatic Stress Disorder (PTSD) and Personality Disorders: Challenges for the U.S. Department of Veterans Affairs," hearing of the House Committee on Veterans Affairs, Washington, D.C., July 25, 2007, http://veterans.house.gov/hearings/hearing.aspx?NewsID=45.

16. Mark Benjamin, "The V.A.'s Bad Review," *Salon,* October 25, 2005, http://dir.salon.com/story/news/feature/2005/10/26/suicide/index.html.

17. "Post Traumatic Stress Disorder (PTSD) and Personality Disorders: Challenges for the U.S. Department of Veterans Affairs," hearing of the House Committee on Veterans Affairs.

18. "VA Should Revise Its Methods for Evaluating and Rating PTSD in Veterans," National Academies press release, May 8, 2007, www8.nationalacademies.org/onpinews/newsitem.aspx?RecordID=11870.

19. "Post Traumatic Stress Disorder (PTSD) and Personality Disorders: Challenges for the U.S. Department of Veterans Affairs," hearing of the House Committee on Veterans Affairs.

20. Associate Press reports on VA bonuses are from Hope Yip, "Senior VA Officials Get Big Bonuses," Associated Press, May 3, 2007, http://sfgate.com/cgi-bin/article.cgi?f=/n/a/2007/05/03/national/w005358D01.DTL&type=politics.

21. Original complaint, *Veterans for Common Sense et al. v. Nicholson et al.,* Case No. C-07-3758, July 23, 2007, U.S. District Court, Northern District of California, www.veteransptsdclassaction.org/pdf/courtfiled/veteranscomplaint.pdf. The case name changed to *Veterans for Common Sense et al. v. Peake et al.* after James Peake replaced Jim Nicholson as secretary of veterans affairs in late 2007. It will likely change again when the next presidential administration appoints a new secretary.

22. Aaron Glantz, "Vets Sue Gov't for 'Shameful Failures,'" Inter Press Service, July 23, 2007, http://ipsnews.net/news.asp?idnews=38640.

23. Ibid.

24. "Defendants' Notice of Motion and Motion to Dismiss Plaintiffs' Complaint," *Veterans for Common Sense et al. v. Nicholson et al.,* Case No. C 07-3758-SC, Document 19, September 25, 2007, U.S. District Court, Northern District of California, www.veteransptsdclassaction.org/pdf/courtfiled/9-25-07-Motion %20to%20Dismiss.pdf.

25. Trial Transcript, *Veterans for Common Sense vs. Peake,* Case No. C-07-3758, U.S.D.C., April 30, 2008, pp. 1385, 1398.

26. The video has been taken down from the Christian Embassy site, but has been reposted in a number of places, including at TruthOut.org, www.truthout.org/ docs_2006/080307A.shtml.

27. Americans United for Separation of Church and State, *Report of Americans United for Separation of Church and State on Religious Coercion and Endorsement of Religion at the United States Air Force Academy,* April 28, 2005, www.au.org/ pdf/050428AirForceReport.pdf.

11   MORE BUREAUCRACY

1. Stella Hopkins and Ted Mellnik, "Some Serious Waiting; Veterans with Severe Ailments Often Subject to Scheduling Lags Observer Analysis: Waits for Appointments are Often Longer than VA's 30 Day Standard," *Charlotte Observer,* October 21, 2007, 1A.

2. Quotations and findings from the VA Inspector General's audit are from Department of Veterans Affairs, Office of Inspector General, *Audit of the Veterans Health Administration's Outpatient Waiting Times,* Report No. 07-00616-199 (Washington, D.C.: Department of Veterans Affairs, Office of Inspector General, September 10, 2007), www.va.gov/oig/52/reports/2007/ VAOIG-07-00616-199.pdf.

12   CRIME

1. The majority of material about Manny Babbitt's case comes from my own notes and audio recordings made while covering Babbitt's clemency petition for Pacifica Radio in 1999.

2. Rachel King, *Capital Consequences: Families of the Condemned Tell Their Stories* (New Brunswick, NJ: Rutgers University Press, 2005).

3. Amnesty International, *USA: The Execution of Mentally Ill Offenders*, 2006, http://web.amnesty.org/library/index/ENGAMR510032006.

4. Ibid.

5. R. A. Kulka, W. E. Schlenger, J. A. Fairbank, R. L. Hough, B. K. Jordan, C. R. Marmar et al. *Trauma and the Vietnam War Generation: Report of Findings from the National Vietnam Veterans Readjustment Study* (New York: Brunno/Mazel, 1990).

6. This and subsequent quotations are from Jonathan Shay, *Odysseus in America* (New York: Scribner, 2002), 26–31.

7. See The VetStage Web site, http://vetstage.org.

8. Tim McGirk, "Collateral Damage or Civilian Massacre in Haditha?" *Time,* March 19, 2006, www.time.com/time/world/article/0,8599,1174649,00.html.

9. "Press Briefing by Tony Snow," White House Office of the Press Secretary, May 31, 2006, www.whitehouse.gov/news/releases/2006/05/20060531-4.html.

10. Tony Perry, "Marine Denies a Role in 12 Haditha Killings; Wuterich Says He Shot Only Five Men at the Site of a 2005 Roadside Blast," *Los Angeles Times,* September 7, 2007, A9.

11. Tony Perry, "The Conflict in Iraq: Marine on Trial; Marines Were Ordered to Be More Violent, Witness Says" *Los Angeles Times,* July 15, 2007, A9.

12. Ibid.

13. Shay, *Odysseus in America,* 224–25.

14. Rick Anderson, "Home Front Casualties: Murders and Suicides by Military Personnel Might Be Part of the Iraq War Toll," *Seattle Weekly,* August 31, 2005, www.seattleweekly.com/2005–08–31/news/home-front-casualties.php.

13   HOMELESS ON THE STREETS OF AMERICA

1. State of California Department of Veterans Affairs, *A Study on the Status of Homeless Veterans in California* (Sacramento: State of California Department of Veterans Affairs, 2002), www.cdva.ca.gov/AboutUs/DocsAndImages/HomelessStudy.pdf.

2. National Coalition for Homeless Veterans, "Background and Statistics: Most Often Asked Questions about Homeless Veterans," 2007, www.nchv.org/background.cfm#facts.

3. Amy Fairweather, *Risk and Protective Factors for Homelessness among OIF/OEF Veterans* (San Francisco: Swords to Plowshares, 2006).

4. For details of the VA's plan for homeless vets, see Department of Veterans Affairs, "VA Announces $24 Million in Grants for Homeless Programs," press release, July 11, 2007, www1.va.gov/opa/pressrel/pressrelease.cfm?id=1356.

5. For quotations from the film, see *When I Came Home,* DVD, directed by Dan Lohaus (New York: Lohaus Films, 2006), www.whenicamehome.com.

6. John Tarleton, "Invisible Soldier," *The Indypendant*, December 29, 2004, available at AlterNet, www.alternet.org/waroniraq/20840?page=entire.

7. Anthony Lappe, "Herold's War: A Homeless Iraq Vet Asks for Respect," GNN: Guerilla News Network, January 10, 2005, www.gnn.tv/articles/article.php?id=1054.

8. Ibid.

9. Stefan Friedman, "Apt Gift for Homeless War Hero," *New York Post,* February 1, 2005, 17.

10. This and remaining Herold Noel quotations are from *When I Came Home,* DVD, directed by Dan Lohaus.

1 4   SUICIDE

1. Quotations from Dena Rand are from Matt Rennells, "Why Did Sgt. Rand die?" *Leaf Chronicle,* April 22, 2007, 1A.

2. This and the following statistics about Army suicides are from Suicide Risk Management and Surveillance Office, Army Behavioral Health Technology Office, *Army Suicide Event Report (ASER): Calendar Year 2006* (Tacoma, WA: Department of Defense, 2007).

3. Erin Emery, "Ex-GI diagnosed with PTSD Dies in Collision," *Denver Post,* February 11, 2007, www.denverpost.com/news/ci_5199139.

4. Amy Forliti, "MN Guard Member Shot Dead by Police Had Been Suicidal in Past," Associated Press, May 30, 2007, available at Veterans for Common Sense, www.veteransforcommonsense.org/index.cfm/Page/Article/ID/7736.

5. This account is from Warren Wolfe and Chuck Haga, "Did War's Demons Follow Iraq Veteran in I-94 Chase?" *Minneapolis Star Tribune,* May 29, 2007, www.startribune.com/local/11587386.html.

6. Forliti, "MN Guard Member Shot Dead by Police Had Been Suicidal in Past."

7. Sgt. Dean's VA evaluation is reported in Dan Barry, "Asked to Serve Again, a Soldier Goes Down Fighting," *New York Times,* May 27, 2007, 18, available at VAWatchdog.org, http://vawatchdog.org/07/nf07/nfMAY07/nf052907-2.htm.

8. "Dean Death Investigation," report from Richard D. Fritz, State's Attorney for St. Mary's County, Leonardtown, MD, May 2007, available at Who's Your Nanny, http://bothwell.typepad.com/whos_your_nanny/files/Dean_Death _Investigation.pdf.

15 SUICIDE AFTER THE WAR

1. Armen Keteyian, "Suicide Epidemic among Veterans." *CBS News,* November 13, 2007, www.cbsnews.com/stories/2007/11/13/cbsnews_investigates/ main3496471.shtml.

2. Exhibit No. P-1283, *Veterans for Common Sense vs. Peake,* Case No. C-07-3758, U.S.D.C. (N.D. Cal. 2007).

3. "Stopping Suicides: Mental Health Challenges within the U.S. Department of Veterans Affairs," hearing of the House Committee on Veterans Affairs, Washington, D.C., December 12, 2007, http://veterans.house.gov/hearings/ hearing.aspx?NewsID=167.

4. Mark S. Kaplan, Nathalie Huguet, Bentson H. McFarland, and Jason T. Newsom, "Suicide among Male Veterans: A Prospective Population-Based Study," *Journal of Epidemiology and Community Health* 61 (June 2007): 619–24, http://jech.bmj.com/cgi/content/full/61/7/619.

5. Department of Veterans Affairs, Office of Inspector General, *Healthcare Inspection: Implementing VHA's Mental Health Strategic Plan Initiatives for Suicide Prevention,* Report No. 06-03706-126 (Washington, D.C.: Department of Veterans Affairs, Office of Inspector General, May 10, 2007), www.va.gov/ oig/54/reports/VAOIG-06-03706-126.pdf.

6. Derek Henderson's story is from Laura Ungar, "Wounds of War; Vet Couldn't Defeat His Demons of War." *Louisville Courier-Journal,* September 2, 2007, 1A.

7. Harry Smith, "Vet Kills Himself after VA Turns Him Away," *CBS News,* March 13, 2007, www.cbsnews.com/stories/2007/03/13/earlyshow/main2562537.shtml.

8. Ibid.

9. Charles M. Sennott, "Told to Wait, a Marine Dies," *Boston Globe,* February 11,

2007, A1, www.boston.com/news/nation/articles/2007/02/11/told_to_wait_a _marine_dies/?page=1.

10. *Kevin Lucey et al. v. United States,* Case No. 3:2007cv30134, July 26, 2007, U.S. District Court for the District of Massachusetts, Western Division.

11. This exchange is recounted in David Capone, "Jeffrey Lucey," Agape Community: Christian Nonviolence, 2005, www.agapecommunity.org/article .php?story=20051122122343394.

12. Department of Veterans Affairs, Office of Inspector General, *Review of Quality of Care Involving a Patient Suicide,* Report No. 05-02562-124 (Washington, D.C.: Department of Veterans Affairs, Office of Inspector General, April 7, 2006), www.va.gov/oig/54/reports/VAOIG-05-02562-124.pdf.

13. Ibid.

14. Shinedown, "45," *Leave a Whisper,* Atlantic Records, 2004.

15. Department of Veterans Affairs, Office of Inspector General, *Review of Quality of Care Involving a Patient Suicide.*

16. Ibid.

17. Democracy Now! "Veteran Who Spoke Out about War's Psychological Affects Commits Suicide," January 30, 2006," www.democracynow.org/2006/1/30/ headlines.

16 A HISTORY OF NEGLECT

1. Peter Schuck, *Agent Orange on Trial: Mass Toxic Disasters in the Courts* (Cambridge, MA: Belknap Press of Harvard University Press, 1986).

2. Ibid.

3. Committee to Review the Health Effects in Vietnam Veterans of Exposure to Herbicides, Institute of Medicine, *Veterans and Agent Orange: Health Effects of Herbicides Used in Vietnam* (Washington, D.C.: National Academies Press, 1994).

4. Gerald Nicosia, *Home to War: A History of the Vietnam Veterans' Movement* (New York: Crown, 2001), p. 387.

5. Associated Press, PM cycle, March 24, 1978.

6. Schuck, *Agent Orange on Trial,* p. 24.

7. Nicosia, *Home to War.*

8. Committee to Review the Health Effects in Vietnam Veterans of Exposure to

Herbicides, Institute of Medicine, *Veterans and Agent Orange* (Washington, D.C.: National Academies Press, 1994), 33–34.

9. Schuck, *Agent Orange on Trial.*

10. Nicosia, *Home to War,* 388.

11. Schuck, *Agent Orange on Trial.*

12. McCarthy's experiences are recounted in Schuck, *Agent Orange on Trial,* p. 40.

13. This incident was reported by Brooks Jackson, Associated Press, A.M. cycle, Washington dateline, May 30, 1979.

14. Nicosia, *Home to War.*

15. Richard Severo and Lewis Milford, *The Wages of War: When America's Soldiers Came Home: From Valley Forge to Vietnam* (New York: Simon and Schuster, 1989), p. 386.

16. Ibid.

17. Ibid., p. 387.

18. Ibid.

19. Nicosia, *Home to War.*

20. "Agent Orange Victims Included in Veterans Law," *Chicago Tribune,* February 7, 1991, 14.

21. Department of Veterans Affairs, Office of Public Affairs, "Agent Orange and Related Issues," January 2003, http://permanent.access.gpo.gov/lps49045/agentorangefs.htm.

22. Seymour Hersh, *Against All Enemies: Gulf War Syndrome; The War Between America's Ailing Veterans and Their Government* (New York: Ballantine, 1998), 4.

23. "Examining the Status of Gulf War Research and Investigations of Gulf War Illness," Hearing Before the Subcommittee on National Security, Emerging Threats and International Relations of the Committee on Government Reform, House of Representatives, 108th Congress, June 1, 2004. Available at www.access.gpo.gov/congress/house/pdf/108hrg/96946.pdf.

24. See Hersh, *Against All Enemies.*

25. Alison Johnson, *Gulf War Syndrome: Legacy of a Perfect War,* (Brunswick, ME: MCS Information Exchange, 2001).

26. John Donnelly, "Iraqi Cancers Offer Clues to Gulf War Syndrome: Uranium Residue a Prime Suspect," *Miami Herald,* April 6, 1998, 1A.

27. This and the following Bush quotation are from R. G. Ratcliffe, "Bush Shores Up South Carolina Support; Military Issues Repeatedly Hit as Contest Shapes Up with War Hero John McCain," *Houston Chronicle,* November 10, 1999, A3.

28. Vicki Brower, "Gulf War Syndrome Revisited," *European Molecular Biology Organization* 4.6 (2003): 551–53.

29. Department of Veterans Affairs, *Gulf War Veterans Information System, May 2007* (Washington, D.C.: Department of Veterans Affairs, June 30, 2007).

17 WINNING THE BATTLE AT HOME

1. Gerald Nicosia, *Home to War: A History of the Vietnam Veterans' Movement* (New York: Crown, 2001), 368

2. Department of Veterans Affairs, Office of Public Affairs, "Facts about the Department of Veterans Affairs," December 2007, www1.va.gov/OPA/fact/docs/vafacts.pdf.

3. Regularly updated figures on campaign contributions and federal lobbying expenditures can be found at www.opensecrets.org, a Web site operated by the Center for Responsive Politics.

4. Michael J. Bennett, *When Dreams Came True: The GI Bill and the Making of Modern America* (1996; Washington, D.C.: Brassey's, 1999).

5. Ibid., 146.

6. Ibid., 153.

7. Press conference announcing the Veterans for Common Sense and Veterans United for Truth class-action lawsuit against the VA, July 23, 2007.

8. Ibid.

POSTSCRIPT

1. "Awareness of Iraq War Fatalities Plummets," Pew Research Center for People and the Press, March 12, 2008; available at http://people-press.org/reports/display.php3?ReportID=401.

2. T. Tanielian and L. H. Jaycox, eds., Invisible Wounds of War: Psychological and Cognitive Injuries, Their Consequences, and Services to Assist Recovery (Santa Monica, CA: RAND Corporation, MG-720-CCF, 2008), 492 pp., available at http://veterans.rand.org.

INDEX

Absent without Leave (AWOL), 93

Abu Ghraib, xiv, 5, 11, 19, 220

Agent Orange, 193–205

Al-Asad Airbase, 62

Alcohol abuse, xvii–xviii, 5, 7, 31, 89–91, 119, 135–136, 146–147, 161, 172, 179, 183–185

American Journal of Psychiatry, xviii

American Legion: President Bush discussing the Walter Reed scandal at, 51; advocating for better TBI treatment, 64; combating poor treatment of wounded WWII soldiers, 70–71; and the GI Bill, 73; employment opportunities for veterans, 108; conservative politics of, 210; money spent lobbying congress, 211; and WWI veterans, 212

American Psychological Association, 2007 study of military mental health, 97

Amnesty International: veterans with PTSD sentenced to death, 146; George Page executed despite mental illness, 147

Amputations: number of Iraq war veterans with, 10; individuals with, 50, 195

Anbar Province, 34

Anti-anxiety medication, 178, 179, 182

Antidepressants, 132, 182

Army Reserve, 3, 23, 29, 55, 61, 79, 119, 171, 172, 188

Army Suicide Event Report, 171, 176

Babbitt, Manny, 143–155

Backdoor draft, 29, 160

Baghdad, xiii, xiv, xv, xvi, xvii, 4, 18, 19, 28, 33, 55, 76, 105, 119, 161, 164, 168, 172, 200, 219, 221, 223, 224

Balad, 106, 161

Ban on photographing coffins of returning soldiers, 208

Bare, Brandon 154–155

Battle of Khe Sanh, 144

Bayh, Evan, 59–60

Beiersdorf, Will and Mary Beth, 23–27, 65–66, 69–70

Benjamin, Mark: and Walter Reed, 51; and the reevaluation of PTSD claims, 123; and veteran suicides, 123–124

Bennett, Michael, 72, 214

Berends, Andrew, xvii–xviii

Bilmes, Linda, 101, 102, 117

Bipolar disorder, 93, 157

Black Veterans for Social Justice, 159, 164

Body armor: and Donald Rumsfeld, 32–33; improvements since Vietnam, 35

Bolles, Gene: on catching brain injuries early, 41; on similarities of TBI and PTSD, 41; recommends TBI screening, 41

Bonus March, 70

Bowers, Todd, 79–80

Bunce, Justin, 36–39

Bush administration: ban on photography of coffins, 208; building case for Iraq war, 3; campaigning on support for troops, 205; Christian evangelicals and, 127–128; criticized for failure to support troops, 32; disregard for the Geneva Conventions, 13; ignoring rise in PTSD, 122–126; opposing benefits for widows of retired veterans, 52; opposing disability compensation for addicted veterans, 119; opposing military health care improvement, 52; opposing military pension funds, 52; opposing post-9/11 GI Bill, 83, 216; opposing prescription drug benefits, 119; politicizing the VA, 120–125; privatizing Walter Reed, 52; refusal to implement predeployment healthcare, 44; refusal to track soldiers diagnosed or deployed with PTSD, 89; response to Walter Reed scandal, 51–52; staffing Wounded Warrior Transition Program, 54; uncapping active duty for Guard and Reserve, 29; understaffing the VA, 120; unprepared to treat returning veterans, 118–128

Bush, George H. W., 199–202

Camp Anaconda, 161

Camp LeJeune, 167, 168

Camp Pendleton, 93, 94, 95, 150, 151

Camp Scania, 55–56

Camp Victory, 18, 19

Campbell, Patrick, xxiii; and GI Bill, 84–85; and TBI, 40–45; and VETS Act, 80–81

Cantu, Ronn, 28–29

Carter, Jimmy 196–198, 209

Cassidy, Gerald, 54–60

Casteel, Joshua, 11–14

CBS News investigation of veteran suicides, 176

Ceramic plated body armor, 35

Cheney, Dick: Halliburton and, 53; military service deferment for, 211; optimistic view of the war, 118

Christian evangelicals, influence in the military, 127–128

Chu, David, 52

Cleland, Max 195, 198

Cleveland State University, 122

Clinton, Bill, 51, 205, 206, 211

Combat skills, 147–148

Cooper, Daniel, 127–128

Cross-generational advocacy, 214–218

Dart Center for Journalism and Trauma, xix

Dean, Sergeant James E., 173–175

Death sentence for veterans convicted of crime despite mental illness, 143–155, 146–147

Defense and Veterans Brain Injury Center: and assessment of severity of brain injuries, 39; TBI Screening Test at, 42–43; treatment at, 37

Defense Policy Board, 118

Department of Defense Health Board Task Force on Mental Health: on administrative discharges, 87; on shortage of mental health providers, 96–97

Department of Homeland Security, 25
Department of Veterans Affairs (VA):
Agent Orange and, 194; bureaucracy in,
37, 105–118; denial of claims and, 74;
failure to diagnose PTSD, 97; fighting
for care at, 61; homeless veterans and,
162; lack of preparation for Iraq War,
118–128; mental health and, 6, 23; politi-
cization of, 120; staff shortages at, 54;
TBI screening and, 41; veteran suicides
and, 177, 178;
Department of Veteran Affairs, Inspector
General: auditing VA patient wait time,
133; delays in medical care, 134; investigation of Jeffrey Lucey's suicide, 184,
187; medical appointments, 133
Depleted uranium (DU) 203
Depression: RAND Corporation study
of Iraq war veterans and, 224; and
suicide, 181; in Vietnam veterans after
start of Iraq war, 122; in war reporters,
xvii–xviii
DeVictor, Maude, 194–196
Dioxin 193–197
Disability claims, 23, 36, 51, 71, 98, 102,
108, 109, 111, 112, 113, 115, 116, 117, 122,
123, 124, 126, 133, 163, 199, 206, 226
Disability percentage, 133
Disabled American Veterans, 68, 109, 121,
211, 213
Dishonorable discharge: to avoid rede-
ployment, 88; personality disorders and,
131; PTSD-related actions resulting in,
93
Divorce, 10, 16, 91, 106
Diyala Province, 4, 76, 223
Dole-Shalala Commission: on military
service and economic stability, 61; recommends merging Pentagon and VA
disability system, 131; and returning veterans, 227

Dow Chemical: Agent Orange and, 197;
class-action law suit against, 196; settle-
ment of Agent Orange claims, 199;
Vietnamese victims of Agent Orange
and, 201
Drug rehab, 137, 161
Drug treatment, 158, 159 (resource box)
Drug use, xx, xxi, 31, 86, 87, 89, 119, 136,
146, 158, 160, 179; and loss of military
benefits, 86–94
Dyckman, Julia, 204–207

East Los Angeles, 75
Edmundson, Eric, 61–70
Eggemeyer, James, 105–111
Erspamer, Gordon, 216
Ethics and PTSD, 153
Execution of veterans convicted of crime
despite mental illness, 143–155, 146–147

Fallujah, xiii, xiv, xv, 78, 79, 164, 223
Fisher House Foundation, 68 (resource box)
Florida, 52, 64, 107, 108, 110, 112, 164, 200
Forgotten Battalion story, 71
Fort Bragg, 105, 107
Fort Carson: investigation of medical
treatment conditions at, 215; medical
staff shortage at, 54; PTSD treatment
at, 99–100; and treatment of TBI, 39–41
Fort Hood, 18
Fort Knox, 56–59
Fort Lewis: domestic violence at, 154–155;
injured troops deployed at, 130–131; losing benefits at, 86–87; medical staff
shortages at, 54; and PTSD, 86–87
Freedom of Information Act (FOIA):
medical records of deceased service
member, 187; requesting military discharge information between 2001 and
2007, 87; substantiating VA claims
with, 114

Germany, 21, 35, 36, 43, 62, 76

GI Bill: building support for, 72, 212–214; Korean War and, 73; Lyndon Johnson and, 209; weakening of, 73–75, 84. *See also* Post-9/11 GI Bill

Good War, 70

Gordon, Nicole, 17–23

Government Accountability Office (GAO): Gulf War syndrome, 206; inadequate PTSD and TBI treatment, 54, 59; Pentagon medical staff shortages, 54, 59

Green Zone, 19

Grieger, Thomas, 6–7

Guantánamo Bay, 25, 26, 65

Guilt: of American public, 209; about the death of an enemy combatant, 34; Herbert Hendin and Ann Pollinger Haas on, 13; Jonathan Shay on, 148

Gulf War, 20, 89, 91, 119, 177, 200–216

Gulf War syndrome 201–207

Haditha massacre, 150

Halliburton, and profiteering, 53

Hanks, Don, 86–87

Harvard University, 73, 101, 117, 119

Henderson, Derek, 178–179

Home for Our Troops, 66

Home to War: A History of the Vietnam Veterans Movement, 209

Homeless veterans, 156–167; age of, 158; custody disputes and, 158; estimations of, 159; inadequate resources for, 162–163; Iraq War service and, 160; number of, 159

House Veterans Affairs Committee, 100

Humvee: accidents in, 40; attacks on, 4, 56, 174; American soldiers killed in, 33; injuries caused by lack of, 130; patrolling in, 78; in raids, 219; rear gunner in, 76; in supply convoys, 105–107; un-armored, 32–33, 134

Husayba, 36

Hussein, Saddam: failure of U.S. to leave Iraq after fall of, 33; invasion of Kuwait and, 200; Iraqi Army and, 200; Iraqis rejoice at the overthrow of, xix; links between 9/11 and, 13; oil fires started by, 203

Huze, Sean, 149–153

IAP World Services: and Hurricane Katrina, 52; and profiteering, 52; and Walter Reed Army Medical Center, 52–53

Improvised explosive device (IED), 10, 42, 36, 61, 114, 212

Indianapolis, 54

Insurgency: attacks by, 33–35; creation of, 19, 33; in Diyala Province, 34; infiltration of, 76; members of, 152; prevalence of, 30; in Vietnam, 144–146

Interceptor body Armor, 35

International Red Cross, 11

Intrepid Fallen Heroes Fund, 68 (resource box)

Iowa, 11, 14, 189

Iraq and Afghanistan Veterans of America, 40, 44, 80, 82, 121, 150, 164–165, 189, 215

Jaffee, Mike, 43

Joshua Omvig Suicide Prevention Act, 189

Journal of Epidemiology and Community Health, 177

Karpinski, Janice, 19–21

Kellogg, Brown & Root, 53

Kevlar, 35, 105

Khe Sanh, 144

Klonopin, 89, 182, 184

Kurdistan, xvi, 30, 224

Kuwait: buildup to the Iraq War, 118; Saddam Hussein's invasion of, 200, 203, 207; rapes committed in, 19–20; supply route to, 55, 106, 161; town hall meeting with Donald Rumsfeld in, 32

Landstuhl Regional Medical Center, 35–43
Listening to veterans, 153
Lohaus, Dan, 165
Los Angeles, 30, 77, 78, 92 (resource box),
  149, 152, 156, 158, 160, 161, 162
Louisville, Kentucky, 178
Lucey, Jeffrey, 180–188; Freedom of Infor-
  mation Act request for medical records
  of, 186

Manuel, Shaun, 89–91, 98
Marine Corps: combat stress program, 88;
  dishonorable discharge for trauma-
  related infractions, 91–96; at Haditha,
  150; mental health care in, 95–96; men-
  tal health stigma in, 88; Navy hospital
  corpsman deployed to Iraq with, 34–35;
  rules of engagement for, 151–152; Second
  Battalion, Fifth Marines Division,
  34–35; suicide in, 180–188; TBI in, 39;
  Wounded Warrior Program, 64
Massachusetts, xxi, 143, 180, 182
Meat tags, 167
Medical care in Germany, 21, 35, 36, 43, 62
Medication, in lieu of treatment, 132
Mental health, military shortage of car
  providers, 96; failure to treat, 97
Meshad, Shad, 30, 153–154
Michael, Durrell, 130–133
Military Religious Freedom Foundation,
  127
Millantz, Jonathan 134–137
Miranda, Cody, 91–95, 98
Monsanto, 196, 201
Multiple deployments, 6, 10, 28, 29, 34,
  45, 79, 80, 88, 89, 91, 101, 160, 168, 169,
  174, 178

Najaf, xiii, xviii, 76
Nash, William, 88
National Cancer Institute, 193

National Council for Homeless Veterans,
  159
National Guard, 23, 24, 29, 32, 35, 40, 55,
  58, 79, 80, 119, 172, 173, 222
National Gulf War Resource Center, 203
National Military Family Association, 27
National Naval Medical Center, 6
National Rehabilitation Hospital, 37
National Suicide Prevention Lifeline, 188
National Veterans Foundation, 15, 153
National Vietnam Veterans Readjustment
  Study, 16, 147
Navy, xx, 3, 25, 27, 34, 36, 88, 96, 98, 151,
  194, 204, 216
Navy Reserve, 25, 204
New Directions, 160–162
New England Journal of Medicine, 4
Nicholson, Jim, 120, 125, 162
Nicosia, Gerald, 209
Nixon, Richard, 209
Noel, Herold 163–167, 216–217
North Carolina, 66, 67, 89, 91, 105, 133,
  146, 167, 168

Odysseus in America, 147
Opensecrets.org, 210

Page, George 146–147
Pain killers, 132
Paralyzed Veterans of America, 68, 211
Percoset, 105
Perle, Richard, 118
Persian Gulf War, 20, 89, 91, 119, 177,
  200–216
Personality disorder: dishonorable dis-
  charge and, 101, 131; length of time
  spent diagnosing, 101; and loss of bene-
  fits, 95–102; as preexisting condition,
  98; unit readiness and, 101
Philadelphia, 5, 7, 10
Pittsburgh, PA, 134

Polling troops on war, 12

Post-9/11 GI Bill, 81–85, 214–215

Post-9/11 veterans, 6, 40, 125

Post-traumatic stress disorder (PTSD): alcohol and, 172, 179; *American Journal of Psychiatry* on, xviii; brain damage and, 41; class action law suit of Iraq veterans with, 125; crime and, 88, 145; definition of, 8 (resource box); deployed with, 10, 30, 45, 88–89; diagnosed with, 56, 93, 136, 157, 174; dishonorable discharge for, 88; education and, 212; federal surveys of veterans and, 16; filing VA compensation claims for, 112; Fort Carson and, 133; investigating treatment of, 54, 215; Iraq and Vietnam veterans' experience of, 122–123; journalists and, xvi–xix; loss of benefits as a result of, 95, 99; low percentage of soldiers diagnosed with, 97; military sexual assault and, 114; National Vietnam Veterans Readjustment Study, 16; number of Iraq and Afghanistan veterans diagnosed with, 6; official psychiatric diagnosis of, 145; prosecuting veterans with, 88; RAND Corporation study of, 224–225; resources for, 112, 203; stigma associated with, 7; suicide and, 123, 172, 179; theater and, 14; treatment for, 7; understaffed medical facilities and, 97; Vietnam veterans and, 6, 122, 145

Prescription drugs: deployment with, 89, 179; treatment of suicidal behavior with, 179; VA benefit program, 119, 121

Principi, Anthony, 120

Profiteering, 52–53

Prostitution, 30–32

Psychotropic medication, 89, 179

Ramadi, 34, 99, 179

Rand, Brian, 168–171

RAND Corporation study on PTSD and TBI, 36, 39, 224–225

Rape, 19–21, 146, 149

Reagan, Ronald, 116, 127, 198–199, 209

Rehabilitation Institute of Chicago, 64–65

Reppenhagen, Garett, 87, 171

Resources: Fisher House Foundation, 68 (resource box); Intrepid Fallen Heroes Fund, 68; (resource box); New Directions, 160–162; Salute Inc., 26–27, 66; TELACU Foundation, 75–77; Texas Veterans Commission, 23; VetStage, 148–151; Veterans Upward Bound Program, 74–77; Wounded Warrior Project, 64, 68 (resource box)

Resta, Patrick, 3–16, 34, 220

Reutershan, Paul, 195–197

Reyes, Jorge, 75–78

Rieckhoff, Paul, 165

Rocha, Alexander, 78–79

Roche, John, 112–116

Rocket propelled grenade (RPG): attacks on US troops from, 34, 76, 157; and traumatic brain injury, 42

Roosevelt, Franklin, signs GI Bill, 72

Rules of engagement, 151–152

Rumsfeld, Donald: and inadequate body armor, 32–33; predicting length of war, 118

Salon, 51, 123–124

Salute Inc., 26–27, 66

Schulze, Jonathan, 179, 188

Secretary of Veterans Affairs, 120, 162

Sexual assault, military, 19–21, 146, 149

Shay, Jonathan: combat exposure and crime, 147; on lack of preparation for civilian life, 147; on listening to veterans, 153; PTSD and crime, 147; on skills learned in combat 147–148

Shrapnel, xiv, 36, 38, 62, 99, 144, 196, 204

Somdahl, April, 167–171

South Carolina, 3, 5, 17, 133, 205

Staffing shortages: cost of addressing, 102; of mental health care providers, 96; at Walter Reed, 53; in Wounded Warrior Transition Units, 54, 59

Stop-loss, 29, 160

Stryker Brigade, 62

Suarez-Diaz, Chanan, 34–35

Suicide, 167–190; *Army Suicide Event Report,* 171, 176; *CBS News* investigation of veteran suicides, 176; suicide by cop, 171

Suicide prevention, 187–189

Sullivan, Paul, 119, 120, 122, 123, 124, 125, 127, 216, 217

Survivor guilt, 34, 148

Swords to Plowshares, 160

Syrian border, 36, 62

Tattoos, 167–168

TELACU Foundation, 75–77

Tet Offensive, 144

Texas Veterans Commission, 23

Tikrit, 90, 105

Town, Jonathan, 99–100

Transitional housing, 162–163, 156–159

Trauma Center of the Los Angeles Institute and Society for Psychoanalytic Studies, 92

Traumatic brain injury (TBI): concussions and, 40; delay in care for, 133; Fort Carson and, 39, 215; mild, 39; number of diagnoses, 10; RAND Corporation study of, 36, 224–225; screening for, 40–45; 59, 93; severe, 39; signature injury of Iraq War, 10; staffing shortages and, 59; treatment for, 64

Troop opinions on war, 12

Undersecretary of Defense for Personnel and Readiness, 52

U.S. Vets Westside Residence Hall, 156

University of California, Berkeley, 40, 80

Vet Center, 135 (resource box)

Veterans: perspectives in theater, 149–153; as voting block, 210; Vietnam, xvi, 6, 13, 16, 20, 30, 73, 74, 114, 121, 122, 123, 135 (resource box), 136, 143, 144, 146, 147, 151 (resource box), 153, 154, 160, 177, 193, 194

Veteran service representatives, 108

Veterans Benefits Administration, 108, 117, 129

Veterans Counsel, 110

Veterans for America, 89, 100, 113, 215

Veterans for Common Sense, 125, 126, 127, 189, 216, 217

Veterans for Common Sense et al. vs. Peake 125–126, 215–217

Veterans for Peace, 90, 221

Veterans of Foreign Wars 64, 110, 210

Veterans Service Officer, 108–112

Veterans Upward Bound Program, 74–77

VetStage, 148–151

Vicodin, 105, 136

Vietnam War: Battle of Khe Sanh, 144; GI Bill after, 73; nature of deployment, 28–45; prostitution during, 32

Walter Reed Army Medical Center: bureaucracy at, 37; Bush administration on, 51–52; investigations of, 61, 131; privatization of, 52; procedures developed since scandal at, 56; recommendation to close, 52; resignations as a result of scandal at, 59; scandal at, 49–53, 212; staff shortages at, 53; study of PTSD at, 4; treatment at, 63

War profiteering, 52–53

War reporting, and trauma, xviii, 13

Washington Post: editors' support for post-9/11 GI Bill, 215; on Vietnam veteran PTSD at start of Iraq War, 122; on Walter Reed, 49–51

Webb, James, post-9/11 GI Bill, 81–83

When Dreams Came True, 72, 214

When I Came Home, 163

Wickenwerder, William, on pre-deployment screenings, 44

World Trade Center, 3, 24, 207; September 11 and, 3, 13, 16, 17, 25, 41, 64, 66, 73, 79, 82, 83, 130, 180, 207

World War I veterans: assistance to World War II veterans, 212; fight for benefits, 70

World War II, 28, 63, 70, 73, 210, 212–214

Wounded Warrior Project, 64, 68 (resource box)

Wounded Warrior Transition Unit: assignment to, 56, 94; staff shortages at, 54, 59

Zogby poll on troops, 12

TEXT: 10.5/15 X 23 AKZIDENZ GROTESK

DISPLAY: AKZIDENZ GROTESK

COMPOSITOR: BINGHAMTON VALLEY COMPOSITION, LLC

PRINTER AND BINDER: MAPLE-VAIL MANUFACTURING